I0884878

REVELATION AND STORY

From the work of Hegel and Schelling to the dialectical theology of Barth, Bultmann and Gogarten, 'Revelation' has developed a long, rich tradition of diverse thought as well as many misunderstandings. Meaning, first and foremost, 'God's encounter with those to whom God wishes to communicate God's own self', Revelation seeks to be recounted and communicated to others. As a theological expression Revelation aims to direct our attention to the modes and areas in which we have a basis for expecting encounter with God – through stories, nature, the world as creation. From a rediscovered emphasis on 'story', narrative theology has emerged – a concept the English-speaking world has welcomed for its neutrality between history and imaginative fiction and stress on narrative rather than doctrinal dimension of biblical text.

Revelation and Story is the first book to bring into relationship a concern with theology of revelation and an interest in the theology of story or narrative theology. Mediating between German systematic theology's concern for revelation and the current Anglo-Saxon interest in narrative theology and centrality of 'story', this book illuminates both traditions. Exploring 'revelation' and 'story' from both theological and philosophical perspectives, this book connects these concepts with questions of the authority of religious and literary texts, particularly the Bible. Believing that God's revelation precedes and forestalls all human perception of God, all speech about God, and every attempt to experience anything about God or know Him, leading scholars from both Anglo-Saxon and German traditions are brought together to present a diverse range of conceptions relating to how God's revelation occurs, resulting in a new theory of the relation of revelation and story which transcends the traditional cultural divide. Stanley Hauerwas contributes the Foreword.

Revelation and Story offers a valuable new contribution to systematic theology, hermeneutics, and the study of the authority of Scripture, as well as presenting insights into important overlaps between British and German theology. This book will be of particular interest to scholars and students of philosophy and theology, and to students of literature and literary theory with an interest in hermeneutics.

Revelation and Story

Narrative theology and the centrality of story

Edited by
GERHARD SAUTER AND JOHN BARTON

Routledge
Taylor & Francis Group
LONDON AND NEW YORK

First published 2000 by Ashgate Publishing

Reissued 2018 by Routledge
2 Park Square, Milton Park, Abingdon, Oxon, OX14 4RN
711 Third Avenue, New York, NY 10017, USA

Routledge is an imprint of the Taylor & Francis Group, an informa business

A Library of Congress record exists under LC control number: 00038101

Typeset by Manton Typesetters

ISBN 13: 978-1-138-73880-5 (hbk)
ISBN 13: 978-1-138-73878-2 (pbk)
ISBN 13: 978-1-315-18458-6 (ebk)

Contents

Foreword

Stanley Hauerwas
The Divinity School, Duke University

This book should not exist. Everyone knows that Germans and the British do not 'get on'. Even less likely is a cooperative venture between German and British theologians. As John Barton observes in his contribution to this book, German theologians are trained to do theology in a manner that almost seems calculated to make British theologians uncomfortable. The Germans seem so sure that they can say things the British are not sure can ever be said. Put crudely, the British may (with some hesitation) be willing to talk about how story might be an informative concept for disclosing the grammar of certain kinds of theological claims; but they would never talk as assuredly as Germans about revelation. At least they would never use the language of revelation in academic contexts as if they knew what they were talking about.

Yet this book does exist, and that it does tells us something important about current conditions under which theological work must be done. At the very least, the book is a testimony to Gerhard Sauter and his Bonn colleagues who have tirelessly worked to make connections with theologians around the world. We have long benefited at Duke from a joint programme with Bonn that involves not only faculty interaction but also student exchanges. Through our interactions those of us at Duke have been enriched by better appreciating the challenges before those working in the German context. Appreciating how they meet those challenges helps us better understand our common work as Christian theologians. The high quality of these contributions testifies to the importance of such collaboration that enables us to learn from one another.

These essays, to be sure in quite different ways, suggest that any account Christians give of the interrelation of revelation and story requires a display of how the content of that which is revealed opens itself out to other stories and voices. That this book is the result of a conversation between theologians who have been shaped by the habits of quite different academic and social contexts is clear from its contents. Moreover, the essays themselves manifest this openness through use of philosophical, literary and historical materials as necessary for the theological enterprise. If revelation is a claim about God's very nature, then it is antithetical to the character of that which is revealed to appeal to revelation to end a conversation. Rather, as these essays witness, the Christian affirmation that our God is revealed is but an invitation to learn from other sources. So the fact that British and German theologians open out, not only to one another but to others whose work may not be explicitly theological, is a small but nonetheless significant sign of hope for our current theological tasks. If nothing else, this volume represents the kind of robust theology possible when theologians recognize the worst theological sin is thinking our task is to protect God.

The existence as well as the subject of this book I believe tells us something about the changing politics for theological work. That politics is not the commonplace that the world is growing smaller and/or that we must now all learn to work in a global context in which we gain an appreciation of stories different from our own. Such a reading, I think, is a profound mistake, given the character of contributions to this book. As one of the early advocates of what came to be called 'story theology', I confess that I have often found myself quite unsympathetic to many of the theological proposals that have flown that flag, because they but reproduce the apologetic strategies of Protestant liberalism in a new guise. The contributors to this book happily avoid that trap to the extent that they make clear that calling attention to the narrative character of Christian revelation cannot be a strategy to avoid questions of the truth of that which is revealed.

Indeed, it is my hunch that the rediscovery of the narrative character of Christian convictions has less to do with the world growing smaller than with the church growing smaller. Once Christians are socially and politically displaced we are then freed to rediscover the particularity of our convictions. That conversations are now not only possible, but fruitful, between Bonn and Oxford is a hopeful sign that God has found a way to rob Christians of the false universalism so characteristic of modernity. Accordingly, we are now able, as this book manifests, to read the Bible without employing reductive methods designed to make us forget that the Bible is a witness to God.

Much silliness has been written about narrative and its significance for theology – which makes this book all the more welcome because the seriousness and complexity, as well as the tensions between narrative and story, are never hidden. As a result, the book opens out to ask us as readers to engage in the work made possible by the collaboration of our colleagues from Bonn and Oxford. Such work after all – like the telling of the story itself – is never finished. That is why, as this book makes clear, it is such good work. So, thank God, in spite of the odds, this book exists.

List of Contributors

John Barton, Oriel & Laing Professor of the Interpretation of Holy Scripture, University of Oxford

Paul S. Fiddes, Principal of Regent's Park College, Oxford

Rainer Fischer, assistant to Professor Sauter

Ernstpeter Maurer, Professor of Systematic Theology, University of Dortmund

Robert Morgan, Reader in New Testament Studies, University of Oxford

Gerhard Sauter, Professor of Systematic Theology, University of Bonn

Caroline Schröder, assistant to Professor Sauter

Graham Ward, Professor of Practical Theology, University of Manchester, formerly Dean of Peterhouse, Cambridge

Michael Wolter, Professor of New Testament, University of Bonn

Introduction

There has been a partnership for 23 years between the Faculty of Theology in the University of Oxford and the Protestant Faculty of Theology in the Rheinische Friedrich-Wilhelms-Universität, Bonn. Undergraduate and doctoral students and lecturers have participated in numerous joint seminars, have become familiar with different ways of working, and have been able to explore the fruitfulness of diversity in styles of thinking.

From these experiences of dialogue there developed a collaborative research project. The participants were, on the Bonn side, Rainer Fischer, Ernstpeter Maurer (now in Dortmund), Gerhard Sauter, Caroline Schröder and Michael Wolter, and, from Oxford, John Barton, Paul Fiddes, Robert Morgan and Graham Ward (now in Manchester). The project was supported for three years by the British Council and the German Academic Exchange Service. The present book contains the results of these researches, involving various different specialist areas within theology.

The participants met twice a year, over three years, each meeting lasting for four or five days, and prepared papers which were discussed in great detail, before reaching their final form and being translated into the other language. Such prolonged contact made us, we believe, more sensitive to each other's traditions than is normally possible in theological conferences, and we hope that the result, while reflecting our differences, also bears witness to our sustained attempt to understand each other and to avoid stereotyped attitudes.

Under the title *Revelation and Story* we are asking about possible ways of speaking about God's action, in all its variety and unfathomableness; and in such a way that this action can be expected anew.

'Revelation' is a term with a long and rich tradition, which is also a tradition of many misunderstandings. Its meaning has always been disputed, and the fact that one hears less in theology and in the church of 'revelation' than was formerly the case certainly does not mean we can put the problem behind us. This is why Michael Wolter's essays sets itself, among other things, to examine texts in which the word 'revelation' appears explicitly. In our discussions we were of one mind in believing that God's revelation precedes and forestalls all human perception of God, all speech about God, and every attempt to experience anything about God or even to know anything about Him. Yet we still have concepts of how God's revelation occurs – conceptions which are diverse but not seriously at variance.

It has often been suspected that the term 'revelation' designates *information* gained through supernatural knowledge: God has made known something which human beings would never, and could never, have known from their own resources. 'Revealed' matters would then be hidden facts which have been disclosed by God's decision, and are accessible on the basis of a divine intervention in the human ability to grasp truth, differing only in degree from other things. But if we were to take this kind of approach, we would have to ask: does this truth come 'naturally' or 'supernaturally'?

Against this it is essential to assert that 'revelation' means first and foremost, and fundamentally, God's *encounter* with those to whom God wishes to communicate *God's own self.* This communication may happen in diverse modes and in various different areas. The theological term 'revelation' is intended to direct our attention to the modes and the areas – stories, nature: the world as creation – in which we have a well-founded basis for expecting this encounter with God. 'Revelation' is not a state of knowledge which these encounters converge to produce. Revelation seeks to be *recounted* and thus *communicated* to others.

At least as early as the religious philosophy of German Idealism (G.W.F. Hegel, *Lectures on the Philosophy of Religion*, 1824–31; F.W.J. Schelling, *Philosophy of Revelation*, 1858) there was agreement on the insight that 'revelation' designates God's *self*-disclosure. God reveals *God*, not something or other else, not even something about God, but God. In the intervening period this conception has become a matter of widespread agreement in theological circles.

In German Protestant theology the concept of 'revelation' took on a new emphasis in the twentieth century through dialectical theology (Karl Barth, Rudolf Bultmann, Friedrich Gogarten). Here 'revelation' means the *event* in and with which God makes Himself known (Morgan). Revelation tells people what they cannot tell themselves. The Bible bears witness to this revelation, which is made known in Christian proclamation. That which is disclosed in this way illuminates human history, and makes it possible to read and understand other testimonies to this history – stories, as we call them – in its light (Fiddes, Maurer).

This concept of revelation is connected to a strong, almost exclusive attachment to the Bible, the so-called 'Scripture principle' (*sola scriptura*). Anything that can be said with theological justification has to be measured against what is addressed to us in the Bible as revelation, that is as God's proclamation. Stories can help to make God's revelation accessible by giving us access to who God is. Stories can open us up to an encounter with God. This mutual relationship of opening up, openness and closure is a leading theme of several chapters (Sauter, Fiddes, Barton). But does that mean, on the other hand, that we encounter God's revelation *only* in reading the Bible? How is this encounter related to the reading of other texts, and not least to the reading of our world as a text? How are biblical stories related to what *we* call 'stories', or tell as our own stories?

Theology in the English-speaking world has found 'story' a useful concept in a number of ways. It is neutral as between an account of actual events (history) and imaginative fiction, from both of which theologians believe important theological truth can derive. It leads to placing the stress, in biblical studies, on the narrative dimension of texts rather than on their 'doctrinal' content. This can be a liberation from too didactic a reading of Scripture. It brings Christian theology potentially closer to Judaism, where the narration of the saving events (above all, in the Exodus and gift of the Promised Land) has a central place in theological understanding. And from a rediscovered emphasis on 'story' has come what is often called 'narrative theology', seen in American writing most clearly in the work of Stanley Hauerwas, whom we thank for contributing a Foreword to our work.

Can *story* be translated adequately into German? At the moment it remains in German as a loan word. In the German version of this book it is generally rendered *Geschichte*, but used in the plural (*Geschichten*) to avoid confusion with *Geschichte* meaning 'history'. Talk of 'stories', *Geschichten*, is meant to point to the *event* of narration. The usage of 'story' in English incidentally corresponds to the derivation of the term from Latin, *historia*. Until the eighteenth century, *historia* meant an individual story, a story that had been related and was to be narrated again. Only later did it come to mean what we call 'history', referring to the whole temporal context of human life.

In Britain and North America there are still many points of contact between the Bible and literature. Theological themes can be encountered, implicitly or even explicitly, for example in novels (John Updike, John Irving), and not merely as a decorative technique. At universities there are courses in the Bible and literature, which is very much the exception in Germany. In Britain and the USA there are journals devoted to this interrelationship. Is this a sign of cultural difference; is it perhaps a sign of theological difference? Liturgical actualization and broad cultural reception have made biblical texts into components of everyday life, differently from the situation in Germany with its long-running, tedious battles over 'reason and revelation', 'revelation and history' and 'natural theology'. These discussions have resulted in deep divisions which do not exist (or not in this way) in Britain and the USA. This is no doubt also the reason why, in these countries, there is a widespread feeling that no fundamental difference exists *in principle* between the Bible and other texts.

What are the reasons for this, and what conclusions can be drawn from it? Does English theology recognize a 'Scripture principle' at all? In Britain there has since the mid-eighteenth century been an interest in the interaction of readers and texts. In Germany this has stimulated many writers to new types of presentation, in which the author interrupts his own narrative (story) and makes it shatter, like light passing through a prism. To what extent is the 'Scripture principle' opposed to this, even in the theological revision offered here by Sauter? One difference between 'stories' in general and the Bible is that no secular story has an ultimate or irreducible character for us, whereas for Christians there is an irreducibility about Scripture. One of the formulas on which all the participants in this project were agreed is that it is not appropriate for Christians to go 'behind' the biblical text, in the sense of treating as authoritative ideas we can derive from it, or our own hypotheses about its origins and component parts, instead of accepting the text we have as the vehicle of revelation.

To this extent a theology of 'story' may well seem incompatible with the principle *sola scriptura*, and hence with a theology of revelation, causing an intolerable tension between our two central terms, *Revelation* and *Story*. However, we are also agreed that, if the activity represented by 'going behind' the text is ruled out when the Bible is read in the Church, there is another – which we call, more or less arbitrarily, 'going beneath' the text (Schröder, Maurer) – which is not only permissible but mandatory for the theologian. This is the attempt to understand the circumstances which produced the biblical 'stories' and hence what they mean: the whole activity usually described as historical criticism. The texts in and through which Christians believe God is revealed are no less anchored in particular circumstances than any other 'stories', and understanding the texts entails investigating these circumstances.

In some forms of postmodernist thinking appeal to a meta-story is ruled out, because the social and historical embeddedness of any account of the world militates against grand explanatory narratives (Foucault, Lyotard, Deleuze). But can Christian theology manage without a meta-story, if it is to speak decisively of God: the story, that is, of Jesus Christ? This story certainly is not to be seen as a narrative stratum set above other stories: rather, it comes across in all our other stories, and holds them all together.

If, then, we begin with the reading of biblical texts, we find ourselves facing the question of what expectation we bring to this reading, what expectation forces us to undertake it. If it is the expectation that we shall discern *God in His action*, then this expectation is concerned not simply with what biblical texts say, but equally with how they say it.

Can the structures of a text give the text the potential for being the occasion for revelation? Sauter and Fiddes, Maurer and Ward, approaching the matter from different perspectives, develop the point that stories 'continue'. But how does this happen? Is it that they contain endless possibilities, and thus turn into a never-ending story, dependent only on our ability to go on making associations with what has been narrated, and so to extend it further? Does it happen by our embedding them in forms of life, in a narrative praxis (Ward)? Or do stories go on and keep developing because the reader is involved in them (Maurer)?

If we assume that revelation unfolds, that reality opens up, how then can we avoid making our own openness to an ever new, unconventional reading full of surprises a criterion for interpretation? This would imply that this openness contained a kind of 'disclosure quality' that could be transferred without more ado to texts. Is reality as a whole meant to produce revelation? Does 'revelation' designate a structure in all reality, insofar as it is from revelation that we understand God's action? Is reality a process with an open future, full of surprises, with repetitions that are not simply action replays? Is it possible that only a theological meta-story (for instance, the doctrine of the Trinity) can keep this open?

These are some of the questions which partly arise from the provocation that the concept of revelation continues to excite, and partly derive from the diverse traditions of thought, and from the differently constituted contexts in which life is led. Above all they make themselves felt when biblical exegetes and systematicians work together and so are obliged to give an account of their way of working. In the process it is possible to see interesting overlaps between British and German theology, which are also manifested by the need for each side to adopt and take further the intellectual approach of the other, and incorporate it into its own work. The accounts that follow are meant to draw attention to ways in which each tradition can be thus augmented and enriched.

The argument of the book develops as follows through the various chapters. The first chapter, by Gerhard Sauter, on the proper use of Scripture in hearing the Word of God, sets out three themes which are to be taken up in turn in the three following chapters: possibility, ethics and conflict. Sauter considers the way that the word of promise in a text opens up possibilities for the future, and this is developed by Paul Fiddes in Chapter Two on the way that stories open up possibilities, and the association of this process with revelation.

Sauter reflects on the proper use of the biblical text in the making of ethical decisions, and this issue is developed by John Barton in his reflection on reading biblical stories 'for life', which he also relates to the theme of open possibilities.

Sauter proposes that proper grounding of belief and practice in Scripture will create conflict among its readers, which is an important preparation for hearing the Word of God. The place of conflict in hermeneutics is taken up in Chapter Four by Ernstpeter Maurer, who also relates it to the distinctions between 'Spirit–letter' and 'law–gospel' sketched by Sauter. Maurer argues that the conflict of intentions *within* the text confronts us with the event of revelation. His contribution not only reflects back to themes which have been opened up by Sauter, but also explores the question of a suitable hermeneutical method. The two following chapters therefore represent complementary approaches to hermeneutics and revelation.

In his chapter Rainer Fischer argues that biblical texts can be apprehended as the Gestalt of revelation, that is, as forming a whole and coherent 'story' in which God's action and speech become apparent. While Fischer therefore emphasizes the 'wholeness' of biblical texts, he claims that the concept of Gestalt has room within it for the 'openness' on which Fiddes and Barton have reflected, and for the tension between 'law and gospel' to which Maurer draws attention. In Chapter Six, Graham Ward concentrates upon the place of allegory and analogy in reading biblical stories; revelation is seen to be inseparable from the act of reading, which constantly requires judgment from readers and so demands participation in the very event of the unfolding of the truth by God. The notion of 'open spaces' for imaginative involvement provided by the text has links to the concept of openness already developed.

At this point, two contributors throw down constructive challenges to the developing argument. First, Michael Wolter takes a different perspective on the relation between story and revelation: whereas the discussion so far has been about the sense in which stories might be the vehicle or occasion for revelation, Wolter examines places in Jewish and Christian apocalyptic where it is claimed that stories themselves *have been revealed*. He concludes that the main function of these 'revealed stories' is less to open up new possibilities than to offer *assurance* in the face of the crisis that confronts the readers. However, there is still some dimension of openness present insofar as confidence evoked in the faithfulness of God enables the readers to perceive that their stories can continue into the future.

Robert Morgan aims to concentrate our attention on the story of Jesus as *the* story about revelation, or a story which contains the deposit of witness to revelation. He issues an important warning against the simple *identification* of a story, whether textual or proclaimed, with revelation; the primary meaning of revelation must be the event of God's self-unveiling in Jesus Christ.

In a final chapter, Caroline Schröder reflects on the process by which the book came into being and comments on the usefulness of the terms 'revelation' and 'story' in theology.

One

'Scriptural Faithfulness' is not a 'Scripture Principle'

Gerhard Sauter

'Do you stand on Scripture?' This, so we are told, is what Gossler, the Prussian minister, asked Adolf Schlatter in 1893 when he sought to call him to a post in the University of Berlin. The distinguished New Testament scholar, dogmatician and ethicist is said to have answered, 'I stand under Scripture.'[1] What is the difference between standing *upon* the Bible and standing *under* it?

People who emphasize *standing upon the Bible* wish to assert their steadfastness and religious accountability. Perhaps they want to affirm that they stand on solid ground, on the eternal Word of God, and not on the shifting views and changing opinions of human beings. But those who speak like this should see to it that they do not place themselves above the Bible and trample on it in the process. The Bible can never be beneath us. That is what Schlatter wanted to say when he turned the minister's question around and phrased it properly. *To place oneself under the Bible* means, on the contrary, to expose oneself to Scripture, to pay attention to what it has to communicate. Standing under Scripture does not mean, however, standing under the Bible in order to feel safe as if it were a shelter or a protective covering against bad weather. That would be something entirely different.

1 What does it Mean 'to Begin with the Bible'?

Images of the Bible as a shelter, a bulwark, secure on every side, erected on a rock-solid foundation and therefore rock-solid itself, emerge frequently when we speak of 'the principle of scripture'. Since the beginning of the sixteenth century, Lutheran and Reformed theologians have appealed to the Bible as a theological principle of knowing (*principium cognoscendi*).[2] They mean that Scripture is an unconditional prerequisite of theology because God reveals God's own self there and has endowed it with the divine Spirit. God acts in God's Word. Therefore Christian doctrine, with which every dogmatician is especially concerned, may not be attributed to any other source. For this reason theology founded upon the Bible considers itself unchangeable and unshakable by anyone or anything. Such a statement sounds almost as though Luther's song of protection, 'A Mighty Fortress is our God', had been rewritten as 'A Mighty Fortress is our Bible', complete with the military metaphors of weapons and shields. Scripture is seen in this way as a fortress and arsenal because theology wants to be as well armed as possible (if not completely armed). In any case, it does not want to be less armed than philosophy with which it compares itself in terms of their principles of knowing.[3] The Bible is studied with these aims in mind: asking what is necessary and sufficient in order to obtain secure knowledge.

In the nineteenth century a different, sharper tone was added. The Bible became the 'formal principle' which was to characterize Protestantism.

> The return to the original revelation in scripture is ... the *formal principle* of Protestantism which presents itself in application as a *critique*, seeking to distinguish between those things which have been presented as Christian truth, but are suspected to be human work and therefore polluted by the admixture of human error, from that which is sifted out of scripture and judged as the unpolluted source of divine revelation.[4]

These are treacherous images! In this approach the 'critique' operates like a chemical process, in which the original revelation acts as a kind of nitric acid which is used to distinguish the gold from all other substances.[5] The Bible appears as a pure source which remains unpolluted as long as no one disturbs it. The goal is that all of Scripture should serve a process of 'justification by Scripture.' But what does 'justification' mean in this instance, if justification by faith alone is, at the same time, defined as the 'material principle of Protestantism'?[6]

It is worth considering here that the appeal to Scripture, indeed to Scripture alone (*sola scriptura*), can have no other ground than the confession of 'justification by grace alone' (*sola gratia*). 'Justification' cannot have one meaning here and a different meaning there. God communicates God's righteousness by speaking with us. Reading the Bible, like prayer, should be done with the expectation that God desires to give God's own self to us. The two are not to be separated from each other.[7] God's unmerited gift is communicated to us nowhere but in the biblical word, and conversely, justification by grace and only in faith (*sola fide*) depends on the expectation of the action of God, an expectation which leads us to Scripture and lets us search in it. We do not search there to find what we already know, what we have been informed about for all time through a biblical instruction, but rather to come upon Christ in the pages and to hear him alone (*solus christus*) among all the voices; we encounter him anew time after time. 'You search the scriptures because you think that in them you have eternal life; but it is they that testify on my behalf' (John 5:39).

In contrast, every 'justification' which is produced with the help of the 'principle of scripture' understands itself as something completely different; namely as *legitimation and authorization.* It is put forward as the ultimate, valid justification with a claim to infallibility, as an unalterable point of departure and an unshakable foundation. In other words, it is presented as the *final substantiation* of everything Protestantism ever stood for. In this process both justification and scripture are fundamentally misunderstood, as if the Bible serves to *derive* religious values from divine revelation. These are, of course, assumed to be the values of Protestantism which is therefore, for this reason, to be accepted as the purest expression of Christian religion.

To 'begin with the Bible' means, from this perspective, to return to the origin, to the very first moment of religion, because it is here, if anywhere, that God can be found. This means that anything which comes later stands in danger of being all too human additions which taint or completely undermine that which once came purely from God. Such a view appears to be easily compatible with historical inquiry into beginnings, and the search for an 'original event' which must be liberated from every human addition in order to shine in its true splendour. Tradition is thus fundamentally suspected of falsification. In this sense the principle of scripture belongs under the slogan: 'We stand on scripture, the Catholics stand in the Church.'

This is how the supposition of a 'theology versed in scripture' could arise, a theology which sees itself like a dike against the prevailing trends of science and ideology which surge against it. Then the person who is true to scripture has a handy Bible verse ready for any situation in life. 'As it says in Scripture …' becomes a motto on the banner of the 'know all' – or the ignoramus!

Nevertheless, this understanding of a 'principle' contains a measure of truth: *one may not go behind the Bible.* Christian theology begins with the Bible insofar as it seriously takes 'the scripture,' (that is, the canon as the church's confession of God's address to humankind) to be the place for God's self-communication in Jesus Christ. One cannot get behind the assertion that God has decisively spoken in Jesus Christ, that God has addressed us in him. Whoever pursues Christian theology honestly cannot deny this characteristic of 'Holy Scripture' in its unity and wholeness. This certainly does not mean that everything that can be said in Christian faith must always begin with a word from the Bible. But all Christian discourse must be measured by whether it can be cross-referenced to the contingent event of 'God coming to speech in Jesus Christ' – or whether it comes from another source.

This event may not be traced back to anything else. What the Bible says can be substantiated neither in a return to historically secured facts nor in the psychological analysis of the authors of extant texts (certainly not using depth psychology), nor in the sociological reconstruction of circumstances, as informative as all these may be in their place. The Bible is defenceless against such attempts to get to the bottom of its texts, because they intend to use a 'foundation other than the one that has been laid, which foundation is Jesus Christ' (1 Corinthians 3:11). 'To get behind the Bible' commonly denotes other reasons and motives. The reader wants to find the authors out by explaining their unexpressed intentions, their interests or their reactions to discoverable life situations. Whoever tries to get behind scripture will usually miss what the Bible itself has to say.

So 'to begin with scripture' means at least 'not going behind scripture', but what else might it mean? Those who are open to scripture will discover an entirely different beginning, a new beginning, *within* it. In Luther's dispute with Erasmus of Rotterdam, the issue at stake was not centred upon an appeal to the Bible's clarity and its importance for binding theological language. Nevertheless, Luther referred persistently to a *primum principium*, a 'first principle'.[8] In so doing he took up a philosophical category which was the unconditioned presupposition of all further argumentation. By 'first principle' he meant the 'certainty' of scripture, that is its unambiguous communication. On the strength of this certainty one can expect clarity in the important life and death issues. This he contrasted with laws which only order customs and decide controversies.

This 'first principle', however, is not intended to be a 'principle of scripture'. It is not some supernatural quality of Holy Scripture. The Bible is not a starting point for enquiries about life in the world or a key for all life issues. The Bible is not a secure bastion behind which we can barricade ourselves or from which we can launch attacks on others. *The primum principium is God, who steps forth from God's darkness, who confronts us, draws near and deals with us.* Stated more precisely, the clarity of scripture is Christ himself as the light which illumines the dark or, better still, who breaks through the dark – the truth as life. The reason we cannot get behind scripture is because God has drawn attention to God's own self so unambiguously clearly there. Therefore we can begin nowhere else, neither before scripture was written nor after. If we try to begin somewhere else, we attempt secretly *to get behind our trust that it is none other than God who speaks in the Bible*. The search for historical clues in scripture is potentially less serious than an attempt to get behind scripture. Naturally getting behind scripture can be expressed in a flight to the historical, social and psychological limitations of the authors, but it can also be practised in the subsequent, seemingly advanced, co-shaping and reshaping of texts by their readers. For this reason any truly urgent reading of the Bible, driven by life and death issues, begins with the questions, 'Who is the God who becomes audible in scripture? Who is the one of whom I read in the Bible?'

2 Biblical Proof Texts or Biblical Grounding?

It would be the exact opposite of the '*primum principium*' to try to draw attention to oneself (and certainly to assert oneself) by using biblical words. It is because of such attempts, however, that the 'principle of scripture' has lost a great deal of vitality. This is an odd irony, yet unfortunately logical. For a long time the Bible was used to challenge ecclesial authorities, who had treated faith as if it were like a door off its hinges, no longer able to swing freely and function properly. The principle of scripture was used as a kind of Archimedian fulcrum and lever to lift *faith* back to where it belonged. In this way it was hoped that freedom, which ecclesial authority had taken away, could be restored to faith. Later on the Bible itself was classified as being part of the tradition from which enlightened Christians had emancipated themselves, in order to recover scripture's living foundation in an original and unmediated relationship to God – or so people thought.[9] From this critical point of view, the principle of scripture was seen as one of the last vestiges of a mediaeval obeisance to authorities. Though reformation theology continued to adhere to it, the Enlightenment was the first to cast it off completely. Thereafter the Bible was continually used – and misused – to make obligatory what ought to be done, when other motivations were either lacking or too weak to stir people into action.

According to this line of thinking, everything that ought to be done without excuse or complaint must have a biblical 'reason.' It is striking, even treacherous, that today the Bible is so often 'used' as instructions for action. This is not surprising when one considers how much in the field of ethics today is controversial, and how even doing what is most necessary evidently requires stronger motivations than those already present. But it certainly gives one cause to wonder, when biblical precepts or mere motifs taken from the Bible are commonly used – *after the event* – to make obligatory what is already known, that is to sanction what has already been discussed as a possibility for action. The Bible is then no longer studied to find a biblical direction for action *in the midst* of urgent and necessary decisions. Such direction should not relieve us of a decision, but point us beyond the decision to a view of God's promise. It directs our view to God's act which embraces us, an act which cannot be confused with our goals, regardless of how honourable they may be.

Currently, in the German Protestant Church it has become customary to propose 'biblical grounds' for each and every thing. The practice already appears to have a tradition. Did not the Reformers refer to scripture passages when they criticized the traditional sacramental practices, called canon law into question and revised church order? With these actions, however, the Reformers did not pit untouched origins against degenerative developments. They professed, rather, Jesus Christ as the present acting Lord of the Church! They wanted to hear him, not a stranger, when – and this is crucial – they described the nature of ecclesial action.[10] But today 'biblical grounds' are urged primarily when urgent decisions need to be legitimated. Such a process goes like this: Bible verses are brought to bear which correspond to the current theme to be clarified. 'What is there in the Bible on this issue?' prompts a search through thematic similarities, corresponding situations, repeatable tasks, or perhaps simply key words in scripture. All that is found presumably leads directly to 'what the Bible says'. This recitation of evidence is assumed to answer the question at hand. Usually, the answer cuts off all further inquiry.

As a curious but symptomatic example I refer to the debate over 'wine or grape juice at communion' which was conducted some years ago.[11] It began with a concern for alcoholics for whom even a sip of wine was considered to be dangerous. One would think that nothing more or less than a pragmatic regulation would be necessary in order to include these parishioners in the celebration of the 'communion of the body and blood of Christ' (1 Corinthians 10:16), so that they should suffer neither undeserved harm nor discrimination.

Why not use grape juice in exceptional cases, if fellow Christians are endangered by the very smell of wine? But people apparently could not be content with such reasoning. 'Biblical grounds' were required, which were first sought in Jesus' last supper with his disciples. When, with the best of intentions and exegetical acumen, no grounds could be found there (after all, the cup of blessing Jesus shared with his disciples certainly contained wine), the admonition of the apostle Paul to the 'strong ones' in the Corinthian congregation was recalled. The strong should have consideration for the 'weak' members of the community (1 Corinthians 8:7–13; 12:22–24a; Romans 14:1–3). This paved the way for the solution which was apparent all along, namely to vary the celebration according to the needs of the communicants. In this way important biblical texts were quoted as proof without regard for their theological context.

For example, there was no discussion on the point that, in his first letter to Corinth, Paul was not merely urging consideration for others, but fighting to clarify the concept of Christian freedom. The Apostle was appealing to Corinthians who regarded themselves as invincible in the power of their faith. They felt quite strong and free to consume meat which may have been previously blessed through sacrifice ('meat sacrificed to idols'). Paul contrasts the strong with members of the congregation who feared becoming contaminated by meat which was used for idolatry, and would rather do without such food altogether. The admonition not to injure the consciences of the 'weak' cannot, therefore, be easily equated with considerate treatment of the addicted. This admonition presupposes a sharp contrast between the Lord's Supper and the worship of idols. The two are not compatible and are in fact not simply practices of worship but questions of daily living (1 Corinthians 10:14–22). In the Lord's Supper it becomes evident that the congregation of Jesus Christ is not subject to the principalities and powers which it must confront in its rites of worship. The Christian community places itself under its Lord who offers them the freedom of his death. By inquiring into the elements of the meal, Paul wants to subject all eating and drinking, all means of life, to a decisive question: 'To whom do we belong?' Meal-time does not serve merely to satisfy our hunger, it also serves as a reminder of the source of our lives.

'Are we provoking the Lord? Are we stronger than he?' (1 Corinthians 10:22). In my opinion this is the crucial turn in the Pauline argument. We must always keep it in mind, and especially in the matter of fellowship in the Lord's Supper between the sick and those who consider themselves to be healthy. Does this mean that no pastoral word regarding alcoholism may be found here? Certainly not, as long as we refrain from drawing thematic parallels and instead draw on the richness of theological perspective about fellowship in the Lord's Supper, namely fellowship in Christ! If indeed 'the right administration of the sacraments is to be tested repeatedly by scripture and to be governed by the landmarks named in scripture',[12] then we must not restrict ourselves to matters of ritual, and certainly not to the tasteless exercise of relating (even by way of comparison) one element of the Lord's Supper to the meat offered to idols in the ancient world! What is most important is this: when it comes to the relation between the 'strong' and the 'weak', self-evaluation is on an exceedingly weak footing. Paul encourages the 'strong' to share in the scruples of conscience of the 'weak', rather than putting the weak into a state of panic through the strong's expression of their freedom. Could it be that those who feel strong and superior are the truly vulnerable ones? By the very demonstration of their strength, could they be showing that they are relying only on what they are and have in themselves?

Paul calls the 'strong' together with the 'weak' (that is, feeble in the view of the strong) into freedom under the Lordship of Jesus Christ. 'Biblical grounding' only becomes apparent in reference to the ground of this freedom. It has nothing to do with 'suitable biblical texts', whether they are adduced to serve either as a master key or as a kind of clip-on picture frame. Nor does 'biblical grounding' provide a rule to be taken into consideration when shaping a worship service. Rather, this rule leaves room for the freedom of the Spirit who restores the strong as well as the weak. Pragmatic solutions for the problems of our life together must be measured by this.

3 Biblical Grounding Means Conflict

'Biblical grounding' does not therefore consist of a recitation of biblical references, followed by clever ways of bringing them up to date. Insofar as the grounding is the outcome of words and texts, its theological context and connections must be transparent. This 'connectedness' cannot simply be lifted out of the Bible, as a textual structure that can be defined in literary terms. It cannot be established by some sentence taken from its context in the Bible, or by some single biblical theme or concept, as if this could then be applied as a criterion for other texts.

Nonetheless, the clear expression of this 'grounding', in all its theological connectedness, cannot be found except in 'searching the scriptures', since this is bound up with the expectation that God speaks the divine judgment there. This judgment not only weighs what we think, do and say, but also judges what is real: 'This is how it is, and there is nothing else.' Reality exists first when God comes to us, and tells us who we are. Only then do we discern what is real.

In the to and fro of personal opinion, who can do any more than put a heavy foot down? Who is capable of bringing about a decision in the midst of conflicting points? That is, who is capable of offering a word which really resolves the problem? This question was the starting point for the theologians of the Reformation in their reference to scripture, and it was the background of '*sola scriptura*'. *Who makes decisions in the Church* when matters – as they did at that time – concern truth and untruth, life and death?

With regard to this starting point, Luther's line of argument in his controversial treatise of 1521, against the humanistic theologian Hieronymus Emser, is particularly instructive.[13] Emser defends the priority of the Church Fathers over direct recourse to the Bible – for the Bible's sake, as he thought. The multiple voices and meanings of a biblical text require hermeneutical criteria, which first become clear through reflection and scholarly penetration into what is said in disjointed ways in scripture. Emser was concerned about the unity of the Church, a unity which he saw could only be possible if it is not undermined by demands made on the Bible from various sides (and, one can logically conclude, with variable interests). Therefore an authority is required which can guarantee the unity of scripture by authoritatively deciding every dispute which crops up – certainly not without biblical assistance, but by standardizing its interpretation. Emser claimed the Church Fathers to be that authority. Since their theological reflection created clarity about what the Bible said, we must turn to them in questionable cases. They are the 'ideal readers' of the Bible and therefore competent to understand it correctly.

Luther called this a *petere principium*,[14] a pseudo-foundational statement which asserts as a basis what is actually yet to be proved. With this flaw in reasoning towards a logical conclusion, a *principium* worms its way in. This is a devastating critique for anyone who is trained in philosophy, but Luther's accusation is even more radical. He severely damaged Emser's mode of argument which strove to stand on a rationally grounded *principium*. At the same time, Luther wanted to take his opponents seriously in their intention to hold a dispute over the clarity of the Bible. Whether those who seriously wanted to be Christians placed themselves under the Bible became apparent when they engaged with the Bible in their dispute, or argued over their interpretations of it.

It is not only instructive but truly moving to follow how Luther repeatedly came up against new problems, complications, even unresolvable perplexities when it came to taking scripture truly at its word. He was only able to overcome such obstacles by characterizing in different ways what it means to 'hear' the word of scripture. In this approach, he outlines what kind of expectation prompts a particular hearing of a text, and also what must be said about scripture in order to allow room for a hearing which is not obstructed by external demands and false expectations. This train of thought appears more complicated with each step. It requires many fuses to avoid short-circuits, but again and again there are surprising discoveries in the texts, where the clarity of biblical statements is compelling to the reader. This does not happen in the form of conclusive evidence, but in being transparent to the speech of God. There are no authoritative overtones, no coercion of thought or pressures to act. Rather, a consensus of faith begins to emerge. There is a liberating agreement (with a sigh of relief) about what God has spoken and for what God takes responsibility.

Appealing to scripture is not a process of building a logical conclusion, but getting involved in the theological 'connectedness' of what is foundational, and becoming aware of its place within the Bible as a whole. In short, appeal to scripture means reading the Bible with the well-founded assumption that God intervenes here, that the Word of God intervenes. This expectation steps out of scripture toward us, and we perceive it. This is not a circular argument (*petitio principii*). Rather, scripture refers to itself as a living whole, in the same way that every living thing must relate to itself in order to exist. The Bible opens itself out,[15] not in some interminable self-conversation, but through expressing outwardly the way in which it maintains its life. Referring to scripture therefore means getting involved in the liveliness of the Bible and living with it. In struggling to find a criterion – or better, an interplay of normative elements – Luther struggles to be directed by God alone, and not by a rigid norm.

If one can speak at all of a 'principle' of scripture in this instance, then it is a *principle of conflict*. Scripture is not to be used to assert oneself during conflicts over claims to validity. On the contrary, referring to the Bible necessitates a conflict of a principal kind. That is, with what do we begin? How do we allow room for God? These basic questions take us beyond the crises of authority into which the principle of scripture led us, even though the principle was supposed to protect us from such crises.

Dissent in the face of what the Bible says to us – this is the beginning for 'sola scriptura'. When differences of opinion arise in the church over truly fundamental, essential issues, they can only be resolved in a common listening to scripture, when everyone places themselves under *God's judgment* and together seeks to hear what is now being said to them in face of certain tasks, questions and uncertainties. For Christians, the Word of God is the final court of appeal on earth.[16] The court of appeal is not what Christians think or feel about God, nor their inner voice, which might have direct access to God. Nor is it the Church as God's earthly representative, as a spokesperson for Jesus Christ and the embodiment of God's Spirit. Thus *sola scriptura* proves to be an alternative to a final appeal to the Church (*sola ecclesia*), or to one's own conscience (*sola conscientia*), or to reason (*sola ratio*) and especially to one's own good feeling (*solus affectus*).

To emphasize the difference once again: the meaning of *sola scriptura* changes fundamentally if everything the church claims as valid has to be *derived* from biblical texts. In cases like this the Bible becomes a 'source'; but it is a source in an entirely different sense from the *sola scriptura* of the Reformation, where one, so to speak, searches with all one's might in the wilderness and in the quicksand of human differences of opinion for a source which yields the necessities of life. By contrast, something which is a source from which everything can be derived appears to be a reservoir of historical investigation from which one might draw, or a supply of truths on which one may fall back as needed, or an information desk that can be resorted to. If claim is laid to the Bible in this way, then it becomes a formal principle, an ecclesiastically sealed document of its own self-assertion, rather than the primary proclamation in which God addresses us.[17]

4 'It is written' – 'It is said to you'

No sentence in the Bible is actually a final court of appeal in and by itself, as if it were a matter of 'This is the way it is, just as it says.' Only in one place in the Bible is there an explicit appeal to the principle 'it is written': in the story of the temptation of Jesus (Matthew 4:1–13; Luke 4:1–13). Satan, the Bible expert, wants to lead Jesus astray at the beginning of his journey with an 'it is written'. Jesus retorted with words from the Bible. Looked at superficially, the scene seems to operate as an exchange of blows using biblical quotes – similar to a story told by Johannes Peter Hebel:

> A farmer met a schoolmaster in the field. 'Were you serious yesterday, schoolmaster, when you interpreted for the children the text, "If anyone strikes you on the right cheek, offer him the other as well"?' 'I can neither add to it nor subtract from it,' the schoolmaster replied, 'it is in the Gospel.' Then the farmer slapped the schoolmaster on one cheek, and then the other, for the teacher had annoyed him for a long time. While this was taking place a nobleman and his hunter rode by at a distance. The nobleman said to the hunter, 'Joseph, go and see what those two over there are up to.' As Joseph approached, the schoolmaster, a strong man, struck the farmer twice and said, 'It is also written, "With whatever measure you measure, you too will be measured. A packed down and overflowing measure will be thrown in your lap."' Along with this last verse the schoolmaster added a half dozen slaps more. Then Joseph returned to his lord and said, 'It's nothing, my Lord, *they are merely interpreting scripture to each other.*'[18]

Boxing with words naturally has nothing to do with the principle of conflict which says 'scripture alone!' That those arguing continue to refer to the Gospel only increases the irony of the punchline.

In the temptation narrative the devil puts Jesus to the test by enticing him to reveal what it is that he lives on, puts his trust in and shelters under. Jesus accepts the challenge by appealing three times to the words of the Torah. He does this precisely in order to testify that he desires to obey the explicit will of God. At one point the tempter also cites a scriptural word, a psalm, which he assumes offers the promise that God can be pressed into service. By his own use of scripture, the tempter calls into question whether the word of scripture is *God's* explicit will. He whispers that scripture might be a magical trick, which will help solve all life's problems, or might in the end be the most subtle instrument of domination. By offering the tempter other words from scripture, Jesus is not trying to outdo him with a greater quantity of quotations or more convincing ones. Rather, he counters Satan's attack with scripture in order that the 'it is written' could be heard as 'it is said to you, said by God, and therefore it desires only to lead us to God'. With this the text unexpectedly changes into a word which addresses and beckons. It is a sign of the devil when one wants to make scripture into an instrument. Used as a weapon it can only be deadly. But in the mouth of Jesus the word of scripture shows how alive it is, because it is heard as God's address to us. It is here that the *'perspicuitas'* of scripture appears – its clarity, which lets us behold God who now takes hold of the word. Jesus does not seek to demonstrate that he has the right biblical word at his fingertips. His use of scripture is itself worship of God.

5 Search the Scriptures: Encounter the True God

Why do we search the scriptures? Why do we read the Bible at all? Indeed, why do we not just turn to it now and then, when we need some information, or perhaps even instruction, in order to put pressure on those who are not of our own 'Bible-believing' persuasion? Searching in scripture is not just looking up quotes to reinforce opinions and prior knowledge, or using it as a book of oracles. Whoever really searches in scripture hopes that, in the process of searching, God will make God's self audible.

Years ago an engaged couple came to me. They wanted their wedding text to be, 'Do justice and fear no one.' That is unquestionably an appealing saying, but it does not occur anywhere in the Bible. Was it out of the question then to use it for the wedding ceremony? I could have found a way out by suggesting a Bible verse which sounds similar, something like Deuteronomy 6:18, 'Do what is right and good in the sight of the Lord, so that it may go well with you.' Yet when I asked about the reasons for their selection of that particular saying, it soon became clear that the betrothed wanted to hear a wise rule of life – this motto of sincerity – endorsed just once in a solemn setting. They wanted to use this rule to bind their relationship with each other. They wanted to promise each other that neither would do anything which would have to be hidden from the other.

What can be said against that? Nothing, except of course the kind of confidence that would have to be placed in such a promise! This couple were trying to base their confidence on their constancy, their own and that of the other. This is what they hoped for, continually to remain true to each other. On the other hand, the Old Testament commandment, however much it wants to impress similar behaviour upon us, places what is right and good under the direction and promise of God. What people promise each other as a result rests upon God's promise of faithfulness. In God's promise, human promises of faithfulness find their support, and in this alone their future is rooted.

The couple might have selected the Old Testament verse, 'Do what is right and good in the sight of the Lord' instead of their slogan for a confident lifestyle, 'Do justice and fear no one!' But then it is possible that they would still have understood the Bible verse in exactly the same way, as a rule of life. The crucial difference between the two sentences would then have become clear; when all is said and done, one can never 'select' God's command.

Those who 'choose' God's word *profess* that they are addressed by it in an incomparable way. With this profession they want to confirm what they have already heard in other ways and therefore 'know', but now they let it be promised to them anew. In this way they place themselves under the Bible and stay united with it (even if they do not actually express themselves like this) because they want to listen to it. In contrast with much selective listening, not to mention selective exhortation, one must be prepared for surprises if one appeals to the Bible. Thus placing oneself under the Bible does not just mean to stay put, to persevere by oneself. Those who expect to hear requirements for living in the Bible will also experience their endeavours as being reliable and as keeping faith, encircled as they are by God's promise of faithfulness.

The Bible as a whole is news of God's faithfulness. The Old Testament tells of God's faithfulness to God's creation and God's people, who are elected as a promise of blessing for all humankind. God's faithfulness asserts itself time and again against human unfaithfulness, against expectations which falsely understand God's promises because people do not open themselves to God's action but misuse God's promises in order to arrange their lives for their own comfort. In the midst of this human opposition, God expresses his faithfulness. The New Testament testifies similarly to God's faithfulness in the person of Jesus Christ, who secures every promise of God (2 Corinthians 1:20) with his death and his life. At the same time this life expresses how, against expectations, even against every hope, people can experience God's faithfulness. In fact they resist God's faithfulness because they think they already know what to expect from good and evil, and this kind of resistance takes place not least in an appeal to 'the law and the prophets'. Here the words of scripture have to be interpreted with a very wide scope, and their relation to everyday reality has to be explored extremely carefully because, from this point of view, there is no situation in life which has not already been summed up by scripture. But in this process the sense of a living claim of God upon us can wither away. Because God demands nothing from the people of God without already taking responsibility for it, God issues his command in order to draw people into the divine promise of faithfulness.

Jesus' use of scripture makes us attentive to this. His words 'But I say unto you' (Matthew 5:22, 27, 32, 34, 39, 44) strongly oppose the idea that this or that disturbed relationship of life can be put in order, or that even some unacceptable behaviour can be avoided, with a mere 'it is written'. Jesus Christ has the authority to promise a new, immeasurable and unlimited action of God. The words of Scripture are transparent to this unexpected evidence of faithfulness, and this changes their effects. Those who lock up God's call into an obedience to regulations hold the word of God captive, and go behind scripture, withdrawing trust in God.

That is why the expression, 'scriptural faithfulness', has a double ring. In the first place it is the faithfulness *of scripture itself* in which we trust. Scripture's quality does not depend on *our* faithfulness, as might be implied – a truly appalling thought! – when someone describes himself or herself as 'Scripture-faithful', equivalent to the ominous expression 'bible-based'. Yet, in second place, *we* can remain faithful on the basis of the faithfulness of scripture, not only in encountering the Bible from our side, but in a reciprocal listening to 'what is said to you'. The faithfulness we experience makes our faithfulness possible.

Faithfulness is a word for the relationship between persons. When we behave faithfully we show that we rely on the faithfulness of others and others can rely on us. Several things belong to such faithfulness: listening to one another, not cutting the other short or interrupting, but letting each other finish speaking in a way that will reveal our identity. These courtesies also apply to our relationship to the Bible. The Bible witnesses to God's faithfulness, and it does this precisely so that we can put our faith in God. As Michael Beintker aptly comments:

> Faithfulness towards the biblical texts remains because of the basic understanding that, in view of God's relation to us, things really are how the texts themselves try to attest, despite their human brokenness. It is salutary for us to allow their testimony of faithfulness to speak to us. Faithfulness towards scriptural texts thus implies an expectation which is not deterred by ambiguity, or even textual silence. It is an expectation that through the texts we are led to the knowledge and experience of the faithfulness of God, that here there are hidden competencies not at our disposal, indeed that their witness which refers to God's faithfulness is always stronger than their undisputed capacity for error.[19]

6 The Horizon of Expectation in Reading the Bible

'Scriptural faithfulness' in this double sense – faithfulness *of* Scripture and faithfulness *to* Scripture – is the inner foundation of the biblical canon. With this a 'line of sight' has come into being, which allows us to perceive the living nature of scripture together with the horizon of expectation which constitutes it. The horizon of expectation in the Christian canon is the perception of the presence of God and the expectation of Christ in the Spirit.

This horizon distinguishes between a faithfulness which would merely preserve the canon of scripture and place it under its protection, and the actual faithfulness of God by which scripture lives, and with it all its hearers and readers.

It will help to elucidate the boundaries of this 'line of sight' if we remark that it would be something entirely different to look for an organizing principle which holds together the collection of texts which have been assembled into the Bible. Historical research seeks indeed to reconstruct such a principle from the criteria which were authoritative for the emergence of the canon. For the selection and demarcation of the various writings, the authority of the canon's authors was decisive, namely their temporal and especially their personal proximity to the original Christ event. It was this proximity that was thought to establish the authenticity of their testimony. But as important as all this may have been for the formation of the tradition, did not the ecclesial recognition of the texts as canonical scripture stand side-by-side with the process of clarification of the understanding of scripture? The process of canon formation, and above all the inner unity of the canon, can only be understood theologically as part of this complexity.

After historical scholarship demonstrated that the criteria for the early church's formation of the canon were fragile, it attempted to define the mass of texts called 'the Bible' by searching for a 'centre of scripture' or a 'canon within the canon'. Individual texts were classified hierarchically in relation to a centre so that their closeness to or remoteness from the 'essential' could be measured, and so that matters of criticism with regard to deviations could be pursued. But is not all this just a strenuous effort to keep faith with something which people had critically determined beforehand?

On the other hand, scriptural faithfulness takes account of the fact that the Church confirmed, in the process of canon formation, what had been impressed upon it: God's faithfulness, disclosed in a *wide variety of perspectives of expectation* in the Scriptures. These perspectives may neither be traced back to one another nor be modelled on one another. They engage with each other in such a way that perception never comes to an end, and is not reducible to a mere sequence of thought.[20] The textual plane contains several vanishing points which draw attention to themselves in such a way that the view is repeatedly directed anew towards other texts, yet without losing the unity of the whole. Consistency and openness here are not mutually exclusive; the perception is neither arbitrary nor fully traced out. Hans Urs von Balthasar, for example, in view of the 'four-fold form of the Gospel', inquires whether the 'unique, divine plasticity of the living, incarnate Word' could be otherwise attested 'than through this system of perspectives which, although it cannot be further synthesized, compensates for this by offering a stereoscopic vista'.[21]

7 Aids for Preserving Faithfulness

Our faithfulness to scripture is dependent upon a mixture of consistency and openness which emerges from the biblical texts. Therefore there is a need for reliable aids, such as are provided by scripture itself. These are rules, bound up with fundamental distinctions, which will enable us to perceive each biblical text as it was intended to be heard. These rules help us not to cut the texts short, not to 'harmonize' them arbitrarily, and so to use them appropriately.

There are three theologically shaped, doctrinal distinctions which build a structure for perception of a biblical text. These prescribe no exegetical outcomes. They are prepared by biblical insights with which the Bible interprets itself. They are rules for dialogue which assist towards a reading which opens the reader for the structure and perspectives of the text. These distinctions can encourage no interpretation which is supposedly greater than that which the texts themselves freely offer,[22] and by which one might read the text any differently, any more deeply or with any greater consequence.

The first distinction, between *spirit* and *letter*, is the oldest in the history of biblical understanding in the Christian Church, and has a really extravagant story.[23] Origen took two ideas from it. In the first place, and above all, the art of Bible reading is a spiritual perception[24] requiring prayer.[25] His second idea was fraught with implications for the history of biblical interpretation, and had consequences which were highly problematic: 'spirit' was conceived as a human capacity, as a divinely imparted intellectual/spiritual sense which is open to the 'upper world' as this has entered the world through Jesus Christ and now fills it. This anthropological allocation is problematic because it gives the appearance that the 'spirit' does not belong to all Christians, but only to the elect. This leads the Church to make a sociological demarcation of the 'spiritually gifted' from all others. Despite this misleading, special doctrine of Origen, however, the distinction between spirit and letter helped the early church to read the holy scriptures of the Jews as a Christian book. God's Spirit had preceded the law which shaped Jewish history; it is the Spirit which reveals the logical and temporal first sense of each text.[26]

The distinction between letter and spirit goes back to a passage from 2 Corinthians 3, where Paul stresses, in verses 4 and 5, that 'We preach not ourselves, but Jesus Christ.' This is then worked out in a very condensed and tangled discussion about the Torah and its reception by the Jewish faithful. The key sentence reads, 'For the letter (*gramma*) kills, but the Spirit gives life' (3:6). This does not mean, as so often misunderstood, a 'dead letter' in contrast to a living spirit: that would be something written down in which life has been deposited, in which meaning – so to speak – lies buried until our intellectual capacity can raise it up. This is not at all what Paul means, as Augustine makes clear in his essay *De spiritu et littera* (IV:6–V:8). Here 'letter' means the will of God expressed in the law of Sinai. People hide behind this law. In the presence of God they pull back into themselves, paradoxically in their very attempt to penetrate the law, and in so doing they are quite unwillingly but inevitably destroyed by the law. Totally different is Christ, the Spirit, who makes alive and liberates, whom we face standing upright: 'Now the Lord is the Spirit, and where the Spirit of the Lord is, there is freedom' (3:17). He is the living form of the will of God and in him God meets us in God's freedom – in such a direct way that we need not hide.

The distinction between letter and spirit refers to *God's freedom in his speaking*. God is not free, of course, with regard to what God *has* spoken. God communicates the divine freedom to us and breaks open the walls we have built around ourselves, opening us up to listen to God's own self. In this respect the distinction between letter and spirit should guide every reading of the Bible. It should draw attention to the fact that we only hear and interpret rightly when we hope that *God will break us open for God's own self.*

The second distinction, between *law* and *gospel,* connects with the first and seeks in a particular respect to make it more precise without either superseding or completely replacing it. As a theological (not literary-critical) distinction, it does not seek to separate two sorts of texts from each other, that is regulations and words of comfort. It implies rather that *every biblical word can encounter us either as law or as gospel.* In this sense Martin Luther repeatedly called the distinction between law and gospel an art – and it is worth noting in what way he deemed this art to be both indispensable and impossible to achieve.

In a sermon on Galatians 3:23–29 dated 1 January 1532, Luther calls this distinction 'the highest knowledge (*maxima scientia*) in Christendom, an art with which we should be acquainted'.[27]

> Therefore advance whoever is really good at this art and call him Doctor of Holy Scripture, for without the Holy Spirit this distinction cannot be discerned. I experience in myself and observe daily in others how difficult it is. The Holy Spirit belongs to this distinction.[28]

Luther understood law – corresponding to the 'letter that kills' – as God's word of judgment, gospel as God's word of grace. Why are the two so hard to distinguish? It would be much easier if one could count on a 'principle', a starting point for all that follows. Accordingly, Luther's favourite sequence has often been conceived along the following lines: first we are wrecked on God's wrath, and then God's grace helps us up. However, the sequence of 'law and gospel' really means that in no case, and under no circumstances – not even in the face of terrible experiences – can we reverse God's will; that is, we cannot act as though God's revelation of God's own righteousness in the gospel were not God's *final* word.

This sequence must not be be transposed into the scheme, 'first wrecked, then helped'. Nor can we construct the opposite scheme, 'first consolation and then demand', or (certainly not) 'first faith, then morals'. We cannot make a dramatic plot out of the distinction between law and gospel. No one can say that one text is God's word of judgment, and another is God's word of grace.

Law is God's sentence of judgment and gospel is God's sentence of salvation. Both may come upon us with the same word, for one person this way, for another person another way, or for the same person in one way one moment, in another way the next. We can neither determine nor codetermine how or when a text will be law or gospel. What we can 'know', however, is that God is judge *and* saviour. Those who know the difference between God's judging and saving action – and how else can they know it but through the Bible! – will be able to hear the demand of the law where the sound of the gospel prevails, if God so chooses. Or they will be able to hear the message of the gospel and proclaim it when God places demands on them and others. They will understand the one or the other in its time and place and accept it for themselves. As judge and saviour, God is one and the same, or to be exact it is possible that in the same word God takes a different role at different times with different persons.

The intent of this distinction is to prepare all who are ready *to hear the word of the Bible as God's sentence, to expose themselves to the living action of God and to entrust themselves to this action.* They should be ready for these things, no more and no less.

Both of the theological distinctions identified above prepare us to answer the question, 'Who is the God about whom we read in the Bible?' God meets us as personal in God's freedom (spirit and letter) and in God's sentencing (law and gospel). That is why it is out of the question to derive one of these distinctions from the other. That would merely encourage a schematization of interpretation, and unfortunately the history of reception of the Bible provides more than enough examples of that!

The third distinction, *promise* and *fulfilment*, is especially liable to this danger. It deals with the fact that God promises future action, along with God's future, and even God's own self. Who but God could do that? 'The Word of the Lord is truthful, and what he promises he certainly keeps' (Ps. 33:4 in the Luther translation). 'For HIS speech is upright, all he does is in faithfulness' (Martin Buber).[29] In speaking, God opens up an expanse of time in which God acts, and so makes it possible for those whom God addresses to make sense of events as history. Whatever happens is discerned with expectant mindfulness of the promise.

The time–space conception of 'history', however, is especially susceptible to schematization. In an effort to review contexts of events and categorize them for the purposes of historical understanding, persons place themselves in time. They do this by distinguishing everything they can 'already' look back upon, from what is 'yet' to come. Such an attempt at classification has also repeatedly been claimed for scriptural interpretation. Above all, it appears suggestive for the relation between 'the law and the prophets' on the one hand, and 'gospel and apostolic message' on the other. The so-called 'salvation history' theology, of whatever shade, is built upon such a schematization. It divides the Bible into an expectation section and a fulfilment section which are interlinked by a wealth of cross-references. Their interrelational richness allows an access to be found to all the information which is important for faith. Johann Albrecht Bengel presents it this way: 'Holy Scripture in itself is a *systema historico-dogmaticum*, a *Lägerbuch* of God's people in the Old and New Testaments from the beginning of the world until its end.'[30] A *'Lägerbuch'* in Swabian linguistic usage is the 'list of all land holdings of a town or region together with their legal standing'. It might therefore be translated as meaning 'the sum of everything worth knowing'.[31] As bookkeepers, theologians can indicate how far this history has run, and what is yet to come.

In this process the promise of God is transformed into an announcement of future events. Correspondingly, 'fulfilment' means that it is possible to ascertain that this prediction has come true. 'Promise' and 'fulfilment' are then divided into two sorts of textual groups which appear to be contrasted with each other in the course of history.

The theological distinction relates, however, to God's speaking and acting which cannot be separated cleanly from each other. *By fulfilling what God has promised, God displays His promise.* Promise and fulfilment form a unity, and this is why we cannot disassemble them. God does not wait for what God says to come true. God acts *in His own way* to fulfil what God promises. Therefore 'fulfilment' does not mean the filling of a void, but the penetration of all things by the uncreated fullness of God. God keeps what God promises – in just the way that *God Himself* promises. God often fulfils his promise differently from the way we expect. Fulfilment does not mean that God checks something off (perhaps a segment of history) and leaves it behind with the stamp of 'finished' on it. Promise continues to endure as God's pledge for fulfilment. It does not subsist as a kind of remainder which is still unsettled.

The story of Christ is the quintessential paradigm for the richly diverse unity of promise and fulfilment. In Jesus Christ, God confirms the divine promise in such a way that people, in communion with Christ, may hope in God, may expect God anew and may expect something new from God. We can only believe as those who hope. *To read a biblical text as promise means, therefore, to hear it as God's promise of faithfulness.* Thus we become aware that God's faithfulness is not merely a cheque to be paid in the future; God has already spoken the divine 'Yes' here and now and we can cling to that 'Yes'. 'Scripture gives us the divine promise and because of that we hang fast to it,' wrote Adolf Schlatter, who was referred to at the beginning of this chapter.[32] That is why he said he 'stood under the Bible'. In this regard the third distinction to be observed in reading the Bible carries the reading of Scripture to a special level, without cancelling out the other two. Only as they are kept in mutual movement can they work together, increasingly opening up new and surprising perspectives, and in this way all proving to be signs of scriptural faithfulness.

Notes

This chapter was translated by Sarah Mount, B. Maurice Ritchie and Paul S. Fiddes.

1 Adolf Schlatter, *Rückblick auf seine Lebensarbeit* (Gütersloh: Carl Bertelsmann, 1952), p.132.

2 See Carl Heinz Ratschow, *Lutherische Dogmatik zwischen Reformation und Aufklärung*, I, (Gütersloh: Carl Bertelsmann, 1964), pp.71–6. In his *Compendium theologiae*; *De sacrosancta scriptura* (1573; Leipzig, 1587), p.1, Jacob Heerbrand called the Holy Scripture the 'universal and indestructible beginning, origin and foundation of all theology' (*commune et irrefragabile principium, origo et fundamentum totius theologiae*). Johann Friedrich König, in *Theologia positiva acroamatica*, 1664 (Rostock, 1699), p.79, relates the doctrinal statements of the Bible to the principle of knowing, out of which all theological assertions are in the first place derived and in which these assertions are finally resolved (*e quo omnia in theologia primo deducuntur, et in quod ultimo resolvuntur*). Insofar as they are inspired, they are infallible (*quidquid scriptura sacra docet, divinitus inspiratum adeoquo infallibiliter verum est*). But what human person can determine that? Who is capable of distinguishing the doctrinal assertions of the Bible from the rest of the text? The reference to the inspiration of biblical teaching is subject to a reservation which aims to avoid pronouncing the entire biblical text as inspired and thus infallible. The Calvinist, Johannes Wolleb, in *Christianae theologiae compendium* (Basle, 1626), p.3, appealed to Scripture, the Word of God, as a 'principle of the Christian religion' and applied to it the rule of all scientific discourse, that one who denies the principles is not worth arguing with (*contra negantem principia non disputatur*).

3 See, for example, Georg Calixt, *Epitome Theologiae*, 1619, in Inge Mager (ed.) *Dogmatische Schriften*, (Göttingen: Vandenhoek and Ruprecht, 1982) pp.97–9. Granted the fundamental difference between 'faith' and 'knowledge', the one established by divine authority, the other by common sense, still they are both ways of thinking that precede from one principle which is their unconditioned presupposition.

4 August Detlev Christian Twesten, *Vorlesungen über die Dogmatik der Evangelisch-Lutherischen Kirche according to the Compendium of Dr. W.M.L. de Wette*, I, 2nd edn (Hamburg, 1829), p.282.

5 When on the other hand the beginning of the Formula of Concord (1580) says the 'prophetic and apostolic writings of the Old and New Testaments are the only rule and measure, by which all doctrines and teachers may be judged' (*Epitome, On the Summary Concept, Rule and Norm*), this is more than a different nuance. This does not go back to the earliest beginnings in order to measure everything later by that and to judge it atrophied and degraded. The Bible is rather meant to be the touchstone which separates true doctrine from false.

6 Twesten, pp.280f.

7 This is why Martin Luther takes both together: God's justification in his speaking and our justification. Compare his *Lectures on Romans* (1515–16) 3:24 WA 56, Weimar: H. Böhlau, 1928, 213,13f. '*Sic etiam iustificatio Dei in sermonibus suis potius nostri est iustificatio; et iudicatio sive condemnatio eius nostri potius est.*' 'Thus also the justification of God in His words is actually our justification; and the judgement or condemnation of Him actually comes upon us.' (American edition, vol. 25, ed. H. Oswald, St. Louis: Concordia, 1972, p.198.)

8 *De servo arbitrio* (1525), WA 18, 653, pp.33–5: '*cogimur primum probare illud ipsum primum principium nostrum, quo omnia alia probanda sunt, quod apud philosophos absurdum et impossibile factu videretur*'. (*On the Bondage of the Will*: 'We are obliged to begin by proving even that first principle of ours by which everything else has to be proved – a procedure that among the philosophers would be regarded as absurd and impossible' (*Library of Christian Classics*, Vol. 17, *Luther and Erasmus*, ed. P.S.N. Watson and B. Drewey, London: SCM, 1969, p.159).)

9 Compare, for example, Immanuel Kant, *The Conflict of the Faculties* (1798), Engl. trans. (Lincoln, Nebraska: University of Nebraska Press, 1979), p.63: 'The biblical theologian says, "Search in the scriptures, where you think you find eternal life." But since moral improvement is the sole condition of eternal life, the only way we can find eternal life in any Scripture whatsoever is by putting it there. For the concepts and principles required for eternal life cannot really be learned from anyone else: the teacher's exposition is only the occasion for him to develop them out of his own reason' (cf. Kant, *Werke*, VI, ed. Wilhelm Weischedel, Darmstadt: Wissenschaftliche Buchgesellschaft, 1964, pp.301f).

10 For example, The Bern Theses (1528): 1. The holy Christian church, of which Christ is the only head, is born of the word of God, remains in it and does not hear the voice of a stranger. 2. The church of Christ does not create laws and commandments over and above the word of God. For this reason no human laws (as we take church laws to be) any longer bind us, unless they are grounded and commanded in the divine word.

11 See the *Handreichung für Mitglieder der Landessynode, der Kreissynoden und der Presbyterien in der Evangelischen Kirche im Rheinland (Instructions for members of the Regional Synod, the District Synods and the Presbyteries in the German Protestant Church in the Rhineland)*, no. 44. Austeilung von Traubensaft beim Abendmahl in Ausnahmefällen (Distribution of Grapejuice at Holy Communion in special cases) (Düsseldorf: Archiv der evangelischen Kirche im Rheinland 1988).

12 Ibid., p.7.

13 'Answer to the hyperchristian, hyperspiritual and hyperlearned book by Goat Emser in Leipzig', *WA* 7, especially pp.632, 637, 639, 640 and 666 (American edition, vol. 39, ed. E.W. Gritsch (Philadelphia: Fortress Press, 1970), pp.143–224).

14 *WA* 7, 632, 26f: 'you shall not prove the first thing from what comes after; neither must you make a *petitio principii*' (which begs the question).

15 Martin Luther, *Assertio omnium articulorum* (1520) *WA* 7, 97, 24f. (*sui ipsius interpres*). Not contained in the American edition.

16 For this reason the Formula Book of Concord (1580) names the Holy Scripture as the only 'judge, rule and guiding principle' because according to scripture 'all doctrines are recognized and judged if they are good or evil, right or wrong' (*Epitome. On the Summary Concept, Rule and Norm*). The lengthy and laborious building of consensus, which was brought to an end with the Formula of Concord, is itself an important example of the use of scripture to achieve consensus.

17 Cf. Martin Kähler's discussion of his statement that the Bible 'contains the foundational story of the church', and his formulation that the Bible as a whole is 'documentation for the performance of the sermon as founding the church': *The So-called Historical Jesus and the Historic Biblical Christ,* Engl. trans. (Philadelphia: Fortress Press, 1964), pp.49, 128; cf. 136.

18 Johann Peter Hebel, *Schwänke aus dem Rheinländischen Hausfreund* (*Comic tales from a Rheinlandish friend of the family*), I Teil (Stuttgart, 1839; reprinted Dortmund, 1979), pp.87f.

19 Michael Beintker, *Anmerkungen zur Kategorie der Texttreue* (*Comments about the Category of Faithfulness to the Text*) in *Sola Scriptura*, ed. Hans Heinrich Schmid und Joachim Mehlhausen (Gütersloh: Carl Bertelsmann, 1991), pp.281–91. This quotation is found on p.283.

20 Rowan Williams points to this in 'The Literal Sense of Scripture', *Modern Theology*, 7, (2), 1991, 121–34.

21 Hans Urs von Balthasar, *The Glory of the Lord*, Vol. I, *Seeing the Form* (1961), Engl. trans. (Edinburgh: T.&T. Clark, 1982; San Francisco: Ignatius Press), p.32.

22 This is how, in my opinion, the *sensus literalis* of scripture is to be understood.

23 An outline is contained in Gerhard Ebeling's article, 'Geist und Buchstabe', in *Religion in Geschichte und Gegenwart* (RGG) 3rd edn, II (Tübingen: J.C.B. Mohr, 1958), pp.1290–96.

24 Compare Origen, *De principiis*, I 1:9; IV 4:10. (*On First Principles*, ed. G.W. Butterworth, London: SPCK, 1936, pp.14, 327f.)

25 Origen, *Epistula ad Gregorium*, 3 (PG 11:92A).

26 On this, see Heinrich Karpp's article, 'Bible' IV, in *Theologische Realenzyklopedie* (TRE), 6 (Berlin/New York: Walter de Gruyter, 1980), pp.48–93. The quotation here is from p.53. See also his *Schrift, Geist und Wort Gottes. Geltung und Wirkung der Bibel in der Geschichte der Kirche – von der Alten Kirche bis zum Ausgang der Reformationszeit* (Darmstadt: Wissenschaftliche Buchgesellschaft, 1992), pp.11f.

27 Luther, *WA* 36, 8–42. This quotation is from 9.28f. (Not in the American edition.)

28 Luther, *WA* 36, 13, 22–6. (Not in the American edition.)

29 Martin Buber, *Das Buch der Preisungen* (Cologne/Olten: 1963), p.51.

30 Quoted from Johann Albrecht Bengel. See O. Wächter, *Lebensabriß, Character, Briefe und Aussprüche. Nach handschriftlichen Mittheilungen* (Stuttgart, 1865), p.144.

31 Martin Brecht, 'Johann Albrecht Bengels Theologie der Schrift,' *ZThK*, 64 (1967), pp.99–120.

32 A. Schlatter, *Hülfe in Bibelnot*, 2nd edn (Verbert: Freizeiten-Verlag, 1928), p.19.

Two

Story and Possibility: Reflections on the Last Scenes of the Fourth Gospel and Shakespeare's *The Tempest*

Paul S. Fiddes

1 Two Final Scenes

As Shakespeare's play, *The Tempest*, comes to its close, Prospero has been restored to his sovereignty as rightful Duke of Milan. He had been betrayed, rejected, cast out of the city and left to die on the high seas. But now on the island which he rules by his magic arts his enemies and his friends have met him again when they thought he was dead. They have recognized him, and he has forgiven those who had wronged him. As the curtain falls on the brightly-lit stage, he is about to set out on his future life, to return by sea to Milan and reign as lord in his own country. Shakespeare appears to have brought his play to a satisfactory end. We are preparing to clap and make a dash for the exit, to leave the theatre behind to catch a train or find the car. The play is over. Everyday life has begun again.

But at this point Shakespeare springs a surprise on us. Prospero turns away from the other characters on the stage and comes forward to address us, the audience. At first we adjust easily to the unexpected. No doubt the actor is going to employ the Elizabethan stage convention of asking for applause; it is going to be a case of 'Once I was a wealthy Duke, but now I am just a poor actor asking for your approval.' But Shakespeare continues to shock us. Prospero remains in his own character; he asks for our applause as a kind of prayer to release him from the island and speed him on his voyage to Naples and Milan:

> Gentle breath of yours my sails
> Must fill, or else my project fails …

He has abandoned his magic arts, broken his staff and drowned his book of spells fathoms deep, so that he is vulnerable 'unless I be reliev'd by prayer …'

Our applause is to be an expression of our willingness to forgive and show mercy, as he has already done to his enemies:

> As you from crimes would pardon'd be,
> Let your indulgence set me free.

The convention of asking the audience pardon for a faulty performance has merged with the need to live a life of forgiveness. The barriers between art and life are being broken down. We had thought that Prospero was safely locked away on the stage 'in a play', but with a shock we find that he is drawing us into the reality of his own story. We are being invited to participate in the next stage of the story, in the uncertainty of life beyond the charmed island. The drama has not finished after all, and we feel that it never will be.

So a master-craftsman challenges his audience. And in writing his gospel, I suggest that the Fourth Evangelist springs a similar surprise on his readers, or on those who hear the text read during worship. He has been portraying Jesus on the brightly-lit stage of the gospel story. Jesus has performed signs which have enabled the disciples to 'see' his glory. We have watched, we who are 'sitting in the darkened theatre of the future',[1] as Jesus has subsequently been betrayed, rejected, cast out of the city and left to die on the cross. His friends have met him again when they thought he was dead, and recognized him. He has given them his Spirit to enable them to pronounce forgiveness of sins, and he is about to embark on his reign as Lord over all. The congregation begins to reach for its hymn books or to prepare to leave for home to make Sunday lunch, when we discover with a shock that the story is not over. Jesus has turned away from the group of disciples gathered in a first-century house, and is now speaking to us, the disciples who are hearing the story today. He comes to the front of the stage and addresses the hearers of the word, beyond the time of the gospel drama, in years to come. He is giving us a special word of blessing:

> Happy are those who never saw me and yet have found faith. (John 20:29)

We find with a sense of surprise that the drama is still going on, and that we are being drawn into it.

I make this comparison between the last scenes of the Fourth Gospel and Shakespeare's play *The Tempest*, *not* to propose any idea of Prospero as a 'Christ figure'. No doubt there is some truth in typology, as Irenaeus saw it, as a 'recapitulation' in Christ of all typical human experiences of hope and despair. But this is not my concern, and anyway I suspect that this kind of literary exegesis runs the dangers of mere triviality. I have placed these two passages side by side because some similarities between them make them a convenient comparison for raising questions about the reader's relation to a story, and about the relevance of a concept of 'revelation' with regard to *both* canonical and non-canonical texts. I believe that *in principle* what is claimed for the relation between story and revelation must hold true for all literary texts, though I hope to show that this does not reduce scriptural interpretation to a mere subset of a general hermeneutic.

2 The Eschatological Character of Writing

All writing may be said to be eschatological, at least in the sense that it opens up meaning and so defers or postpones the finding of meaning to the future. As Jacques Derrida suggests, 'Wouldn't the apocalyptic be a transcendent condition of all discourse ... of every mark and every trace?'[2] When we categorize certain writings as eschatological, or we detect some eschatological aspect in them, we are thus registering that they are 'an exemplary revelation of this transcendent structure',[3] as they *explicitly* draw attention to a future unveiling of meaning and understanding. But if we only speak of *a postponement* of meaning, we might end up perpetually wandering through the maze of life with endless interpretations and no destination at all. To the scattering of meaning we must add that writing is also eschatological in opening up *possibilities* and so hope for the future. As Paul Ricoeur puts it,[4] the world of the text, or the sort of world the text 'unfolds before itself ... as its reference', expresses possibilities rather than actualities. The world to which the text refers is 'mimesis' of life only in the sense that writing creates as well as imitates; the text refers, not to what is, but to what might be. The world to which it refers is not the present world behind the text but a projected world in front of the text.

In this sense, both these pieces of writing we are considering are self-consciously eschatological. They draw the reader towards the future, with a promise that truth will be unveiled and that possibilities will be fulfilled, though only in order that the fulfilment may become further promise in its turn. In John 20, the blessing formula in the words of Jesus (v.29) alerts us to this orientation to the future, as it recalls the form of blessing used seven times for eschatological promise and warning in the Apocalypse of John.[5] The saying itself, addressed to future believers ('Blessed are those who have not seen and yet believe') makes clear that Thomas himself could have been the first member of the future generation of those who believe, not through seeing the signs Jesus performed, but through relying on *witness* to the signs. His faith could have been grounded in hearing the testimony of disciples who say, 'We have seen the Lord' (v.25), and so he could have been part of the audience of the text. But he insists on being among those who see for themselves and for this earns the rebuke of Jesus. The evangelist then ends his Gospel by inviting the readers to be among those who – unlike Thomas – do believe on the basis of the witness of his text to the signs of Jesus (v.31). Perhaps the reference to the 'many other signs' originally stood at the end of the 'Book of Signs' in chapter 12, as a means of transition to what is often called 'The Book of Glory'; but whether the evangelist has transferred it to this point or newly created it, the effect is to include the resurrection appearances of Jesus among the signs which witness to the glory of Christ. The term 'sign' thus acquires a 'striking elasticity',[6] which the addition of chapter 21 and the concluding comments of the redactor(s) in 21:24–5 are to widen further.

At the same time, this opening up of the idea of a sign reflects back on the nature of the signs recorded earlier. Rudolph Bultmann does not seem to be fair to the text when he finds an outright *opposition* between sign and belief. The relation between the sign and the word that leads to faith is more complex; the point is not that future believers should reject signs set up by Christ in history as irrelevant to faith (or even disregard them as being 'of only relative worth'[7]), but that they should be interpreted as pointers to the glory of Christ rather than as rational proofs. However, Bultmann has, I suggest, faithfully picked up a note of self-deconstruction in this chapter. It is striking that, no sooner has the Gospel recorded the resurrection appearances and included them in the notion of a sign, than we are told to believe on the basis of the witness of others and the proclaimed word rather than 'seeing'. While the event behind the text is not disparaged – it must be there for the text to represent it – there is at least a discouragement of direct reliance on the event itself, and encouragement to make the witness to it our own. The verbal signs in the text which represent the sign-event have become signs of glory in their turn, inviting our participation and so the reproduction of the content of the sign in our own lives in a multiplicity of ways. We will find out what resurrection appearances mean (what the signifiers signify) as we engage in the story and recognize the glory of Christ and the possibility of a glorified creation.

The impression we gain from chapter 20 is confirmed by the appending of chapter 21 and its concluding verses. The addition of a sequel (Jesus by the lakeside in Galilee) makes clear that the story is open and not closed; the 'many signs' invite expansion, normally by interpretation (see on v.25 below) but even, more daringly, by extension of the narrative ('After this Jesus appeared again to his disciples…'). Perhaps the occasion for this extension was the unexpected death of the Beloved Disciple (whose identity does not matter for our present purposes) and the crisis this caused in the early church community. The writer deals with this on the one hand by asserting that Jesus spoke of the Beloved Disciple's remaining to the parousia only as a hypothesis, and on the other by affirming that the disciple's witness remains despite his death (v.24). Indeed, the redactor is claiming that the Gospel is based on this witness. But this is tantamount to saying that the writer himself is a true witness; there is an overlapping of witnessing voices – the Beloved Disciple, the evangelist, the editor(s) – akin to the multiple witnesses at the beginning and end of the Apocalypse of John, in that case including Christ, angels, 'John', Christian prophets,[8] the Spirit and 'the Bride'. As R.E. Brown comments, 'The Johannine notion of true witness goes beyond an eye-witness report. ... it includes the adaptation of what happened so that its truth can be seen by and be significant for subsequent generations.'[9]

The theological justification for this expansive notion of witness lies in the concept of the Paraclete as supreme witness (15:26–7, 14:26), at work in disciples as well as in Jesus himself. Verse 25 extends this work to disciples of all ages, placing the readers in the succession of witness, called to internalize and represent the text of the Gospel in themselves. This, at least, I take to be the impact of what seems at first to be an exaggerated claim that, were all that Jesus did to be written down, 'the world itself could not contain the books that would be written'. There is an echo here of the earlier statement about the many unwritten signs Jesus performed (20:30), but we are now to read this renewed claim in the light of the repeated command of Jesus to Peter in the appended scene (vv.19, 22); disciples obey the injunction to 'follow me' by the imitation of Christ (vv.18–19), so that the life of the community is shaped by the story, and the representing of Christ is a matter of action (praxis) as well as reflection. Through the signs of the text the disciple is drawn into a following of Christ that leads to a limitless exploration of the glory of God in the face of Christ,[10] and the continual making of a new world with its own signs that challenge the actuality of the present.

As the original end of the Fourth Gospel invites sequels, so does the end of *The Tempest*. All writing, I have suggested, is eschatological, but certain writings make this explicit and thereby invite expansion of meaning and even of narrative. *The Tempest* has attracted commentary, not by professional critics alone, but by other creative artists who have wanted to add interpretation through verse and drama. Among many examples, Fletcher wrote two plays based on the world of Prospero (*The Prophetess* and *The Sea Voyage*, 1622), Milton used it for his masque, *Comus* (1634), Dryden and Davenant adapted the play in *The Enchanted Island* (1667), the minor dramatist F.G. Waldron provided an entire sequel called *The Virgin Queen* (1797) and W.H. Auden in our time created an extended verse meditation in which the major characters reflect on their natures and their destinies ('The

Sea and the Mirror'). While all these fill out the play itself with further insight and meaning, it is significant that several offer accounts of what happens 'after the island'. This is, no doubt, partly because Prospero is left at the end of the play poised to leave his island kingdom and to embark on the voyage back to resume his dukedom in Milan. As with any good story, the reader wants to know what happens next. But it is also because this play throws all conflict forward into the future, and so leaves us in an eschatological anxiety as well as expectation.

This forward projection of threat and tension comes from the fact that during the period of the play's action itself Prospero has complete mastery of what happens on the island, or at least control of all outward events. He is magician, dramatist and stage-manager in his island kingdom, and his visitors can do harm neither to him nor to each other as they could in Milan or Naples. By his magic arts, Prospero is inevitably going to foil all plots laid against him, and require his wicked brother Antonio to restore his dukedom to him. We are assured from the beginning that no external power can withstand him on the island since the first scene has shown us what is apparently a fearsome storm at sea, which we then discover to be a piece of theatre, a dramatic illusion directed by Prospero with the spirit Ariel as his stage-hand. Prospero is more in control of events than any character Shakespeare ever created. The conflict in this play that keeps our interest alive is not opposition that arises during the course of the action, but the betrayal in the past (in 'the dark backward and abysm of time'), and the threat that the future holds as Prospero renounces his magic arts and leaves the enchanted isle for daily life.

We feel the impact of this threat as Shakespeare evokes various hostile forces that are present on the island but which have no power at present over Prospero. There are, for example, the elemental forces of nature embodied in the resentment and the near-rebellion of Ariel; there is the power of evil which resists all the arts of civilization, and which is embodied equally in the primitive Caliban and the sophisticated Antonio; there is the onset of time and death which evil places a sting within and makes destructive of the energies of life. This last is brought strongly to our attention at a moment when Prospero appears to be disturbed by remembering Caliban's plot against him. He breaks up a pageant he has just been presenting for the entertainment of Miranda and Ferdinand (on the theme of fertility!), a little piece of singing and dancing whose actors were spirits of the air. He offers some consolation to Ferdinand for this interrupted performance:

> ... be cheerful, sir.
> Our revels now are ended. These our actors,
> As I foretold you, were all spirits, and

Are melted into air, into thin air:
And, like the baseless fabric of this vision,
The cloud-capp'd towers, the gorgeous palaces,
The solemn temples, the great globe itself,
Yea, all which it inherit, shall dissolve,
And, like this insubstantial pageant faded,
Leave not a rack behind. We are such stuff
As dreams are made on; and our little life
Is rounded with a sleep. (IV.1.147–58)

There is a multi-layer reality about this speech. The revels that 'now are ended' or, as Prospero warns, will end, are fivefold: first, they are the little pageant which Prospero has just presented for the lovers; second, they are the events on the island which Prospero has also stage-managed to bring about the reconciliation he wants; third, the revels are the play of *The Tempest* itself, and here the play-writer speaks with Prospero; fourth, they are the end of a person's life, which will surely come to all of us: 'we are such stuff as dreams are made on'; and fifth, the revels are the whole world, 'the great globe itself' which will dissolve on the day of judgment. As Prospero speaks, he is not really worried about Caliban's trumpery plot against him; this is not the cause that puts him into a passion and 'works him strongly'. His anxiety derives from what *will* happen when his island kingdom comes to an end, when he has abjured his magic arts and returned to Milan. Then he will be truly exposed to such hazards as the plot of Caliban points to. Conflict awaits *in the future* from the forces of nature and the evil in the human heart, and the enemies of time and death ('all which it inherit shall dissolve') make evil even harder to deal and bear with. Prospero brings the pageant of the spirits to an end as a sign that he will break his magic staff and drown his book of spells. The magic arts are symbolic for all the human arts, which have their limits, as life itself has the limit of death.

The conflict is thrown into the future, and we as the audience are drawn into sharing it. We have seen how at the end Prospero engages us by inviting us to participate in his voyage to Naples and Milan. This breaking down of the boundary between art and life has already been prepared for in Prospero's great speech about the ending of the revels. For the image of the island runs through its various levels of meaning. Prospero is about to leave his island theatre, but we ourselves are about to leave the theatre where we have been watching the play, an island of light and music, and go out into the dark streets. We go to continue our daily life which is itself a kind of island set in the sea of the unconscious ('our little life is rounded with [surrounded by] a sleep').[11] As the characters in the play come out of the sea onto the island and then at the end enter the sea again ('sea-swallowed'), so our life is a dream surrounded by a sea of sleep ('We are such stuff/ as dreams are made on'). The dream of the island ('when I wak'd/ I cried to dream again'), the dream of the play and the dream of life merge into one focus. The result is that we are drawn into participation in the eschatological conflict that Prospero faces.

The text opens up a possible world. It promises a world in which there is not only the threat of evil but the healing power of forgiveness, and in which neither are amenable to control by the arts. For all his power, Prospero has only been able to arrange outward circumstances; he cannot manipulate the human heart. He can encourage, but not coerce Miranda and Ferdinand to fall in love. When those who have wronged him are powerless before him he offers forgiveness rather than revenge, but Antonio remains silent in the face of this offer, declining to choose the good. The modern poet W.H. Auden makes him speak thus:[12]

> Your all is partial, Prospero,
> My will is all my own:
> Your need to love will never know
> Me: I am I, Antonio,
> By choice myself alone.

Through the experience of this play we come to see that, even if a man might control nature and his own passions, he could not force love and forgiveness upon other persons. These remain 'a most high miracle', as Sebastian exclaims on seeing Ferdinand and Miranda together. In the four hours space of the play Prospero uses the dramatic skills of his spirits, music, sleep and enchantment in order to give his enemies space and opportunity to learn repentance. Alonso does repent his part in the supplanting of Prospero; he restores his dukedom, receives his son Ferdinand back from the dead and gains a daughter in Miranda:

> I am hers:
> But, O, how oddly will it sound that I
> Must ask my child forgiveness.

Prospero had played at being god on the island. But he cannot arrange repentance and love. When he resigns the role of God he is only making clear what has been true all along. He never did have control at the deepest level of human life. A future world is promised in which forgiveness and love will overcome the threat of evil, and we are invited to participate in making this world ('as you yourselves would pardoned be ...'). But it must be promised and not planned or predicted; there is something open about the future which belongs to the freedom of human personality. We can understand why the rather minor dramatist Waldron wrote his sequel to the play (*The Virgin Queen*) in which Antonio and Caliban conspire to kill Prospero on the voyage home to Milan, and Prospero consequently retrieves his book from fathoms deep in the ocean and mends his broken magic staff! This catches the openness of the future, but not the vulnerability of human life which is expressed by Prospero's abandoning of book and staff. As we leave the theatre and the revels are ended, these can never be retrieved. But we are invited to face the dark unknown with forgiveness in our hearts.

I have placed an exegesis of the ends of the Fourth Gospel and *The Tempest* side by side, but not to claim that there are strong parallels in their content. In the first we are drawn into an ongoing *witness* in order to reproduce the signs of Jesus; in the second we are drawn into an ongoing *dream* in order to engage in the conflict of life. Despite the common thread of the possibilities that forgiveness brings (see John 20:23), there are profound differences here. But we *can* see that the effect of all stories is to draw the reader in to make new meaning which does not yet exist, and to make a world of new possibility in which the subject–object split of Antonio and the world around ('I am I') is overcome. Our two texts are eschatological in that they make explicit what is true of any story. Thus any declaration about the part revelation plays in this disclosure of a new world cannot ignore the fact that the phenomenon happens in non-scriptural texts. Shakespeare is as open to this kind of commentary as the Fourth Gospel.

3 The Opening of Possibility: Two Proposals

I have suggested that both pieces of writing refer to a world of possibilities, and so open hope for the future. But where do these possibilities come from, and how can we have any assurance that they are any more than a dream themselves? We may find two different answers to these questions in the thought of a philosopher, Paul Ricoeur, and of a theologian, Eberhard Jüngel. While both wish to establish the priority of possibility over actuality, I believe that the difference between them is highly illuminating for the relation of revelation to story.

As I have already indicated, Ricoeur maintains that stories and poems do not refer *directly* to the world around us; they are no mere imitations. But they do nevertheless refer to the *real world*, that is to the world as it can be. The world of the text is referring to a world not so much 'beyond' it as 'in front of' it.[13] Stories describe, not how things are, but how they might be. They point to a way of being beyond the greediness of the ego, and so beyond the split of the consciousness between subject and object. Here Ricoeur is deliberately picking up from Jacques Derrida the idea that there is always a 'surplus' or 'excess' of meaning in verbal signs. Derrida draws attention to the chain of reference of signifier to signifier within a text ('since the signified always already functions as a signifier')[14] which means that final meaning will be suspended or postponed as it is dispersed down the series of signs in their 'difference' from each other.[15] But Ricoeur gives this expansion of meaning another direction from the endless straying and playing which Derrida commends, and which throws doubt on whether a text can ever represent anything outside itself.[16] The result of the *surplus in a text*, Ricoeur suggests, is not only to defer meaning, but to give us hope.[17] This is because there is an overflowing *surplus of being* in human existence itself, from which we are oriented forwards in a passion to be, and this is the true basis of hope.[18]

As narrative 'configures' the different moments of past, present and future into a new temporality,[19] so metaphor configures dissimilar objects in the world into a new whole. Both story and image '*redescribe* reality', and there is a fictive experience which we can only call 'seing as'.[20] When we say 'this is and is not', we see the world 'as not yet', and we open up the play of possibilities. Ricoeur thus understands texts as eschatological, but not merely in the sense that they defer meaning forwards; in their very meaning, in their sense (structure) and reference (creating a new world) they present a hope by which human beings can live.

For Ricoeur, human being is *possibility itself*, and out of this fecund capacity the imagination can create genuinely new possibilities which are not simply repetitions of the past and present; symbol and myth refer to a reality which is yet to come and which they help to create. 'Fiction changes reality,' maintains Ricoeur, 'in the sense that it both "invents" and "discovers" it.' Imagination offers possibilities to the will which adopts them and forms *projects* which are not dependent upon conditions in the present. Such projects are not unreal just because the contingent conditions for them do not exist here and now, as the world includes 'what *is to be done* by me'. Human existence means that 'the possible precedes the actual and clears the way for it'. Possibility is more than an extension of the present; it challenges and contradicts present reality. Yet possibility for Ricoeur is still in a sense immanent within human life, since humanity has by its very nature 'a passion for the possible'. Here, however, we can detect a significant difference from the notion of possibility in the thought of Eberhard Jüngel, a theological conversation partner with Ricoeur.

In a study on 'metaphorical truth' copublished by Jüngel and Ricoeur, Jüngel argues that religious language calls actuality into question as the ultimate referent. Metaphor brings to speech states of affairs that are 'more than actual'; metaphor refers not to the world as it is, but as it is coming to be.[21] Jüngel affirms, moreover, that metaphor can refer to the coming of

God to the world, and so *in* metaphor God also comes to worldly speech.[22] In finding that being embraces possibility as well as actuality, Jüngel, like Ricoeur, seeks to reverse the long Western intellectual tradition of making actuality prior to possibility.

However, in so doing Jüngel launches a direct attack on the idea of the possible as the 'not yet', as found in Ricoeur as well as in Ernst Bloch and Jürgen Moltmann. In another essay, 'The world as possibility and actuality', he urges that the radical eschatology of the New Testament cannot be contained within the well-worn formula of 'the already and the not yet'.[23] He argues that, if we define the 'possible' as that which is 'not yet', we are simply subordinating it once more to actuality (as not yet actual) and reducing it to mere 'potential for actuality'. 'Not yet' defines the possible merely in negatives, and 'not yet being' is a kind of ghostly being. We will only make possibility prior to actuality if we understand it exclusively as that which God creates, and cease to define it by any tendencies in the present. 'That which God makes possible in his free love has ontological priority over that which he makes actual through our acts.'[24] Possibility thus belongs with our justification as a free gift from God. The language of metaphor testifies to a possible world for which we can hope, but this is established by the external agency of God on whom the world is contingent.

For Ricoeur, as we have seen, possibilities are rooted in the human *capacity* for surplus of being and meaning.[25] By contrast, Jüngel wants to cut off any continuity of the 'possible' (as distinct from the not yet actual) with existing structures of human life. Possibility can only begin from a human reduction to nothingness. Along with justification by God, hope in the possible is a creation *ex nihilo*. Jüngel points out that the Christian experience of justification is that possibility is prior to actuality; we *become* righteous in God's sight before we *act* righteously. But this justification follows from a participation in the cross of Jesus where all our actuality is brought to nothingness under the divine 'No' against human life, which is spoken for the sake of the creative divine 'Yes'. Here we find the hostile 'nothingness' of a loss of relationship with God and others revealed for what it is, and we find it negated by God.[26] Those who are justified have faced up to the blank nothingness revealed in the death of Christ, and have trusted in the promise of the resurrection that God alone will bring new possibilities to the world.

Ricoeur, to be sure, also recognizes the judgment on present actuality that the cross of Jesus represents; he finds that the cross of Jesus symbolizes the 'reality forsaken by God', which is to be replaced by the 'how much more' of hope in the resurrection.[27] The cross is, as it were, God's verdict on mere actuality which leads us towards the light of a possible world. But the crisis of the cross speaks into a kind of receptivity in the human heart, which is the passion for the possible.

4 Possibility and Revelation

These two proposals about the grounds of possibility, as exemplified by Ricoeur and Jüngel, have implications for the way that story and revelation may be seen to be related. For Ricoeur, because of the human passion for the possible, all stories have the power to challenge our perception of present reality and to project a new world in front of the text. He regards this manifestation of a new world as a kind of 'a-religious revelation'. Poetics 'obliterate the normal referential function' of a descriptive kind, and restore to us a participation in, or a belonging to, 'an order of things which precedes our subject–object distinctions'.[28] Stories and poems incarnate a concept of truth which is nothing to do with verification, but rather manifestation – letting be what shows itself. And what shows itself is a proposed world of new possibilities. While Ricoeur does not explicitly state the matter like this, he implies that the experience of cross and resurrection (judgment on actuality, manifestation of possibility) has an analogy in all poetics.

He does assert that the phenomenon of revelation in all literature is 'capable of entering into resonance with biblical revelation', though the religious meaning of revelation cannot be simply 'derived' from it. The biblical witness to revelation is about encounter with the 'Name of the Unnameable' which 'moves among all the forms of discourse', and to which all biblical discourse finally refers. Like all poems and stories, the Bible unfolds a world in front of itself which is full of possibility, but this world is inseparable from the presence of the one who unveils himself while remaining hidden. Thus Ricoeur claims that, while the biblical hermeneutic is 'one regional hermeneutic within a general hermeneutic, it is also unique'.[29]

By contrast, like his mentor Karl Barth, Jüngel centres all revelation in Jesus Christ to whom scripture witnesses. Jüngel is not interested in any general concept of revelation (religious or not), but begins with the particular revelation of God in the cross and resurrection of Jesus Christ which brings us possibility as a sheer divine gift. This particular event has, however, a general validity in that it can illuminate the whole world;[30] once we have experienced revelation in Christ, we can 're-experience' all our experiences.[31] Revelation thus releases us from the constraints of actuality. Jüngel agrees with Ricoeur that texts have a kind of externality, distance or objectivity in themselves; this is primary to any intentionality of the writer or the reader. In the speech-acts of the New Testament understood like this, which testify to the event of revelation in Jesus Christ, 'God comes to human speech.'[32] God makes God's own self available in the objectivity of language in order to draw human existence into the divine life. So the Kingdom comes to speech in worldly narratives or parables. Once we have experienced the Kingdom through scriptural parables, we find that the natural order can also become a parable of the Kingdom.[33] When God comes to the world from beyond, the familiar is expanded,[34] and what is already interesting in itself (the world) becomes even more interesting.

Jüngel thus implies, though does not make explicit, that non-scriptural narratives, poems and stories can also become parables of the Kingdom.[35] What is not clear is how this might be related to revelation. Might it then be feasible to combine the best insights of Ricoeur and Jüngel? Can we keep Jüngel's focus of revelation in Jesus Christ and his insistence that all possibilities derive from a new creative act of God, while at the same time acknowledging with Ricoeur a 'passion for the possible' in human nature and the phenomenon of something that looks like revelation in all literary texts? Can we develop a comprehensive understanding of revelation that will do justice to the new world manifested by stories of all kinds, while avoiding a general hermeneutic of which scriptural interpretation is merely one subset? I believe that we *can*, and the remainder of this chapter will make at least an attempt in this direction.

I believe that we *must* make the attempt, given the effect upon us not only of such texts as John 20–21, but Act V of *The Tempest*. The audience of the Fourth Gospel has been brought to face the bringing of actuality to nothing in the story of the cross of Jesus. Like the disciples, in the face of God's verdict on human reality, we sit in a locked room in fear and trembling (20:19) from which we can only be liberated by the joy of resurrection life and the new possibilities this unfolds. But the audience of *The Tempest* is also made to face a judgment on all reality which the human arts can create; we are brought to recognize human achievement as an 'insubstantial pageant' and to confront the final end to 'the baseless fabric of this vision'. We are left vulnerable in a hostile world, without being able to justify ourselves by the book of the dramatist or the staff of the theurgist. We cannot create either love or forgiveness in others, but are dependent upon receiving them as a gift. Only when we accept this negative judgment on life as it is can we achieve liberation from an island which has become claustrophobic, and set sail for a world of new possibilities. I do not mean that the end of *The Tempest* is an allegory of cross and resurrection, but that it calls into question the kind of reality offered by the world around, and opens up the promise of participation in a new kind of existence.

It seems to be a mark of revelation to disturb established expectations, to bring the surprise of something new. In John 20 the saying of Jesus, 'Blessed are those who have not seen and yet believe' has an unsettling quality within it. Perhaps it is the reversal of a well-known logion found in the Synoptics (Luke 10:23, 'Blessed are the eyes that see what you see'; Matt. 13:16).[36] In a similar way, Prospero in his epilogue upsets the expectation that the player will, in asking for applause, doff his disguise and appear as himself. Both shocks point us forward to something unexpected, not simply an extension of the present. While the contrast Jürgen Moltmann makes between 'epiphany' and promise' is rather polarized,[37] revelation does seem to be a contradiction of the present by a word of promise rather than by the disclosure of some kind of Platonic heaven, a parallel higher world.

Any understanding of story and revelation should have something to say about the presence of this kind of challenge and promise in a text like *The Tempest* as well as the Fourth Gospel. I suggest that, oddly enough, it is Jüngel with his vision of God who comes to (all) worldly speech who leaps the gap between scriptural and non-scriptural stories, while Ricoeur's distinction between 'a-religious' and 'biblical' revelation keeps the gap open. Yet Jüngel does not relate the coming of God outside scriptural texts to a concept of revelation, as I believe we must. When we talk of a text 'opening up' new possibilities, or being creative of new meanings, we are using the language of disclosure. Something is being unveiled. The question is whether this is 'revelation' in the biblical sense, or something analogous to it, or nothing like it.

Some closer definition of revelation must be ventured, however, before this question can be answered. I take it as axiomatic that associating revelation with the biblical text cannot mean a direct communication of propositions by God. Apart from the critique that no proposition can be unconditioned by culture and language, if the Word of God were simply the same as a human proposition or concept this would undermine the freedom and the mystery of God. Revelation can surely be nothing less than the self-unveiling of the God who remains hidden. Barth's lapidary phrase that revelation is 'God's speaking person'[38] – that is, God's own self in the very act of speaking – is helpful as long as we do not forget that 'speaking' is a metaphor. The idea of a 'voice' behind or within the words of scripture is modelled on the prophetic form of discourse, and (as Ricoeur has pointed out)[39] there are other forms of language which also become the occasion for revelation in scripture. Notably, the wisdom saying is not about hearing a voice but observing patterns in the world, and through this 'seeing' being brought up against limits through which God makes God's own self known. A whole semantic field of metaphors for revelation may be appropriate here, self-utterance being complemented by self-opening, self-offering, self-expression and self-coming.

The gracious self-opening of God enables a human response (as God does not speak into the void but for a purpose), and this response will employ a spectrum of verbal signs, from the more imaginative forms of story and metaphor to the more reasoned forms of concept and analogy. Here I suggest that it is useful to distinguish between 'disclosure' and 'revelation'. We might keep the word *revelation* for the very act of God's self-offering, and use the word *disclosure* for the result of the interaction between divine self-opening and human response. This result will be a sense of something being unveiled or uncovered. As Barth puts it, revelation seizes the human word and makes it capable of *corresponding* to reality.[40]

If our vision of God is of one who has freely chosen to be committed to the material creation, then we will understand that in a self-opening to human persons God takes some object in the world through which to make God's own self available. The Christian confession has been that the humanity of Jesus Christ is the primary sacrament of God's objective presence, the Word of God in the full sense or the primary 'parable' of God. The verbal signs in scripture are secondary witness to this Word. In this sense, the speech-acts of scripture are both *response* to revelation, and *occasion* for revelation, as God takes and uses these secular objects as a place for the repeated divine self-opening and self-offer here and now. As Jüngel puts it, God 'comes to speech'.

5 Revelation and Trinity

The experience of revelation is that the God who opens God's own self to us veils the divine self at the same time. The revealed God is the hidden God. The God who names God's self remains nameless. Various theological reasons can be found for this spiritual experience of the hiddenness of God. If God takes objects in the world to become objective to us, since God is not himself an object like other objects, the result will be ambiguity and mystery. Finite and sinful reality is not a suitable medium for the self-revelation of God ('the veil is thick': Barth),[41] while God also retains the divine freedom to be unveiled as well as veiled. This hiddenness at the heart of revelation is a theological reason why meaning remains open to the engagement of the reader, and can never be finally closed. From a literary critical point of view, there will always be a gap between the sign that signifies and what is signified, and (as we have already noted) this gap is only widened by the fragmenting of meaning down the chain of signifiers in a text. These theological and literary factors may interact to produce what is often felt to be a 'crisis of representation'. As Graham Ward points out in a study of Mark's Gospel,[42] there is an elusiveness about the way that the historic Jesus represents God, and about the way that the text of the Gospels represents Jesus. This 'crisis' draws us into participation in the whole process of representation, as we in turn become witnesses to the Word. But this means nothing less than being drawn into the life of God, and in this sense 'revelation is the root of the doctrine of the Trinity'.[43]

For the church doctrine of God as Trinity attempts to model the conviction that God's life is relational, that the depth of God's personal being can only be expressed in terms of a dynamic interweaving of personal relationships. We can be drawn into participation in God because there is already a movement of relationship going on, in which we are invited to share. We call God 'Father' because within God there is already a movement of relationship like that of a Son speaking in humble obedience to a Father, and we can share in that eternal 'conversation'. At the same time we find that there is a third movement within God which is always provoking and opening up the conversation in new ways, moving it towards future fufilment. This then is the experience of prayer 'to the Father, through the Son and in the Spirit'. The concept of the Trinity is not about *observing* God, but about *participating* in God. The self-opening of God in revelation entices us into engagement with God, to share in movements of speech, suffering and mission (sending) which are already there, but which take on new depth with our participation in them.

This interweaving or perichoresis of relationships can be expressed in a narrative way: God has a story within God's own self – the story of a Father who sends out a Son in a Spirit of love and openness to the future. The story of the eternal birth of the Son from the womb of the Father continues in the historic story of the sending out of Jesus Christ on his mission within Galilee and Judaea in the power of the Spirit, finally treading the road to the cross in Jerusalem. The story of the eternal glorifying of the Father by the Son continues in history in the story of the resurrection and the raising of Jesus Christ to be Lord of the cosmos, 'to the glory of God the Father'. This is the 'meta-narrative', into which we are invited to incorporate our own stories. We are invited to let the reconfiguration of time in this Grand Story, its particular integration of past, present and future, shape the way we see past history and expect what is to come. Postmodern criticism has been suspicious of all meta-narratives, that is stories which claim to explain the whole of reality (though Derrida himself never thought they could be entirely erased), since they easily become ideologies which oppress persons in the name of absolute truth. But we have seen that there is an openness in the way that a reader participates in *this* narrative, which has hiddenness at its heart. As a modern literary critic, Valentine Cunningham, puts it, 'biblical logocentricity is already deconstructive';[44] the Word makes himself heard in ambivalence and silence.

To return to the story of the resurrection appearances of Jesus to his disciples in the room of John 20, we can see how this provides a place for the 'coming' of God to human speech, to draw the reader into the story of his trinitarian life. The risen Christ invites his disciples to participate in his own story of relationship to the Father, saying, 'as the Father has sent me, so I send you' (v.21b). What they are sent to do is to offer forgiveness and acceptance into the Kingdom of God as he has been doing in his own mission (v.23), but what this will mean for disciples in future times and places is necessarily open, as the endings to chapters 20 and 21 make clear.

But what can we say of the final Act of *The Tempest*? I believe that we cannot follow Ricoeur in distinguishing between a general 'a-religious' revelation and a special 'biblical' revelation, as we cannot step outside our Christian perspective on the world. If we want to speak of revelation at all with regard to non-biblical texts (and I agree with Ricoeur in affirming that we do), we must still say that 'God comes to speech'. Whenever people are drawn towards a new world of possibility which enhances truly personal life, they are being drawn into the life of the triune God. That is, the images and stories of all creative literature can be a response to the self-unveiling of God, and an occasion for the self-offering of God here and now. Ricoeur makes a strong point that the reader can only recognize the unfolding of a new world of possibility, because human nature is already characterized by a 'surplus' of meaning and a 'passion for the possible'. However, this ought also not to be detached from revelation; with Karl Rahner, we can say that the human spirit is open to an infinite horizon and oriented towards the final mystery which is God, only because God has opened God's own self to all his creatures in the first place.[45] There is no nature without grace, creating and recreating. Human beings have a passion for the possible because they live in the presence of a God who is always encouraging new possibilities to develop.

In this way we may begin to do justice to two insights: on the one hand, possibility is more than a 'not yet' in human existence – it is a creative act of God (Jüngel); on the other, human existence is oriented forwards in hope (Ricoeur). But what is the content of this possibility? We may certainly affirm that, as well as envisaging possibilities for the world from all eternity, God is free to conceive new possibilities from the divine imagination as the work of creation continually proceeds;[46] such a freedom of God begins to account for the openness of the future, and the biblical witness to promises that are fulfilled in unexpected ways[47] rather than in exact prediction. But I suggest that, to do justice to the openness of meaning in a text and its promise of future fulfilment, possibilities must also arise from God's partnership with creation.

This is in accord with revelation as an invitation to participate in the story of the triune God. A God who loves will allow those who are loved to make a contribution to the relationship between them, and so to share in the divine creative project. As soon as love is understood to be more than a 'doing good' to the other, and to involve mutuality and passions, space must be made for genuine human response to the purpose of God. So we may envisage new possibilities as not only conceived by God in the divine mind, but emerging from the interaction between the creator and the created.[48]

This is the theological basis for what happens when a reader engages with a text; while the text may unfold a possible world 'in front of it', this future world will not be realized except through its impact upon the reader who will help to make it. The creative mimesis of the text needs to be matched by the creative mimesis of the readers, representing what the text represents within their life and the life of their community. The configuration of past, present and future within a story must be appropriated by the reader, whose own sense of time and history is thus reconfigured by it.

I have been arguing that stories such as *The Tempest* may be occasion for revelation, for the unfolding of a future world of new possibility. But the question then arises: what is the particular place of Holy Scripture? The answer begins with the belief of Christians that the self-unveiling of God is focused in Jesus Christ, though not, as we have seen, without ambiguity and crisis for the beholder. All self-opening of God is relational, drawing us into the story of God's triune life, but we must also affirm that the 'Son-like' movement of relation within God is – by God's free decision – forever inseparable from a human son; for this reason, *no* revelation can be said to be outside Jesus Christ. This is the case wherever revelation happens, but the Bible has the authority of being first-order witness to Christ (though not necessarily eye-witness), since it is bound up with the historic event of Jesus and his context in the history of Israel in a more intimate way than any other text.

Scripture is also distinctive because its writers are conscious of revelation, explicitly aware that they are offering witness to an encounter with God through many different verbal forms (prophecy, narrative, wisdom, psalm, law, letter, gospel). It has been no part of my argument that Shakespeare designed *The Tempest* as a deliberate reflection on religious themes, or that any critic worth his salt must find witness to revelation within it. Employing the distinction I made previously between 'disclosure' and 'revelation', we may say that any reader can speak of a play such as *The Tempest* offering a *disclosure* in which something previously hidden is unveiled. But it requires belief in a self-offering God to speak of *revelation* as the initiative behind this experience of disclosure. This leads us to a final reason for the special authority of the Bible: the church is a community of faith which has been shaped by reliance upon the text of scripture, and which has made scripture the foundational witness in its life. As long as we regard ourselves as members of this community, we have an obligation to relate to scripture and to wrestle with it for meaning. We must always be in dialogue with the story of scripture, while there is no *requirement* to make Shakespeare such a part of our life.

This relation of text to the community and its tradition has some bearing on a final issue that arises from our comparison of two 'final scenes' in literature. If meaning is always open, and shaped by the engagement of the reader, are there any limits to expansion of meaning? Can we distinguish fullness of meaning from inflationary and arbitrary reading?

6 Limits to Meaning? Story and Concept

Throughout this chapter I have laid stress on the openness of the two stories from the Fourth Gospel and *The Tempest*, deferring the making of meaning to the engagement of future readers and promising future fulfilment which has room for the unexpected within it. But we also ought to note features of closure within them. Indeed, the critic Gabriel Josipovici goes so far as to find the New Testament characterized by closure in general, in contrast to the Old Testament which he finds marked by openness; he maintains that, while the Old Testament writers tell us stories and urge us to remember, the New Testament insists that we should *understand*, with Paul and the Fourth Gospel as the worst offenders.[49] This chapter offers, I hope, a support for the claim that the Fourth Gospel along with the whole New Testament text is indeed open to expansion of meaning, but we should take account of Josipovici's observation that texts also have ways of closing meaning at the same time. One way is through the placing of conceptual statements which 'urge us to understand' alongside story and image. In John 20 we find this in Thomas' confession when he sees the risen Christ, 'My Lord and my God', followed by the concluding statement of the evangelist:

> ... these are written that you may believe that Jesus is the Christ, the Son of God, and that believing you may have life in his name.

In Prospero's epilogue, alongside the open image of a voyage to be embarked upon, there stands a statement which is quite didactic: prayer for forgiveness frees from all faults.

I have already suggested that response to revelation takes a spectrum of verbal forms, ranging from metaphor to proposition. While story and image tend to open meaning, concepts tend to delimit meaning, to hedge it around, and to reduce the playful multiplicity of images to a system. It is the work of theologians within the community of the Church to develop doctrine which aims to talk responsibly about God, and to develop as precise concepts as are possible in the light of the nature of transcendent reality. The doctrine of the Trinity, using the quasi-philosophical language of 'three hypostases in one ousia', is perhaps the prime example of the reasonable reflection of the Early Church. Now, I certainly do *not* want to be understood as suggesting that, unlike metaphor, doctrinal concepts are a literal way of talking about

God.[50] To the contrary, neither metaphor nor proposition can be a univocal description of God or the life of faith; there is always hiddenness and 'crisis' in representation. Nor ought concepts to be allowed to control images. But some verbal forms are more characteristic of closure and some more of openness, and I suggest that we need to be faithful to both in our interpretation of a text, and to allow the one to interact with the other. In the process of relating them and correcting one by the other, merely 'inflationary' exegesis may be avoided.

That this is a *process* is well illustrated by the verbal forms which 'urge us to understand' in John 20. The confession of Thomas contains concepts of belief, in that it takes ascriptions in the Septuagint belonging to Yahweh the God of Israel and applies them to Christ. Bultmann points out that various combinations of *kurios* and *theos* are found in the LXX, especially in address.[51] By means of these terms, Bultmann concludes, this confession 'makes clear that Jesus is the Logos who has now returned to the place he was before the incarnation, and who is glorified with the glory that he had with the Father before the world was'.[52] But we should notice that this conceptual confession interacts with the story, to bring some indeterminacy of meaning. The confession is made, not as a dogmatic statement, but as an act of worship in the context of 'seeing' Jesus. So Thomas is confessing that in Jesus he *sees* God (cf. 14:9); in the Son he *sees* the glory of the Father. What he sees we are to believe on the basis of witness. But the way that Jesus represents the Father, so that we see them together in one focus, is left quite open. The experimental nature of this confession is followed by the concluding statement, where already known terms are brought together to qualify each other. We are to believe that Jesus is 'the Christ', but the Jewish understanding of Messiah is to be modified by the confession of Thomas, and by the meaning which the evangelist gives to the title, 'Son of God'. The evangelist's use of the latter title is evidently moving beyond the Jewish sense of merely human 'sons of God' who (like the Davidic King) represent God and act for him. But the use of the title is moving from the area of mere function to that of being (ontology) in an experimental way, assisted perhaps by the idea of Logos in the Prologue, and it cannot be loosened entirely from its Jewish roots.

Taking these 'urgings to understand' seriously will not therefore remove the openness of meaning in the text, or undermine the effect of the story which calls us to participate. But it will provide some parameters within which meaning can expand. Any inflation of meaning which does not help us to understand the designation of Jesus as 'Lord, Christ, Son of God' will not be doing justice to the text: that is, the intention of the text itself and not of the author or authors. Similarly, we might say that any exegesis of the final Act of *The Tempest* which undermined the concern of Prospero for forgiveness (presenting him, for example, as a power-hungry tyrant) would not be doing justice to that text.

In this chapter I have been exploring the way that a story unfolds a world of new possibilities, and how this might be related to the Christian concept of revelation. The very notion of 'possibility' has openness within it, yet it also has some boundaries insofar as it is God's purpose for human life. Christian eschatology has a note of closure in that it is confident in a consummation of God's purposes for creation, but it also has an openness for the content of that fulfilment to be shaped by human participation in God's project for creation. Prospero sets sail for Milan, 'where every third thought shall be my death'. By contrast, the risen Jesus Christ will never die again, and is on his path towards receiving his final glory. But through their stories, in different ways, we are invited to share in the humble pilgrimage of the triune God.

Notes

1 Raymond E. Brown, *The Gospel According to John (xii–xxi)*, The Anchor Bible (New York: Doubleday, 1970), p.1049. I am indebted to Brown for suggesting the theatre analogy for this scene in John 20.

2 Jacques Derrida, 'Of an apocalyptic tone newly adopted in philosophy', trans. J. Leavey (1982) reprinted in H. Coward and T. Fosby (eds), *Derrida and Negative Theology* (New York: SUNY Press, 1992), p.57.

3 Ibid. See also Derrida, 'No Apocalypse, Not Now', *Diacritics*, 14(2) (Ithaca, NY: Cornell University, 1984), pp.20–32, esp. p.28.

4 Paul Ricoeur, 'Towards a Hermeneutic of the Idea of Revelation', in Lewis S. Mudge (ed.), *Essays on Biblical Interpretation* (Philadelphia: Fortress Press, 1980), pp.99–100.

5 So Rudolph Schnackenburg, *The Gospel According to St. John*, vol. 3, trans. D. Smith (New York: Crossroad, 1990), p.334. He cites, for promise, Rev. 14:13, 19:9, 20:6, 22:14; and for warning, Rev. 1:3, 16:15, 22:7.

6 So W. Nicol, *The Semeia in the Fourth Gospel. Tradition and Redaction* (Leiden: Brill, 1972), p.115.

7 Rudolph Bultmann, *The Gospel of John. A Commentary*, trans. G.R. Beasley-Murray (Oxford: Blackwell, 1971), p.696.

8 See Richard Bauckham, *The Climax of Prophecy. Studies on the Book of Revelation* (Edinburgh: T.&T. Clark, 1993), pp.85–6.

9 Brown, *supra*, n.1, p. 1129.

10 So Origen, *On First Principles*, Book II.6.1.

11 Shakespeare uses a similar image in *Hamlet*: 'to sleep, perchance to dream' (III.i.56f.).

12 W.H. Auden, 'The Sea and the Mirror', II in *Collected Longer Poems* (London: Faber, 1974), p.212.

13 'Towards a Hermeneutic of the Idea of Revelation', *supra*, n.4, pp.98–9.

14 Jacques Derrida, *Of Grammatology*, trans. G. Spivak (Baltimore: Johns Hopkins University Press, 1976), p.7.

15 Jacques Derrida, 'Structure, sign and play in the discourse of the Human Sciences', in *Writing and Difference*, trans. A. Bass (London: Routledge, 1978), pp.278–94.

16 See Roland Barthes, *The Pleasure of the Text*, trans. R. Miller (Oxford: Blackwell, 1990), pp.27ff.

17 See Ricoeur (1969), 'Freedom in the light of hope' in *Essays on Biblical Interpretation*, pp.163ff.

18 Here see especially Ricoeur's book *Freedom and Nature. The Voluntary and the Involuntary*, trans. E. Kohak (Evanston: Northwestern University Press, 1966), pp.48f., 54ff.

19 Paul Ricoeur, *Time and Narrative*, vol. 1, trans. K. McLaughlin and D. Pellauer (Chicago: University of Chicago Press, 1985), pp.54ff.

20 Paul Ricoeur, *The Rule of Metaphor*, trans. R. Czerny (London: Routledge, 1986), pp.209–11.

21 Eberhard Jüngel, 'Metaphorical truth. Reflections on theological metaphor as a contribution to a hermeneutics of narrative theology', in *Eberhard Jüngel, Theological Essays*, ed. and trans. J.B. Webster (Edinburgh: T.&T. Clark, 1989), p.32.

22 Ibid., pp.59–60.

23 Jüngel, 'The world as possibility and actuality. The ontology of the doctrine of justification', in *Theological Essays*, *supra*, n.21, p.103.

24 Ibid., p.116.

25 Ricoeur, 'Freedom in the light of hope', *supra*, n.17, pp.165–6.

26 Jüngel, 'The world as possibility and actuality', *supra*, n.23, pp.112, 120.

27 Ricoeur, 'Freedom in the light of hope', *supra*, n.17, p.163.

28 Ricoeur, 'Towards a Hermeneutic of the Idea of Revelation', *supra*, n.4, p.101.

29 Ibid., p.104.

30 Eberhard Jüngel, 'Das Dilemma der natürlichen Theologie und die Wahrheit ihres Problems', in *Entsprechungen: Gott – Wahrheit – Mensch* (Munich: Kaiser Verlag, 1986), pp.175f.

31 Eberhard Jüngel, 'Gott – um seiner selbst willen interessant. Plädoyer für eine natürlichere Theologie', in *Entsprechungen*, pp.196–7.

32 Eberhard Jüngel, *The Doctrine of the Trinity. God's Being is in Becoming*, trans. H. Harris (Edinburgh: Scottish Academic Press, 1976), pp.11–15.

33 Jüngel, *Entsprechungen*, *supra*, n.30, p.7.

34 Jüngel, 'Metaphorical truth', *supra*, n.21, pp.68–9.

35 This might be seen as an expansion of Barth's view of Jesus Christ as the Light of the World: *Church Dogmatics*, IV/3, 69–72.

36 So C.H. Dodd, *Historical Tradition in the Fourth Gospel* (Cambridge: Cambridge University Press, 1963), p.354.

37 Jürgen Moltmann, *Theology of Hope*, trans. J. Leitch (London: SCM, 1967), pp.42–4.

38 Karl Barth, *Church Dogmatics*, I/1.5, trans. G. Bromiley and T. Torrance (Edinburgh: T.&T. Clark, 1975), p.136; also I/1.8, p.304.

39 Ricœur, 'Towards a Hermeneutic of the Idea of Revelation', *supra*, n.4, pp.76ff.

40 Barth, *Church Dogmatics*, I/1.8, p.340; I/1.9, pp.362, 372–3.

41 Barth, *Church Dogmatics*, I/1.5, pp.166ff.

42 Graham Ward, 'Mimesis: The Measure of Mark's Christology', *Journal of Literature and Theology*, 8/1, 1994, 9.

43 Barth, *Church Dogmatics*, I/1.8, p.310.

44 Valentine Cunningham, *In the Reading Gaol. Postmodernity, Texts and History* (Oxford: Blackwell, 1994), pp.400–402.

45 Karl Rahner, *Foundations of Christian Faith*, trans. W. Dych (London: Darton, Longman and Todd, 1978), pp.126–33.

46 So Keith Ward, *Rational Theology and the Creativity of God* (Oxford: Blackwell, 1982), p.154.
47 The phrase is from Walther Zimmerli, 'Promise and Fulfilment', in C. Westermann (ed.), *Essays on Old Testament Interpretation*, trans. J. Mays (London: SCM, 1963).
48 This is stressed by Charles Hartshorne from a process perspective: *Creative Synthesis and Philosophic Method* (London: SCM, 1967), pp.63–5.
49 Gabriel Josipovici, *The Book of God. A Response to the Bible* (New Haven and London: Yale University Press, 1988), p.274.
50 See Paul S. Fiddes, *Freedom and Limit. A Dialogue between Literature and Christian Doctrine* (Basingstoke: Macmillan, 1991), pp.13–15.
51 Bultmann, *supra*, n.7, p.695, n.2.
52 Ibid., pp.694–5.

Three

Disclosing Human Possibilities: Revelation and Biblical Stories

John Barton

It is easy to draw sharp contrasts between the characteristic features of systematic theology in the English- and German-speaking worlds. Anglo-Saxon systematicians, it may be said, typically begin with questions that belong to the philosophy of religion: the existence, nature, goodness and omnipotence of God. Only then do they go on to discuss the nature and work of Jesus Christ, the Church, doctrines such as justification by faith or the atonement. For, such theologians would ask, what do these other things matter unless we begin by assuring ourselves that there is a God who can be known and who is both powerful and good? To many German-speaking theologians, indeed to theologians in any continental European tradition, this seems perverse. Not only are they often opposed to the idea of natural theology, which seems to be inherent in the Anglo-Saxon way of doing theology, they also question what point there is in thus investigating God in an abstract way. Unless God is the God and Father of our Lord Jesus Christ, the God who welcomes sinners and sets our fallen human nature free, the attempt to discuss him is empty: any 'knowledge' we acquire as a result is empty knowledge, knowledge of a theory or an abstraction. The correct place to begin is with what we already know of God through his self-disclosure in Christ: more abstract questions can then fall into their proper, subordinate place.

In writing the present book we are of course aware of these tensions, and discussion has focused on them time and again. We have discovered, however, that they do not correlate precisely with an English/German divide. There are of course German philosophers of religion who have much in common with the Anglo-Saxon tradition. More importantly for our present project, the British participants in the *Revelation and Story* project all share a sympathy for the idea that theology can and should begin with the givens of Christian tradition, rather than with the questions that are traditionally defined as the task of natural theology. Whether or not natural theology is possible and licit is a question over which we might indeed disagree; where we agree is in thinking it not the best starting-point for theological enquiry.

There is an interesting illustration of this in a recent discussion by Sarah Coakley of the kenotic tradition in Christology. She writes:

> What one sees so interestingly in writers such as Moule, Robinson (and to some degree in Davis) is a primary commitment to the given *narrative* of the New Testament, and especially of the gospel accounts of Jesus' life; and this takes precedence even over philosophical questions of apparent coherence, or of traditional *a priori* assumptions about the unchanging divine attributes. Such narrative commitment is a feature of post-war theology in general (especially continental theology), and indeed could be said to be the point at which contemporary theology and analytic philosophy of religion divide most painfully in their fundamental assumptions.[1]

The two salient matters here for our purposes are: (1) 'home is where we start from' (T.S. Eliot): our theological enquiries, wherever they may end, *begin* with the givens of the Christian tradition, with those matters that Christians have always held to be 'revealed'; and (2) these givens are inextricably linked to what the Bible communicates to us in the form of *narrative*, pre-eminently the narrative of the life, death and resurrection of Jesus of Nazareth. We begin, not with an enquiry into the possibility of knowing God in principle, but with the conviction that we have been told something we could not tell ourselves. And what we have been told has the shape and character of a narrative. This is why we have given our work the title *Revelation and Story*.

1 How Stories Work

How do stories 'work' in communicating to us the revelation of God: that is, God's revelation of himself? Paradoxically perhaps, they do so by showing us who we are ourselves, by opening up to us the possibilities and the problems of being human in God's world. A writer I have found particularly illuminating here is the American philosopher, classicist and ethicist Martha C. Nussbaum. In her two books, *The Fragility of Goodness* and *Love's Knowledge*,[2] Nussbaum argues that works of fiction can disclose vital insights into the question how we should live precisely because there is no fixed boundary between the 'fictional' characters who appear in stories, plays and poems and the 'real' people we meet every day. When literary critics this century have taken an interest in 'literature as a guide to life', they have generally done so by arguing that well-drawn characters in novels or plays are almost real and so can offer insight to real people like ourselves; and Nussbaum does argue along those general lines at times. More characteristic, however, is her suggestion that literature can offer a guide to living because 'real' people – we ourselves – are actually just as fictional as the characters in a novel. What she means by this is that all our encounters with other people depend on our ability to 'fictionalize' them: to 'read' them as persons of this or that sort, with predictabilities and unpredictabilities in various parts of their personalities, and capable of interacting with us only because they in their turn can see us as 'characters' too. It might be said that some personality disorders, and extreme states such as autism, amount to an inability to interpret other people as characters in a story with a plot, and a consequent perception of them as bundles of random actions and emotions. Thus the possibility of turning to literature for insight into life rests, not on the closeness of good fiction to reality, but on the closeness of any reality we can grasp to fiction. And this suggests, Nussbaum argues, that we can read 'for life'. Stories can disclose for us the possibilities of being human.

We learn from stories how to live because we discover from them how voluntary decisions interact with unpredictable occurrences to generate moral character. Nussbaum is interested in how moral agents can shape their destinies in a framework established by forces that are not themselves moral, but random or malign. Stories disclose human possibilities by helping us to imagine ourselves in complex situations not of our own making, and envisaging the room for free action that such situations might leave us, and the kind of people we would have it in us to be when confronted with such complexities.

Nussbaum's examples are taken from Greek tragedy and modern fiction, especially the works of Charles Dickens and Henry James. She analyses characters in these works at great length, and shows how the interplay between character, decision and chance produces the humanity that we recognize in them as similar to our own. The tragedians' characters are not invented to illustrate some general principle or other, but are conceived as complete human beings woven out of many strands. Similarly, the protagonists in sophisticated novels can train us in moral perception by presenting us with complex models of what human beings are capable of, both for good and for ill. We are drawn into their story in imagination, we measure ourselves against them, and more and more truth about what it is to be human becomes apparent to us as we read on.

2 Biblical Stories

Could biblical narrative texts be brought into contact with Nussbaum's approach?[3] It seems to me that many stories in the Old Testament are quite similar to the events of Greek tragedies, and could readily be treated in a similar way. By drawing the reader into the story, narrative texts achieve a disclosure of human possibilities (and human limitations) which is arguably not available in any other way. Obvious examples of such stories would be the Joseph Story (Gen. 37–50) and the 'Succession Narrative' (2 Sam. 9–20; 1 Kings 1–2). These stories are not reducible to a set of ethical principles, as if they were sermon *exempla*. Principles can certainly be seen as exemplified by the stories: in the Joseph Story, that envy is evil, forgiveness is to be encouraged and bearing grudges is unworthy of mature humanity. But the story cannot be *replaced* by a statement of the principles, which are disclosed through the interplay of characters and situations and not in any other way. The Succession Narrative, altogether a darker text, discloses how one sin (David's adultery with Bathsheba) results in a whole chain of evil consequences, partly through divine judgment, partly through accident, partly through the interplay of characters who owe their own character to their biological descent from David himself. In this, very like a Greek tragedy, the Succession Narrative illustrates the operation of nemesis (though a nemesis distinctively Hebrew in character). We learn by reading it, but it is not easy to say what we learn. We begin, after all, as experienced Bible readers and as Christians or Jews by knowing the moral principles against which the actors in the drama offend: so we cannot be said to 'know' more about ethical obligation at the end of the story than we knew at the beginning. What we see through the story are the unfathomable consequences of a single immoral action, at the same time as we realize that its perpetrator is not at all a moral monster but a human being with the same potentialities that we have ourselves. David is not inhuman, superhuman or subhuman, but all-too-human and therefore susceptible to temptations and disasters, just as we are ourselves.

Just as, in Paul Fiddes' account above, Shakespeare draws us into the world of *The Tempest* and invites us to see ourselves as part of its continuation in a never-ending future, so the biblical narrators draw us into the world of David or Joseph and ensure that we will never again be quite the same people that we were before we read these classic stories. There is an irreducibility about the narrative character of these works. The narratives disclose realities that cannot be disclosed in any other way and, equally, cannot (even after their disclosure) be restated in such a way that the narrative can then be discarded as having accomplished its task. Having got 'the point' of the narrative, we do not then ignore the narrative and think simply about the point; on the contrary, we go back to the narrative better equipped to read it.

An analogy that could be useful here is that of the icons used in Eastern Orthodox tradition. It is said that icons work with a technique of perspective the opposite of that normal in Western art since the Renaissance. In a Western picture the lines of perspective converge on a point which has to be imagined as behind the surface of the representation. Icons, on the other hand, are constructed so that the lines converge in front of the picture, and the point of convergence is the worshipper standing before the icon. The icon does not invite us to enter its world, still less to penetrate behind it; it challenges us to allow ourselves to be the recipient of its 'message', to be worked on by the icon rather than working on it ourselves. Thus icons, which to many Western Christians seem so smooth and bland and two-dimensional, can be perceived by the Orthodox as reaching forward to the worshipper, who constitutes the picture's third dimension and who is needed to complete its effect. Interpreting icons involves a kind of 'reader response' criticism; the icon opens up fresh possibilities for each 'reader'. Instead of aiming at closure, an icon is inherently and by its very definition open, designed to become part of a dialogue with each fresh person who seeks God by contemplating it.

It is the same with some biblical stories. The lines of perspective in the story seem at first to converge behind it, giving it a satisfying aesthetic shape and a satisfactory closure. It is only as we read it more deeply and grasp its 'point' that we realize they really converge on us, the readers, so that the story leaps at us out of its frame. This is what happens to David in 1 Samuel 12 when Nathan tells him the nicely rounded parable about the poor man and his little lamb and then destroys its closure by revealing that it is a story in which David himself is deeply implicated; and this effect, whereby the story denies its own fictivity, is then replicated in us, as we hear the prophet's word, 'Thou art the man', addressed to ourselves. The Succession Narrative as a whole is thus like one of its component parts, and what works at one level within the text works also at another level in the relation between text and reader. Just as, within the story, Nathan's parable has the effect of making David realize his guilt, so the story of the succession as a whole challenges us, its readers.

3 Openness and Closure

I have written so far as though the disclosure of human possibilities is linked to the openness (lack of closure) of a story. This is certainly the reason why *The Tempest*, as analysed above by Paul Fiddes, has the effect it does on us: instead of the curtain falling between us and the actors when the play ends, the action moves as it were in front of the curtain and transports itself from art to life. Some biblical stories are clearly open in this sense. The book of Jonah, for example, does not end with the sparing of Nineveh, which would represent closure, but with God's dialogue with Jonah – his challenge to the prophet to believe in the mercy God has shown to the city, and to let this become part of his general perception of God. If there were to be another

Nineveh, then the reader of Jonah would have been equipped by the story to understand the divine compassion and not gloat over its ruin. Jonah turns into Everyman, with his prejudices and hatreds and yet also with his ability to know the God who is 'gracious and merciful, long-suffering and of great goodness', and who 'repents of evil'. Similarly, the stories in Daniel end with an actual or implied invitation to worship the God of Daniel: the story does not stop when the narrative stops, but continues into the reader's present.

However, not all plays or stories are open in the way that *The Tempest*, Jonah and Daniel are. The Succession Narrative ends with the firm conclusion, 'So the kingdom was established in the hand of Solomon'; the Joseph Story ends with the deaths, first of Jacob and then of Joseph himself, and though we know that the story will continue in Exodus, nothing in the end of Genesis itself even hints at this continuation. These are stories which exhibit closure in the traditional sense that this term has in the analysis of novels. A point is reached where the plot is clearly complete, and though the novelist may add a chapter telling us what happened to all the characters afterwards, the story is by then already rounded off and finished. We are not meant to see ourselves and our own lives as a continuation of the novel, since the novel is now an aesthetic object to be contemplated from outside as a finished product.

This raises the question whether we should really link *disclosure* to *lack of closure*, as I have been doing. For this seems to lead to the conclusion that only 'open' stories have the potential for disclosure. Only 'eschatological' writing, that is writing that is open to the future, has the power to disclose human possibilities to us. If this is true, then it has the odd effect of elevating some biblical stories to the status of disclosures, and leaving others as merely historical records or old tales. And this seems intuitively implausible.

Part of the answer might be that openness and closure are not entirely objective features of stories or plays or novels, but lie partly in the reader's own perceptions and use of narrative material. There may be stories which in themselves appear to be open but which I perceive as closed. This can be a matter of cultural distance. Many Greek tragedies are closed for the uninitiated reader who fails to see the universal humanity of the characters because he or she cannot penetrate beyond the archaic cultural vehicle of Greek drama. Conversely, stories which appear on analysis to be really closed can function as open stories for particular readers.

Gabriel Josipovici, in *The Book of God*,[4] argues controversially that Old Testament narratives are open, but New Testament ones closed: the New Testament mentality does not tolerate loose ends or unfinished plots, with the result that New Testament narratives are stories unequivocally about the past, which do not resonate in the present. Old Testament narrative, by comparison, is always open-ended, and draws the reader into itself. It is literature whose genius is to mirror real life, in its lack of closure and in its openness to many different resolutions. It seems to me that Josipovici is certainly onto an important contrast here, though I do not believe it is a contrast between Old and New Testaments. Openness and closure lie to a considerable extent in the eye of the beholder, and depend on our willingness to see the story we are reading as open for ourselves, whether or not it is 'open' or 'closed' in a technical literary sense.

What this comes down to is that 'openness' is a kind of literary *metaphor* for the way in which biblical narrative – and many great literary texts too – operate on the reader who is prepared to be open to it. In the biblical narrative, possibilities are disclosed when the reader acknowledges the correctness of the verdict 'You are the man!', when the story strikes home into the reader's own heart and mind. This is *analogous* to what happens when a text is perceived as 'open' from a literary point of view, just as it is analogous to the way icons work on us. The point is more than a literary or aesthetic point, but the literary or aesthetic comparison does much to illuminate it.

4 Story and Revelation

In speaking of 'disclosing human possibilities', I have intentionally remained within the range of readings that might be undertaken by Christian or non-Christian alike. *The Tempest*, on Paul Fiddes' analysis, does not disclose the possibilities of human choice and experience only to the Christian, but to anyone who approaches it with the right kind of expectation. This is equally true of the biblical stories I have been discussing. Just as with Martha Nussbaum's examples from Greek tragedy and from modern novels, stories in the Bible speak about the human condition from one cultural context to another, and in their openness (or in their ability to be read as open) they communicate human possibilities and human experiences of good fortune and disaster, of love and hate, to readers in any century and any country: *cor ad cor loquitur*.

What then is the relation of story to *revelation*? Caroline Schröder observes in Chapter 9 that seeking revelation through the biblical text is not a matter of looking for texts that (happen to) describe alleged revelations of God and ignoring others that do not. Rather, seeking revelation means adopting a particular hermeneutical expectation, a way of reading *all* the texts in the Bible (and possibly others too). Revelation does not occur just because a text alleges that its author received a revelation (as, for example, in apocalyptic texts). But nor does it occur just because a particular text becomes a point of (what I have been calling) disclosure. Revelation occurs where *God addresses us*, breaking through our expectations and suspending our own judgments about what is or is not a true disclosure. There is a danger of eliminating this element of revelation coming from beyond human expectations, by stressing too strongly the similarity (or even suggesting an equivalence) between divine revelation and human disclosure through narrative texts. Yet it is essential to see that there is a similarity. In both cases we are challenged by something beyond ourselves, something we did not make or discover ourselves, to open our minds and welcome alien truth. This is the heart of what we mean by linking revelation to story: that God reveals himself by telling us new things, things that turn us upside down and remake us.

Notes

1 Sarah Coakley, '*Kenosis* and Subversion', in Daphne Hampson (ed.), *Swallowing a Fishbone: Feminist Theologians Debate Christianity* (London: SPCK, 1996), pp.82–111; this quotation is on p.100.

2 Martha C. Nussbaum, *The Fragility of Goodness: Luck and Ethics in Greek Tragedy and Philosophy* (Cambridge: Cambridge University Press, 1986); *Love's Knowledge: Essays on Philosophy and Literature* (Oxford: Oxford University Press, 1990).

3 For some suggestions along these lines, see John Barton, 'Reading for Life: The Use of the Bible in Ethics and the Work of Martha C. Nussbaum', in John W. Rogerson, Margaret Davies and M. Daniel Carroll R. (eds), *The Bible in Ethics: The Second Sheffield Colloquium, Journal for the Study of the Old Testament* supplement series 207 (Sheffield: Sheffield Academic Press, 1995), pp.66–76.

4 Gabriel Josipovici, *The Book of God: A Response to the Bible* (New Haven and London: Yale University Press, 1988).

Four

Reading the Bible Theologically

Ernstpeter Maurer

My own preaching leads me to suspect that philological analysis and theological interpretation are linked immediately. The most interesting ideas for a sermon emerge in reflecting on the biblical *text*, and often in translating it. It is exactly the concentration on the *letter* that confronts us with the manifold movements in the biblical language and texts, that is, with the vivid and powerful dynamics of the *Spirit*. Of course, this concentration on the letter confronts us with philological problems, such as the gap between methodological questions in recent literary criticism and the hermeneutical search for understanding the text. Some literary criticism does not *interpret* the texts, since the implications of *reading* texts are more interesting.[1] Meditations on 'horizon', '*Geschichtlichkeit*' and 'existence' – the traditional key words of German philosophical hermeneutics – do not contribute anything to the analysis of textual structures, and we may even ask whether they are irrelevant to the range of critical historical methods. Obviously, these methods do not need any philosophical reflection or legitimation. This insight will be important for us, because any philosophical mediation between reading and understanding the text may obscure the theological dialectics of letter and Spirit.

In this chapter, I will try to give a precise description of the direct link between philological analysis and theological interpretation. This exercise may have nothing to do with the relation between 'story' and 'revelation'. The conceptual connection 'story and revelation', however, lies at the core of a full account of *theological* hermeneutics, at least in a Protestant context. Martin Luther describes the power of biblical texts in the phrase '*scriptura sacra sui ipsius interpres*' ('Scripture interprets itself'). Of course, this remark is Luther's alternative to the Catholic principle that Scripture has to be interpreted by tradition. But there are more and deeper implications: the clarity of Scripture confronts us with our sinful presuppositions concerning the relation between God and human persons. Scripture thus frees us from our sin, in a confrontation which is always a struggle of incommensurable readings of a biblical text. Therefore Luther's insights have implications for the analysis and for the reading of texts, possibly even on the philological level. Scripture may disclose aspects of reality which otherwise remain hidden, thereby provoking and exposing our sinful blindness, manifest in any all-too-simple reading of biblical texts.

Luther's strange idea of 'self-explication' refers to an event in which the biblical text is stronger than our sinful presuppositions, where the scriptural disclosure is more powerful than our human attempts to harmonize it with seemingly self-evident experience. At that point, the immediate link *and* the subtle difference between theological interpretation and philological method converge with the distinction of letter and Spirit: it is precisely the *literality* of Scripture confronting human presuppositions with the biblical testimony. The *disclosure* liberating us from our sinful blindness arises from the structures of the text and yet is not identical to these structures.

The powerful and liberating disclosure arising from biblical texts is at least one aspect of the theological concept of 'revelation'. The stress on liberation implies that Scripture does not reveal just anything, but fundamental and otherwise inaccessible features of *our* identity and personality. Scripture provokes and exposes *conflicts* of identity and personality, which is a very important aspect of the Reformers' distinction between law and gospel. At the same time, the question of personal identity is one of the characteristics of the rather vague concept, 'story'.[2]

The precise description of the immediate link between theological and philological hermeneutics must look for the *application* of this theological connection between disclosure and personal identity, revelation and story. Are there any traces of such a connection in a single biblical text, so that philological analysis immediately results in a theological interpretation explicating the actual relevance of the text *for us*? The advantage of such a link may be the methodological clarification of the theological concepts, 'revelation' and 'story', by reference to the analysis of limited linguistic entities. The mediation between biblical texts and twentieth-century experience by reflections on 'existence' or 'universal history' may turn out to be superfluous. These reflections legitimate the reference to biblical texts on a highly general level only.

The basic problems of *philological* hermeneutics may be illustrated by the commentaries on texts written in a foreign language. The text must be (a) translated and (b) interpreted by the hypothetical reconstruction of the authorial *intention*. Both aspects converge on the question, 'What does the text mean?' Any answer is at least related to the problem, 'What did the author mean by this formulation?' (b) and results in a possible paraphrase (a), even if there is no translation in the strict sense. Both problems are rather complex. In order to explicate this complexity, I will follow Friedrich Schleiermacher's 'Lectures on Hermeneutics', which is a classical attempt to describe hermeneutics as an *art*.[3] The philological interpretation is outlined as a craft. This access to hermeneutics has been the immediate background for developing the methods of literary criticism, especially by August Boeckh. Unfortunately, Hans-Georg Gadamer's misinterpretation of Friedrich Schleiermacher's 'Hermeneutics' became standard in the German discussion.[4] A reassessment was provoked by Manfred Frank, who treated Schleiermacher's insights as anticipations of recent tendencies in structuralism and post-structuralism.[5]

Nevertheless, I will concentrate on Schleiermacher for mostly *heuristic* reasons. His idealist foundation of all knowledge, including hermeneutics as 'art of understanding', in the immediate self-consciousness is exactly the point of difference and conflict with theological hermeneutics in the Protestant account as sketched above. Any liberation of the person from sinful blindness will exactly and necessarily attack this person's immediate self-consciousness. This difference and conflict, however, does not diminish the relevance of Schleiermacher's refined explication of hermeneutics as an art. His philosophical arguments – especially in the 'Dialectics', but also in the 'Hermeneutics' – anticipate some insights of recent analytical philosophy, which eliminate the idea of a transcendental subject altogether. This rather surprising 'dialectical' feature in Schleiermacher's philosophy converges with Frank's references to the 'structuralist challenge to the hermeneutical subject'.[6] In the following, such anticipations will be explicated as steps in the dramatic development of the aporias in philological hermeneutics – aporias marking the point of connection *and* difference, where theological interpretation discovers traces of revelation and liberation within the texts, including their philological analysis. In short, the fundamental problems in Schleiermacher's account of hermeneutics converge with the theological elimination of a continuous transcendental subject.

1 The Problem of Translation

1.1 The problem of translation raises the question of *structures* of language in general. For Schleiermacher, the 'grammatical interpretation' is one of two complementary hermeneutical tasks: the text must be understood as mental fact ('psychologically') *and* as modification of thought by language ('grammatically'). The given structure of any language shapes the text, but any linguistic entity may affect that structure.[7] Grammatical interpretation, therefore, has to solve two problems: the structure of language must be described as precisely as possible, as a *system of rules*, generating an infinity of different utterances from a finite set of elements. Against this background of general rules, there emerges the *individual use* of language – and vice versa: any attempt to describe the structure of the language must refer to individual utterances. Such a circular movement makes it impossible to give *mechanical* rules for any language, and for that reason interpretation is already an *art* at the fundamental level of grammar, 'since given rules do not give mechanical rules for their application'.[8] The language as a whole at a certain time and the single utterance are interdependent. They provide an example for the circular relation between any organism and its individual parts. This is the basic formula for the so-called 'hermeneutical circle' in Schleiermacher's version.

Schleiermacher's celebrated phrase that the interpreter must understand the text initially as well as, and later on even better than, its author, belongs here. 'For since we have no immediate knowledge of his inner consciousness, we must try to make conscious a lot of his unconscious intuitions. ... Objectively, he has no more data than we have.'[9] The problem is: we have to find and to explicate the linguistic *rules* unconsciously followed by the author.

The results of grammatical interpretation as semantic analysis are found in a dictionary; syntactic analysis results in the rules of grammar. Both are in the first place limited to the language of a particular author. The manifold meanings must be explained as a hierarchy of oppositions. In order to get at ordered sets of oppositions, 'we must combine the method of *confrontation* with the method of continuous *transformation* of the meaning'.[10] The confrontation becomes especially clear when the author explains an idea by giving its opposite in the same context.[11] This antithetical linguistic structure determines the unity in the use of words *externally*, that is, distinguishes one lexeme from other lexemes. At that point grammatical interpretation intersects with logical analysis: 'Words referring to concepts derived from the same more general concept are interrelated, if coordinated. This coordination presupposes an emergence of ideas by confrontation within a more general sphere.'[12] *Internally*, the semantic nuances must be explicated by reference to the different use of the word in different contexts. Transferring a word to other contexts presupposes that analogies can be perceived. These analogies are fixed by the differentiated use of one and the same word.[13] Therefore, the use of the word must be described as unity in movement, with manifold changes and transfers.

This unity in movement is the ultimate limit for logical analysis as an attempt to give mechanical rules for the structure of language. The method of confrontation cannot determine the distinctions within the use of a given word created by analogy.[14] Moreover, as soon as the function of logical and constructive *thought* gets to the limit marked by the *perception* of analogies, the individual subject appears in language: 'as there are different perspectives, so there are different ideas of one and the same object'.[15] Individual use of language creates new transfers again and again, metaphorical varieties in the use of the same word. That is true especially of discoveries.

'Every revolution in thought forms language.'[16] The following anticipates Thomas S. Kuhn:

> Scientific revolutions as well as revolutions in the realm of ethics produce new systems and reject the old ones. ... It would be misleading to compare single aspects in the new system with single aspects in the old one, for the relation between single aspects and the whole is different in each system.[17]

The semantic analysis of a given language has to be completed by the syntactic analysis (and conversely). The latter deals with given phrases in their context. The two are interdependent, for the determination of sense and reference relies on the comparability of contexts. Conversely, the precise translation of conjunctions and prepositions may be difficult and end up with a level of analogical transfer. The German '*aber*' ('but') does not always express opposition (cf. the Greek '*dè*'). The semantic analysis, however, often relies on oppositions in the use of words and must therefore presuppose the adversative meaning of the conjunction in a given case. In order to give reasons for such a presupposition, the semantic analysis must be presupposed. So we may be confronted with a new instance of the hermeneutic circle.

1.2 Schleiermacher's account of grammatical interpretation is not simply 'romantic hermeneutics' or 'aesthetics of genius' stressing the intuitive empathy between author and interpreter.[18] Rather, Schleiermacher's discussion converges with structuralist methodology and with insights of recent analytical philosophy. The stress on the limits of logical and mechanical reconstruction of sense and reference implies the *indeterminacy of translation* as demonstrated by Willard V.O. Quine.[19] Quine's argument for the indeterminacy in principle of translation starts with the ideal situation of unambiguous reference *and* absence of any cultural link between two languages. Even if both the native speaker and the first translator see a rabbit, the native speaker's utterance 'gavagai' does not necessarily mean 'rabbit'. In order to check such a one-to-one translation, we must have words for the difference between 'one and the same x' and 'x and y similar in all respects' in the hitherto untranslated language. This distinction is a necessary tool for semantic analysis, because what seems to be the word for an object in this language may refer to strange ontological aspects. These can be discovered only by the comparison of different contexts referring to the *same* object. But the translation of the words for identity and difference in turn depends on paradigmatic situations and contexts.

Translation remains indeterminate in principle, but indeterminacy is not arbitrariness. Rather, there must be simple and repeatable *rules*. So, even if there is no mechanical application of these rules, following the rule is self-evident in most cases. Moreover, the rules can be made explicit because they are simple and repeatable. On the other hand, there will always remain an irreducible plurality of such explications, and this exposes the indeterminacy of translation.

1.3 Of course, Schleiermacher would not have taken the last and radical step. Indeterminacy of translation may be seen as a trace of subjectivity in language and, at the same time, it may lead to a theological rejection of this concept of subjectivity: we are confronted with the problem of non-linguistic entities and their possible relevance. The relation between word and object, concept and extension in the simple sense of reference and correspondence has been replaced by a plurality of perspectives embedded in language. That is the philosophical consequence of the circular references in grammatical analysis, implicit in Schleiermacher's account, explicated by Quine. The result is a complicated web of identity and difference on both sides, in language and perception. So the difference between word and object is no more fundamental than other differences, and may be described *within* the web of identity and difference:

> Structuralist linguistics aims at listing pre-signitive entities, whose material distinctness ... is relevant only as a necessary condition for the correlation between the system of strictly distinctive values (*signifiés*) of a *langue* emerging from diacritical and interdependent profiles and the system of equally distinctive material *média* (*signifiants*).[20]

The structuralist analysis, then, does not identify the *signifié* with any non-linguistic entity.

At this point, it is possible (1) to insist on at least one *signifié* in the strict sense of a reality inaccessible to language. This is Schleiermacher's position, since the *transcendental subject* always constitutes the perspective discerning between identity and difference. The *ego* stays at the centre of language. The alternative (2) insists on the relevance of extralinguistic reality in a quite sophisticated way. Quine's argument for non-translatability presupposes exactly the possibility of elementary reference to *objects*. There is no determinate translation, because any statement referring to that object will imply presuppositions concerning the possibility of pointing to the *same* object in a different situation. And there will be always more than just one adequate set of presuppositions. This argument converges with Wittgenstein's remarks on following rules in the context of 'language games'.

The relevance of the transcendental subject in Schleiermacher's argument must be challenged on *theological* grounds. The liberating power of biblical texts is effective in questioning my personal identity and continuity, exposing my ego as the source of sinful presuppositions destroying the relation between God and human persons. Against this background it is clear that the concept of the transcendental subject cannot have the last word in biblical exegesis. Interestingly, ambiguity is a characteristic philological feature of biblical texts. The words and phrases are not only translatable in various ways, so that we have to decide between two or more versions: the plurality of versions is *constitutive* and *irreducible*. In biblical contexts, we often find antithetical structures, where several meanings of a certain word or phrase are mutually exclusive, but nevertheless suggested by the same context. Such antithetical structures disturb the egocentric character of language, which is responsible for the indeterminacy of translation. Normally, we try to balance these perspectives by a 'fusion of horizons' in order to reduce the indeterminacy by interpretation. But this balance collapses as soon as mutually exclusive perspectives are inscribed in the text.[21]

If the continuity of immediate self-consciousness is just questioned by theological hermeneutics, this attack on personal identity leaves traces at a philological level. The attack even involves the reference relation between word and non-linguistic object. Quine and Wittgenstein argue for a certain privilege of medium-size physical objects, since we can point to these objects using ordinary language. Certainly, this aspect is fundamental for the *development* of language, but the proliferation of more and more linguistic contexts and systems indicates the metaphorical dynamics of language. Of course, the emergence of an indefinite plurality of more or less 'objective' language games is the background of the complicated arguments in the 'philosophical investigations', with the dialectical consequence that we can explain the meaning of the word 'object' only *within* the language game. So the antithetical structure in biblical texts may be the result of intersecting language games preventing any definite reference to a certain kind of object. Therefore non-linguistic 'reality' becomes as problematic as the transcendental subject.

2 The Problem of Intention

2.1 The quest for authorial intention is characteristic of historical criticism, taking this as standard for philological hermeneutics. Schleiermacher's discussion of the *technical and psychological* interpretation exposes the methodological problems implied in the question of authorial intention.

Interpretation of a text as '*mental event*' has to distinguish two aspects: the production and the construction of ideas. In some sense, interpretation has to repeat both, 'as if' the interpreters transformed themselves into the authors.[22] Nevertheless, Schleiermacher does not mean 'empathy', although the formulation may be misunderstood. He concentrates on investigations which can be described methodologically. As in grammatical interpretation, texts have to be compared, and again there emerges a circular structure. What are the points of comparison? What makes certain poetic forms belong to a certain genre? What makes particular motifs make up a coherent tradition? We need some intuitions of *relevant* similarities – Schleiermacher calls these intuitions 'divination' – but they must be controlled in order to exclude crazy ideas and arbitrariness. 'Divination is confirmed only by comparison ... but comparison never establishes continuity.'[23] Clearly, 'divination' aims at the problem of selecting the most interesting and productive aspects of comparison from an infinity of possibilities. This is not exclusively a hermeneutical problem. It is present behind all inductive theory construction.

Psychological interpretation is the attempt to understand 'any given complex of thought as a moment in a particular person's life'[24] and concentrates on the development of the fundamental ideas. *Technical* interpretation analyses the composition as 'a certain connection of thoughts and direction of the exposition producing chains'.[25] Again, the methods are complementary, since there are no ideas without form. First, the intention has to be clarified as decision: such a decision gives unity to the text and defines its proper direction. Secondly, the composition has to be analysed as *objective* realization of the decision. Therefore we must reconstruct the author's 'meditation' (Schleiermacher's term for the structure of basic ideas determining the composition). Finally, the deviations have to be distinguished from the mainstream of thoughts, since these deviations are the *trace* of the author's situation.[26]

The psychological interpretation has to situate and to integrate the unity of the text in the author's life. What is the reason, the background of the decision – of the 'authorial intention' – and its aim in the context of the author's life? The intention may be described by motifs and tendencies rooted in the author's historical situation. The situation is relevant for the interpretation only if there are traces of the situation in the text:

> The problem is solved as soon as I have recognized that every detail has its function in the unity of content and form in analogy to any work of art. But if there are details which cannot be harmonized with the unity of content and form, so that these details are interconnected, there lies the hidden unity in the author's secret goal.[27]

We may compare the technical interpretation to the grammatical analysis: the interpreter has to reconstruct the explication of the basic ideas down to the details in order to expose a quasi-deductive structure. This explication concentrates on content and form. As a first step, we try to give a table of contents.

> Is it possible, however, to follow the author's inner process of thought by describing chapters and paragraphs in general? It is possible by observation confirmed by self-observation. You must have some experience in meditation and composition in order to understand these processes behind another person's texts.[28]

Schleiermacher does not say 'empathy': the point is the analogy between author and interpreter. Again hermeneutics is characterized as 'art'. Interpretation needs practice and experience in the production of texts, because only these create the sensitivity – the 'taste' – for another author's style.

Dividing a text into sections corresponds to the grammatical analysis of semantic oppositions. The main sections of the text reflect the basic ideas, these sections must be analysed in detail by describing subsections and so on, 'down to the mere context'.[29] Obviously, Schleiermacher presupposes a hierarchy of interrelated and distinct arguments. Wittgenstein's '*Tractatus logico-philosophicus*' would have been an ideal example. The 'mere context' which remains stable is the background of self-evident convictions and implications 'between the lines' and between the steps of the argument. To explicate this continuity of plausible convictions corresponds to the grammatical analysis of metaphorical developments in the use of a certain word, which complements the logical construction of a precise definition by opposition. This complementary method converges with the idealist distinction of thought and perception (see above, section 1.1) leaving its traces in a given text: the hierarchical structure of basic ideas and subsections represents the intersubjective medium of argumentation, whereas the *deviations* reflect the author's personality and his or her self-evident convictions. Therefore they have to be taken into account separately. Moreover, the deviations may create a continuity between clearly defined forms of literature – between the extreme possibilities of a strictly logical exposition without any deviation (where meditation and composition are the same) and a poem without any deductive relation between basic ideas and details (and without any distinction between basic ideas and deviations).

2.2 The methodological precision *together with* the insistence on the relevance of structural breaks is one of the advantages of this hermeneutical account. We could even say: only the search for structures which are as clear as possible gives significance to the inconsistencies in the text. In a certain sense, the psychological and technical interpretation comes closer to theological hermeneutics than does the structuralist analysis of the production of texts aiming at processes which may be described mathematically and even mechanically. The psychological–technical interpretation looks for the individual and characteristic features of the particular text, locates this particularity in the textual features which cannot be reduced to any structural regularity *and identifies such features as traces of the subject in the text*. The question remains, however: why should individuality be revealed in the breaks? *Do the inconsistencies disclose the individual person, just because they cannot be reduced to general structures*? And is the irreducible 'remainder' always an inconsistency? In many cases, yes, but inconsistencies are neither the sufficient nor a necessary condition for the disclosure of personal intentions. They may result from the antithetical structure in biblical texts (see above, section 1.3). In the breaks, then, the power of the content is stronger than the author's control of the form, so that the text surpasses authorial intention. In this respect, the breaks do not disclose any authorial intention, whereas a text without breaks may exactly reflect the author's intention.

At this point, the exploration of the author's subject is limited in principle: there is no necessary correlation of characteristic features in the text and individual subjectivity. Certainly, we may find the traces of the author: linguistic hints, such as particles, or deviations. But these traces do not disclose an *intention*. We may produce more and more refined analyses of the relation between form and content, but this refinement will not necessarily be what the author has in mind. The degree of complexity may be the result of the inner dynamics in the form–content relation, possibly in conflict with, rather than corresponding to, authorial intentions. Again, as in the case of the structure of language, we must admit: *the author's ego remains inaccessible*. We may remember an important aspect in Wittgenstein's rejection of 'private language': the word 'mean' has many meanings, but we do not always and necessarily refer to some internal and mental act. Rather, there are characteristic contexts in which the use of the word is relevant.[30]

Any inference concerning intentions will remain theoretically questionable, since there is no intention *without* manifestation and articulation in language. That does not imply, however, that they have to be eliminated as theoretical concepts. That would be necessary only if any reference to the structure of self-consciousness was superfluous in the precise description of texts. But this structure may certainly be traced within the text, in a theoretical framework necessarily implying the concept 'intention'. That is the condition for the non-redundant use of theoretical concepts: they must define a theoretical structure which informs our precise perception of reality. This holds true for the structure of self-consciousness, if we can show that the relation between ego and self as dialectical distinction-in-unity is irreducible and explicable in a productive way. Certainly, my use of language is one of the models – theoretical applications – for this structure. I may recognize my individual self in my texts or not. In either case, the difference between the text and the original intention is presupposed. This difference describes the meaning of 'intention' without presupposing anything concerning the ontological status of intentions[31] – not even the existence of a transcendental subject.

Once more, biblical texts radicalize the quest for authorial intention because, already at the low level of single paragraphs, philological analysis will distinguish different tendencies in conflict. Of course, the conflict may be eliminated by literary criticism distributing the textual segments to different authors. But if we do not accept this rather harmless solution, the search for traces of subjectivity confronts us with antithetical structures.

3 The Theological Depth of Philological Problems

We will try to demonstrate the indeterminacy of translation and the aporia of authorial intention in biblical texts: the basic problems of philological hermeneutics and their radical version in theology. This radical version may be summarized in two fundamental statements reflecting the basic insights of Protestant hermeneutics (see above, p.61). First, Scripture resists determinate translation. Biblical texts are not vague; rather, they confront the interpreter with an irreducible plurality of possible readings and translations. This plurality may be described very precisely, provoking a history of interpretation. Luther's statement '*scriptura sui ipsius interpres*' is metaphorical. On the other hand, the concept of a transcendental subject has become questionable; there is no self-consciousness 'behind' language. So the metaphor may lead to the disclosure that, if there are only spoken and written texts interpreting each other, the plurality of interpretations *within* the text illustrates the process of self-interpretation.

Second, the search for determinate authorial intentions is questionable just because Scripture is letter. But this insight may liberate the author from his or her intention. The concentration on the written text will disclose a plurality of intentions, a vivid dialogue rather than a one-to-one relation of intention and expression. This dialogue *within* the text reflects the Spirit *in* the letter.

3.1 As an example, we will analyse some aspects of Romans 10:1–13. Here we find two philological problems closely connected: (1) What is the meaning of '*télos*'? (2) How does Paul integrate Deuteronomy 30:11–14? The word '*télos*' means 'end' or 'fulfilment'. Even if the New Testament scholar does not look for a determinate translation, he will ask for the best paraphrase. The version 'end' raises the following problem. Paul gives a self-refuting argument for the statement, 'Christ is the *télos* of the law' by quoting a basic passage from the Torah. On the other hand, 'fulfilment' is a difficult version because it harmonizes Paul's rather violent use of the Old Testament quotation. There may be a wise solution in the middle: Christ is the *point* of the Law. But this middle way gives a metaphorical interpretation and so transposes the problem to another level.

Paul changes the Old Testament quotation in a very interesting way. Deuteronomy 30:12 reads: 'Who will ascend to heaven for us in order to bring [the commandment] and to proclaim it to us, that we may follow it?' Paul replaces the commandment with Christ: it is not necessary to bring Christ, who is already near to us, down. So Paul sees an analogy – however qualified – between Christ and the commandment. This analogy is illuminated by Deuteronomy 30:14, proclaiming the intimate relation between us and the Word of God, which may be immediately transposed from the commandment to Christ. But Paul simply eliminates the threefold 'that we may follow it'.

Christ *literally* is the limit here, the end and the point of the quotation, which has lost its original point. The result is a significant gap, provoking the question: what is the meaning of '*ᶜāsāh*' in Deuteronomy 30:12–14? Is it *necessary* to follow the commandment as an imperative, so that we have to fulfil God's will? In that case, human action would be the last resource, and the reference to God's will would be superfluous. Such a reduction contradicts Deuteronomy 30:11–14, because the point of this text is that the commandment is *close* to us, and it is *easy* to follow it. Paul does not misuse the quotation, but explicates its implications by complicating it: the passage, Romans 10:6–8 demonstrates a liberty from the Law which is *free* for the Law, referring to the Law and suspending the aspect of action in the Law in order to gain an adequate perspective on one's own action. So the point, the '*télos*' of the Law is exactly the antithetical movement between the versions 'end' and 'fulfilment'. Paul demonstrates in language what he is proclaiming: we are free from the Law as a medium of salvation. But the point of this liberty is the proclamation of God's liberating action prior to any human action.

3.2 It is important that we do not simply avoid the decision between two possible translations of '*télos*'. The antithetical relation between 'end' and 'fulfilment' is rooted in the complication of language and reality, because the reality described converges with the process of describing it, so that the linguistic web or texture is not simply disturbed by a logical contradiction, but rather remains in process because of the antithetical tension. Of course, this tension *disturbs* the subject and his or her attempts to find a determinate perspective in language, concentrated in the ego. The ego could eliminate the tension by a clear distinction between object language and meta-language or between Paul's intention and the intention of the author of Deuteronomy 30:11–14. But this elimination is prevented by the structure of the quotation. So there is no determinate perspective left. The ego is liberated from the attempt to grasp the totality of reality.

Such incommensurability in the text provokes the interpreters. If they do not distinguish meta-language from object language they have to bear the tension, to specify it, adding new versions of the antithetical structure. So *Scripture provokes its own interpretation and* (in a certain sense) *its translation*, again and again. Furthermore, the biblical text provokes new proclamation, because the tension in the text generates good ideas for the sermon. And in Romans 10, the tension, as the trace of the dialogue between Paul and the author of the quotation, provokes a movement from this biblical text to other biblical texts, generating new versions of the word 'Law', for example the manifold use of '*nómos*' in Paul's letters.

3.3 The tension also affects the question of authorial intention. The example is of special interest, since a biblical text interprets another biblical text. Every quotation presupposes an agreement, and at the same time it is a productive extrapolation. The quotation defers my own intention, but precisely against this background my intention may become clear.

Therefore quotations are a special example for the *structure of self-consciousness* in texts. The quotation is a very simple form of redaction. The author refers to another authorial intention, whether he interprets it adequately or not. In either way, the intention of the author using the quotation is manifest, because we can hardly quote another text by accident. Moreover, we quote a text, an intention that has been made objective by language. The agreement is fundamental, because otherwise the author could avoid the quotation. There must be a reason for using another person's text. The author *recognizes his own intention* in the quotation – and may be wrong, but that does not matter in the present argument. Rather, it is important that both authorial intentions may diverge and yet throw into relief the intention of the author using the quotation, perhaps exactly by the divergence: the author could have avoided the quotation, if his intention was completely different. Obviously, he tries to throw into relief his intention just by confronting it with a divergent intention.

The interpretation is prevented from determining Paul's intention in Romans 10:1–13. Obviously, *his intention cannot be disconnected from the confrontation with another intention*, with Deuteronomy 30:11–14. But it is important that this indeterminacy is not a loss of precision in interpretation. On the contrary: intentions in conflict may become the background for each other. It is even possible that the quotation discloses a conflict of intentions *within* the quoted text. There is a dialogue between Paul and the author of Deuteronomy 30:11–14 clarifying the intentions step by step. It is relevant for theological hermeneutics that authorial intentions become explicit dialogically and must be specified dialectically. Luther's statement '*scriptura sacra sui ipsius interpres*' is operative even in the micro-structure of texts referring to other texts, thereby exposing the difference of subjective intentions in the text *without distinguishing them in a subtractive way*. If quotations are that important, the literality of the text becomes relevant: the letter may be full of life.

3.4 It might be interesting to pursue these aspects of Romans 10:1–13 in the context of Romans 9–11. At the end, Paul refers to a mystery (Rom. 11:25): the obduracy of a part of Israel has a function within God's economy of salvation aiming at the plenitude including the Gentiles and Israel. Michael Wolter mentions this passage as an example for the Pauline disclosure of esoteric revelation as story.[32] What remains a mystery, can be disclosed only by revelation and told as a story: the relation between Israel's justice and the justification by faith remains incommensurable. Therefore the conflict is explicable only by a lot of Old Testament quotations. The promise has not become invalid – it is still valid as a *scandal* (Rom. 9:33) and provokes the hardening of God's People except for a remnant. This distinction precisely keeps the story going, as already in the Old Testament. This disclosure of God's mysterious depth (Rom. 11:33) may be traced even on the linguistic level. The passage Romans 10:1–13 is just one example.

4 The Subject of Theology and Theological Hermeneutics

This analysis of Romans 10 may raise the question whether we can find equally complex structures in other than biblical texts, for example in poems. Presumably, the answer will be 'yes'.[33] Therefore, we are confronted with the following problem. We have concentrated on 'traces' of revelation in the structure of the texts referring to the event of revelation. If these structures are found in poems and plays as well, poetical texts must be related to revelation in some way. On the one hand, we must not level out the irreducible originality of biblical texts. On the other hand, it is not sufficient to assert the exceptional position of Scripture dogmatically.

It is possible to solve the problem by making a strict distinction between the *event* of revelation and the *texts* referring to revelation. The event is witnessed to by the texts, and this order is irreversible. The structural characteristics of the texts may be relevant, but they will never exhaust the concept of revelation. They are relevant, because, at least in the context of Christian faith, there is no revelation without a human response, and there is no response without language. Describing and analysing the structure of this particular language is a philological task and theologically legitimate, if we do not submit the originality of biblical texts to general categories. But there is no mechanical method to prevent such a mistake. There are only paradigms for the structure of biblical texts challenging our expectations and preparing the way for the power of the event of revelation. We have to describe these paradigms as precisely as possible in order to find some regularities, and in order to become sensitive to the power of revelation.

In this account, theological hermeneutics is not reducible to literary criticism. In terms of philosophy of science, we may compare such a cooperation with the connection between physical theories and mathematics. Physical theories presuppose the mathematical description of physical objects. Nevertheless, the Newtonian mechanics is not reducible to geometry or analysis, although particular mathematical structures, such as functions, are characteristic features of physical laws. The physical description does not *add* anything to the mathematical description of one and the same experiment, but rather discloses interesting and surprising *connections* between seemingly disparate experimental constellations.[34] Correspondingly, a biblical text is received as witness to revelation only if such a reception is moved and supported by the story which has been initiated by the event of revelation. This movement will never be discovered by the structural analysis of a single text, but it will provoke and keep alive the quest for the structure of our human response to revelation. This connection is irreversible.

Against this background, there is no reason to deny the structural analogies between biblical and non-biblical texts. Historical reconstruction will never explore the depth of the event of revelation witnessed to by Old and New Testament texts, but it may clarify the place of a text within the story of revelation. In most cases, historical criticism discovers non-biblical linguistic and literary structures which have been used to articulate the new experience disclosed by revelation in a particular situation. Why should we exclude the possibility that other non-biblical texts are drawn into *our* story initiated by the revelation of God in Christ? Because we always start with revelation, we may well discover irritating structures in poetical texts, which become 'traces' of revelation only for us, as far as we make non-theological language serve the purpose of articulating and reflecting God's revelation. In that case, non-biblical analogies will improve and refine the theological interpretation of biblical texts. Furthermore, the antithetical and reflexive structure of biblical texts will remain significant even if we find it in non-biblical texts as well, because this structure is not in a logical sense the necessary and sufficient condition for using the concept 'revelation'. The antithetical and reflexive structure would lose its significance only if discovered (almost) anywhere, which is highly improbable because of the complexity presupposed.

The antithetical and reflexive structure of biblical texts is no sufficient condition for a text as witness to revelation; rather, it is a rule for theological interpretation making the biblical text transparent for the event of revelation. This rule corresponds to the basic insights of the reformers' theology (see above, section 3), which in turn are special versions of the axioms describing the 'subject matter' of theology: the triune God and God saving the *homo peccator iustus*.

First, on the one hand, the biblical witness to God refers to an ultimate reality which objectifies itself in the strict sense as far as the biblical witness interrupts the linguistic structure created by human subjects. The human subject's activity is manifest in the continuous changes of semantic nuances in the use of a word and in the irreducible indeterminacy of translation. These are traces of the subject and his or her perspectives and perception. But as soon as the continuous changes are intensified and become *antithetical* complications, as soon as mutually exclusive readings prevent any decision in favour of a determinate translation, there is a limit to these traces: God is present in language as irreducibly resistant divine subject. On the other hand, God witnessed to in Scripture liberates us from the obsession of a language which is determinate and enables us to grasp the totality of reality in a definite sense. This subject does not only interrupt our activity in language, but creates it anew. We *are* enabled to translate and interpret biblical texts again and again: as a reflex of the divine abundance and creativity.

Interpretation, then, is not simply incomplete. Rather, interpretation extrapolates the process which is already present in the biblical texts and God-talk: As the biblical texts interpret each other, the proclamation of the Church interprets biblical texts and is illuminated by other biblical texts. Interpretation of biblical texts aims at proclamation and finds its fulfilment in a sermon which enables the listeners to explicate new ideas concerning the interpretation of the text. This threefold structure of God's irreducible and resistant objectivity, of the divine subject's liberating presence and of God's life-giving spiritual creativity in language, describes the trinitarian structure of theological hermeneutics.

Second, the characteristic extrapolation and proliferation of interpretations without reference to any intention as a common measure is not arbitrary; the inner structure of the texts is a constraint, and there is a certain pattern in this structure: I will be confronted with my own subjectivity by the structure of the text. This complicated structure is very often specified by a difference of authorial intentions. Therefore the question of literary criticism is productive: we should analyse these intentions, but without insistence on any homogeneous or fundamental intention. Biblical texts interpret each other in the conflict of intentions *and* in the agreement concerning the striving for adequate God-talk. Therefore the difference of intentions must become explicit, because just at this point the texts disclose the trace of the subject's liberation from the obsession of subjectivity – which is the point of justification by faith.

Moreover, justification does not only affect the biblical writers but the listeners as well. The subject's liberation from the obsession of subjectivity may as well be described as self-consciousness without *criteria for identity*. My critical remarks concerning Schleiermacher's hermeneutical argument may have exposed a certain alienation – the subject's alienation in language. The problem is that the subject leaves his or her traces in the breaks and gaps of language and texts, but at the same time is unable to connect these defective aspects of linguistic entities with self-cognition or self-consciousness. However, this is a pseudo-problem presupposing a naïve one-to-one-relation 'mapping' the subject to the linguistic entity. These naïve connections between the 'inside' and the 'outside' are inevitable obsessions as long as we ask for *criteria* for self-consciousness in language. But we could as well read the traces simply as a stimulating hint without determining self-cognition. The decisive question then remains: does the ego insist desperately on criteria for self-consciousness – which are principally lacking in language – or does the ego enjoy the liberation from these restrictions, because biblical language provides an abundance of possibilities for linguistic self-objectification?

Notes

1 Cf. Lutz Danneberg and Friedrich Vollhardt (eds), *Wie international ist die Literaturwissenschaft? Methoden- und Theoriediskussion: kulturelle Besonderheiten und interkultureller Austausch am Beispiel des Interpretationsproblems (1950–1990)*, (Stuttgart: Metzler, 1996).
2 This aspect is also referred to by Michael Wolter in Chapter 7 of this volume.
3 F.D.E. Schleiermacher, *Hermeneutik und Kritik. Mit einem Anhang sprachphilosophischer Texte Schleiermachers*, 5th edn, ed. Manfred Frank (Frankfurt: Suhrkamp, 1993).
4 Cf. Hans-Georg Gadamer, *Wahrheit und Methode. Grundzüge einer philosophischen Hermeneutik*, 6th edn (Tübingen: Mohr, 1990), pp.188ff.
5 *Das individuelle Allgemeine. Textstrukturierung und – interpretation nach Schleiermacher*, 2nd edn (Frankfurt, Suhrkamp, 1985).
6 Ibid., p.48.
7 Schleiermacher, *supra*, n.3, p.79.
8 Ibid., p.81.
9 Ibid., p.94.

10 Ibid., p.107.
11 Cf. ibid., p.137.
12 Ibid., p.144.
13 Cf. ibid., p.108.
14 Cf. ibid., p.144.
15 Ibid., p.145.
16 Ibid., p.115.
17 Ibid., pp.139f.
18 Gadamer (*supra*, n.4), p.196 tries to demonstrate the transfer of 'Genieästhetik' to hermeneutics by Schleiermacher.
19 Cf. Willard V.O. Quine, *Ontological Relativity and Other Essays* 2nd edn (New York and London: Columbia University Press, 1971).
20 Frank, *supra*, n.5, p.52.
21 Cf. Gerhard Sauter, Chapter 1 of this volume (esp. pp.14–16).
22 Cf. Schleiermacher, *supra*, n.3, p.169.
23 Ibid., p.170.
24 Ibid., p.178.
25 Ibid., p.181.
26 Cf. ibid., p.183.
27 Ibid., p.188.
28 Ibid., p.214.
29 Ibid., p.176.
30 Cf. Philosophical Investigations (PI), Oxford: Basil Blackwell, 1963, §§ 243ff, esp. 335ff.
31 That is the difference between a *metaphysical* behaviourism denying the reality of psychical phenomena, and a *methodological* behaviourism denying any access to these phenomena by introspection; cf. Wolfgang Stegmüller, *Hauptströmungen der Gegenwartsphilosophie*, 6th edn, vol. 1 (Stuttgart: Kröner Verlag, 1978), p.639; for Stegmüller, Wittgenstein's 'private language argument' is an example of methodological behaviourism.
32 See Chapter 7 of the present volume, p.128.
33 Paul S. Fiddes gives an instructive example by comparing the epilogue of Shakespeare's *The Tempest* with the ending of the Gospel of John in Chapter 2 of the present volume.
34 A mathematical function is not completed by additional determinations to formulate a law of physics, it is simply read differently: as a rule we have to follow in order to find interesting similarities between physical constellations. Cf. Wolfgang Stegmüller, *Theorienstrukturen und Theoriendynamik. Probleme und Resultate der Wissenschaftstheorie und Analytischen Philosophie*, Bd. 2/2 (Berlin, Heidelberg and New York: Walter de Gruyter, 1973).

Five

Revelation as Gestalt

Rainer Fischer

1 Points of Orientation in Determining the Concept of Gestalt

In the first of his five books on the 'Refutation and Contradiction of Gnosis falsely so called', Irenaeus of Lyons (*c.* AD 180) illustrates the appearance of the Holy Scripture(s) by means of a remarkable comparison. He accuses gnostic exegetes of having changed the true order of the Scriptures and altered the true sense by falsifying the way the books are assembled.[1] This treatment of the Scriptures, he continues, seems to him to be

> as if someone were to destroy the basic human shape of the image of a king made by a wise artist out of many-coloured stones, misplace and change around the stones, make the image of a dog or a fox, and at the same time try to explain and assert that this was still that beautiful image of a king which the wise artist made.[2]

It is remarkable that Irenaeus draws on a comparison from the world of visual perception for the reading and understanding of the Bible; remarkable, too, that he narrows the treatment of texts down to the problem of the ordering of the individual components in relation to the whole by using the example of mosaics, and admits that there are many possibilities for such a relationship. His insistence on a single 'correct' ordering which does justice to the appearance of the Scriptures may take us aback, because our exegetical and communicative perception is characterized by the manifold variety of the biblical texts and of the possibilities for their reception. But, precisely in the context of these varied ways of understanding texts, and an increasing preference nowadays for a 'patchwork' hermeneutic, Irenaeus' mosaic image reminds us of *the need to examine our overall picture of the biblical texts and to ask whether there is a particular Gestalt from which revelation – that is, God's self-manifestation – emerges.*

This task also arises because the perception of the biblical texts is not connected with the visual perception of a pictorial Gestalt merely in the sense of an illustrative 'as if'. On the contrary, reading and understanding the Bible occurs in a way that *really* corresponds to seeing and composing a picture. It is no accident that the formulation 'I *see* it differently' surfaces when people try to understand each other's divergent interpretations of biblical texts, or the biblical basis for different points of view. There is more behind this way of speaking than simply a visual illustration of differing standpoints in an argument. Different viewpoints may derive from the fact that different aspects of the object under discussion are being perceived. But the reason may also be that there are totally different ways of seeing the matter about which agreement is being sought. In any case the perception of Gestalt plays a decisive role.

Hence, in the 'dispute about interpretations' (as Paul Ricoeur has observed), the attempt to solve the hermeneutical problem by an extensive ontological recourse to the question of the being of the understanding subject and the appearance of being does not go far enough.[3] Ricoeur prefers a different phenomenological approach. He unlocks the hermeneutical problem as a semantic one,[4] asks about psychological processes in the interpretation of texts,[5] and concentrates on the process by which the formation of meaning takes shape, describing it as a threefold *mimesis* (prefiguration, configuration, refiguration) in its extension through time.[6] Instead of seeking to simplify the 'dispute about interpretations' by placing it within the frame of a philosophical overview, Ricoeur dissects the problem phenomenologically. We intend to continue along this path and to ask about the aesthetic constitution of hermeneutics. How is the Gestalt of a text appropriated?

The term 'Gestalt' describes a perceived coherence. The Gestalt, as a narrated, coherent entity, takes linguistic form in a *story*: it forms the *plot* and at the same time the *scopus*. In relation to the perception of the Bible this coherence is extremely complex, because in it there is a convergence between the effect of the biblical texts and their perception by their recipients.[7] To put it differently, the impression which the biblical texts mediate, and the way this impression is structured within our grasp of it through sense perception and reason, converge on the claim that here something of God's speech and action becomes clear. In an attempt to penetrate the complexity of this coherence we begin by borrowing some ideas from Gestalt theory in psychological aesthetics.

From an epistemological point of view the term 'Gestalt' is 'a basic term in aesthetics and as such (like all basic terms) undefinable, that is not capable of being equated with a combination of terms "more familiar" than itself'.[8] The founder of Gestalt theory, Christian von Ehrenfels, introduced the term 'Gestalt' in order to describe complex wholes (such as melodies) which are so perceived from the beginning. In his treatise *Über Gestaltqualitäten* (1890), Ehrenfels identified two criteria of perceived

Gestalten. First, the Gestalt as a psychological whole is *more and other than the sum of its parts*; secondly, it is distinguished by its *transposability*, that is, its distinctive characteristics remain the same in a variety of constellations, like a melody transposed into different keys.[9]

In his later work (*Kosmogonie*, 1916) Ehrenfels – like his pupil Max Wertheimer in his studies of how we see movements (1912) – drew stronger attention to the process of shaping, the activity that precedes the formation of a Gestalt, and in this acknowledged the key role of transformations (*Umgestaltungen*: called *Übergänge* by Wertheimer).[10] Wolfgang Köhler, who introduced the term 'Gestalt' into the Anglo-American vocabulary (*Gestalt Psychology*, 1929), saw at work in the processes of transformation what he called a 'tendency to pregnant meaning'. According to this principle the appropriation of a Gestalt tends to the closed and regular configuration of a 'good *Gestalt*'.[11] But as against Ehrenfels's first and second criteria, this feature is in no way essential to the perception of Gestalt.[12]

The decisive matter is the *integrated definition of the term* 'Gestalt', not only in relation to what is perceived but also in relation to the perceiver. In relation to the thing perceived the initial stages of perceiving a Gestalt reject an analytical dissection concentrating on the appropriation of individual elements; for this runs the risk of losing sight of the structure of relationships *between* these elements, which cannot be reduced to the sum of all the parts. The Gestalt is not the result of a brain-teaser: it does not arise through the human mind's first collecting sense impressions and then working these up to make a coherent, rational whole.[13] Rather, human perception is determined in advance by a smaller or larger number of Gestalt complexes, which form the connecting links between sense impressions and rational perception. Hence the 'priority of the coherence of *Gestalten*' is just as valid for sense perception as it is for the emotional and rational appropriation of facts.[14]

Accordingly, the priority of Gestalt-type perception provides a key to understanding human cognition in general as an integrated process, embracing both sensuous and rational knowledge. This wholeness of the human grasp of reality is not in the least the realization of a sensory whole, for the complexity of a Gestalt always rests on a selective perception.[15] As Rudolf Arnheim demonstrated, 'grasping substantial general characteristics' stands at the beginning of the process of human cognition.[16] The perception of 'general characteristics' rests, however, on an abstraction which (contrary to a widely held opinion) does not represent a 'departure from immediate experience'. On the contrary, only abstraction can open up an ordered route into the world of experience (cf. Arnheim, 1972, pp.153ff., 181), and thus form the 'bridge between perception and thought'.

2 Clues for Differing Perceptions of the Gestalt of the Bible

What clues are there that might lead us to suppose that the different ways in which the Bible is understood really rest on different perceptions of its Gestalt? With our limited framework we cannot present a comprehensive phenomenology, but only a few shafts of light. *First*, we should note *the choice between methods of exegesis and interpretation, and the way they are focused on particular dimensions of the biblical text.* If, for example, we observe the much-criticised fixation on the facticity of the text which is to be found in historical-critical exegesis, with the concomitant far-reaching neglect of (among other things) its spiritual dimension, then we shall have to agree that 'the problem of the theological legitimacy of historical-critical exegesis … is at its core a problem of theological aesthetics'.[17]

A *second clue* is provided by *the use of the categories 'abstract' and 'concrete'* in understanding the Bible. Appeals for a 'literal' understanding of the Bible generally claim to be defending the 'concrete' sense of the biblical texts against exaggerated or critically distanced interpretations – interpretations which abstract from what 'is really there', thus leaving the door wide open for texts to mean anything you like. As a brief glance at the insights of Gestalt psychology has shown us, the dividing line between 'abstract' and 'concrete', which looks so clearly drawn, is really a blur of fluid transitions. In the beginning the appeal to an immediate, 'concrete' correspondence of wording and revelational Gestalt looks conclusive; but in the concrete case it proves to be itself an abstraction, and in drawing a clear dividing line it fails because of the way letters, seen as reflections of reality, break down.

Quite apart from the changes in meaning which affect the Hebrew and Greek texts of the Bible through translation (since every translation is also an interpretation),[18] the relation of the letters on the page to reality is rendered inadequate and peculiarly broken by the fact that the letters do not designate objects in an immediate way but are only 'signs for [auditory] signs for objects'.[19] Between letters and reality stands the wording.[20] In a special theological sense the relation between the letters of the biblical text and the revelational content which is ascribed to them also breaks down because no utterance can express God's truth fully and finally. Hence the reality of God cannot be ascribed a one-to-one relation to the words of the Bible. Otherwise, God would be reduced to an object among the other objects that lie in the catchment area of human cognition.

Here is a further reflection. We have seen that there can be a superficial evaluation of the literal meaning of the words of Scripture as 'concrete', and of the meaning of Scripture applied to a particular situation in which it is to be used as 'abstract'. But this is actually less obvious than it seems at first sight. Johann Georg Hamann (1730–88), a friend and critic of Kant and other intellectual luminaries of the time, went so far as to defend the thesis that the reverse is true: the 'literal meaning of Scripture' is abstract and the applied understanding of the Bible extremely concrete.

On the assumption that the biblical texts reveal God's speech and action, understanding them is inseparable from applying them to the life of the recipient (it is *this* that is signalled in 2 Tim. 3:16). Therefore, according to Hamann, the 'literal meaning of Scripture' conceals hidden beginnings, which to start with are still abstract, and which grow in concreteness only through further knowledge, experience and application.[21] Anyone who still asserts that the literal meaning of Scripture allows only a single interpretation is not only turning 'literal understanding' into a bloodless abstraction without 'spirit and life', but is also overlooking the 'beam of popery in his own eye',[22] in other words the authoritarian claim to represent the one correct meaning which is bound up with abstraction.

A *third clue* to perceiving the Gestalt of the Bible consists in *the way the 'central issue' and the 'side issues' in the Bible are determined and set in order*. In an essay entitled 'Unser Streit um die Bibel', Martin Kähler put forward the thesis that for understanding the Bible it was enough to concentrate one's interest on the 'main issue', and only to pay as much attention to the 'side issues' as was absolutely essential.[23] In this he describes the hermeneutical scheme of the 'canon within the canon' as a formal phenomenon, saying that perceiving the Bible as a whole does not mean understanding it as 'a whole all of the same kind, in which every piece and every part has the same value' (Kähler, 1967, p.57); rather, a holistic understanding of the Bible requires a sharpened perception, whose surrounds may legitimately have a certain lack of sharpness without thereby becoming completely indeterminate.

Kähler is opposing in this thesis a development of the doctrine of verbal inspiration which began from the opposite point of view:

> There it is argued: 'Because all the side issues are in order, I can rely on the central one, *and not otherwise*.' My argument is: 'Because the central issue is in order, the same will be true of the side issues, *but the former does not depend on the latter*.' (ibid., p.47)

Such a view of the Bible can easily be exposed to the danger of understanding it chiefly by contradicting opposed positions, and thereby it gets entangled in the same set of problems that it denounces in historical–critical research: the fragmentation of a holistic understanding into unconnected questions of detail (for example, about dating or authorship). Against this, Kähler represents a doctrine of inspiration which is equally open at its edges, and this is an immediate consequence of his understanding of the 'central issue': justification through faith in Jesus Christ, who relieves the person forming a judgment about the text of the necessity of constituting his relationship to the Bible through a comprehensive understanding which is his own work (cf. ibid., pp.73, 79).

3 Hans Urs von Balthasar's Perception of the Bible as a Gestalt of Splendour

Apart from occasional examples,[24] no theologian in modern times has handled the question of spiritual perception of Gestalt so comprehensively as Hans Urs von Balthasar. In an interview, Balthasar identified the concept of Gestalt as the clue to his theology: Gestalt in the sense of *a structure of perception, within which there is no conflict between determinacy and multiplicity of meanings:*

> I have tried to see Christianity or the figure of Christ first of all as a *Gestalt*; and together with Christ, his Church. One can walk around a *Gestalt* and look at it from all sides. Again and again one sees something different – and yet sees the same thing.[25]

The first part of his theological aesthetic (published with the overall title *Herrlichkeit*) Balthasar entitled *Schau der Gestalt*. In it he deals with the 'total witness of history as Scripture presents it to us ... with the sign of the concept of *Gestalt*',[26] and with the basic theological question how God's revelation is perceived in history, as 'a question of seeing the *Gestalt*' (Balthasar, 1961, p.166). Accordingly, consideration of the '*Gestalt* of revelation' forms the pivot of his theological aesthetics, into which the perception of God in history is compressed:

> The experience of God in the Bible, in the old and new covenants, is completely characterized by the fact that the God who is by nature 'invisible' (John 1:18) and 'unapproachable' (1 Tim. 6:16) ... becomes, through his own action, visible to his creatures; the one who is without *Gestalt* in the world and in history takes on *Gestalt*, and in this *Gestalt*, chosen and clothed by himself, can be encountered and experienced by all mankind. (Ibid., p.290)

Gestalt here means first and foremost a perceived whole;[27] for Balthasar the 'indissolubility of the *Gestalt*' is always 'the first consideration', and the fact that it is 'qualified by many prerequisites' is secondary (ibid., p.23). Here he rejects a historical criticism of the Bible that 'seeks to "understand" what lies before it by actually beginning by dissecting it into sources, psychological goals, and influences from its sociological milieu, before ever the *Gestalt* as such has been truly identified and read with the meaning that attached to the *Gestalt*' (ibid., pp.28f).[28] With this research by dissection he contrasts the primary demand to let what is perceived 'be what it is', and to refrain from 'mastering it and using it up' (ibid., p.145).

The explanation for Balthasar's sometimes violent polemic against a 'dissective' style of biblical research lies in his belief that the perception of a coherent Gestalt is a universal human trait, and that the 'fact of aesthetic *Gestalt*-vision' is an 'incontrovertible fact' (ibid., p.144). 'The meaning [Gehalt] does not lie behind the *Gestalt*, but in it. Anyone who manages not to see and to read the *Gestalt* is bound also to miss the meaning' (ibid.). This mode of argument, in which an opposition is set up between the analytical procedures of scientific research and the givenness of ordinary experience in Gestalt psychology, does not seem at all conclusive; for surely scientific procedure is aiming at a gain in knowledge precisely by stepping outside the old established ways of ordinary experience!

Equally inconclusive, at first sight, is Balthasar's transition from the understanding of the text-Gestalt of the Bible as a perceived whole to a personal understanding of the Gestalt: that is, to the 'perception of the objective God-*Gestalt* of Jesus Christ', which for him is the 'central form of evidence on which all else hangs' (ibid., p.196).[29] It seems like a philological trick when Balthasar uses the linguistic space offered by the term 'Gestalt' in the German language[30] to present the Bible as hanging together only when given a Christological centre. However, within his aesthetic theory this transition is actually consistent, since it rests on the relation of Gestalt (*species*) to splendour (*splendor*) in the sense that one transcends the other aesthetically.

The revelational quality of the Gestalt results, for Balthasar, from the fact that, when it is perceived, it becomes possible for a 'deep dimension between ground and appearance' (ibid., p.145) to become visible, a dimension which he summarizes under the term 'the beautiful': 'The beautiful is above all a *Gestalt*, and light does not fall from above and outside onto this *Gestalt*, but breaks forth from within it. In beauty *species* and *lumen* are one and the same' (ibid., p.144). In selecting *species* and *lumen* (or *splendor*), Gestalt and splendour, as the basic relation of the beautiful, Balthasar is referring back to the doctrine of transcendence in mediaeval scholasticism,[31] especially in Thomas Aquinas, in whose work the terms '*species*' (as a synonym for *pulchritudo*) and '*splendor*'[32] as a defining characteristic of beauty alongside *integritas* and *proportio* are juxtaposed in the framework of a consideration of Christology.[33] This is the source of Balthasar's statement that in Christ *species* and *lumen* coincide (ibid., p.226).

What is decisive for him in the special 'revelational *Gestalt*' of Jesus Christ is 'that this *Gestalt* proclaims himself to be the revelation of the inner depths of God' (ibid., p.165), and that this extraordinary claim of Jesus Christ becomes accessible only in the perspective of the promises of the old covenant:[34]

> The *Gestalt* of Christ ... appears in the world with such an abundance of meaning ... that as a divine, divine-yet-worldly synthesis He is bound to be simply too much for humanity, seeming dark from an excess of light. This eschatological culmination of all absolutes would inevitably seem a pure contradiction, if it were not broken down through an historical prism: the prism of the old covenant. (Ibid., pp.620f)

Balthasar bypasses metaphysical explanations of Jesus' claim to reveal (which on the ordinary view of things is opaque) by explaining them from the relation of the old to the new covenant: Jesus Christ, as the 'place where that which was not a *Gestalt*, from an eschatological point of view, becomes a *Gestalt*' (ibid., p.628), brings together in one the things that in the old covenant 'were disclosed serially' (ibid., p.617).

The Gestalt of Holy Scripture as a perceived unity thus consists in its transparency to the Gestalt of Jesus Christ. Balthasar speaks of the 'mutual reflection' of the old and the new covenant giving 'the greatest transparency to the mirror' (ibid., p.202), and emphasizes 'that Scripture does indeed have a *Gestalt*, but that this is theologically significant only insofar as it is a pointer and a witness to God's revelational *Gestalt* in Christ through the Holy Spirit' (ibid., p.524). Here he is using the same principle of transcendence to determine the relationship of the *Gestalten* of Scripture and revelation that lies at the basis of his determination of the personal and revelational *Gestalten* of Jesus: the transcending of the 'beautiful' Gestalt by a splendour which does not fall suddenly upon it from without but breaks forth from within it. Beginning with the analogy of such a transcending within worldly and historical existence, Balthasar is here pursuing a 'path from below to above' (ibid., p.31), which the idea of Gestalt provides him with the methodological means to develop.[35]

That the Gestalt of Jesus Christ transcends its historical context follows, not from the (salvation) historical development of the old and the new covenant, but from the relationship of cross and resurrection. It is only with his resurrection that Jesus Christ acquires that *Übergestalt*[36] which is the completion of the 'beautiful' Gestalt; the 'shattering' of the Gestalt in the event of the cross is 'removed' (*aufgehoben*) in the Thomist sense.[37] The 'categories of aesthetics' are 'not simply destroyed, but (in an inconceivably positive way) are raised above themselves [*non destruit, sed elevat, extollit, perficit naturam*], in order to provide lodging for something which is infinitely greater than they' (ibid., pp.586f).

This transition from a secular aesthetic to a divine one resting on grace is, according to Balthasar's understanding, fixed irreversibly by God, and it requires a 'conversion from seeing to being seen by God' (ibid., p.467). On the other hand, its outlines are to some extent blurred because it picks up the bias to the transcendental that Balthasar derives from the original phenomenon ('*Urphänomen*') of the aesthetic. According to this a certain splendour, a certain radiance is always given 'simultaneously' with the Gestalt (ibid., p.18); it is precisely in its radiance that the Gestalt – the form of the beautiful that appears – transcends itself, even inwardly (ibid., p.20). This is particularly apparent, Balthasar argues, in the spiritual Gestalt of the human being, that is his or her spiritual–physical identity (cf. ibid., pp.18ff).[38]

The perception of the transcendental tendency of the Gestalt is, however, by no means so self-evident as its designation as an '*Urphänomen*' leads one to expect. Balthasar indirectly admits this when he reproaches Gestalt psychology for having surrendered the 'transcending centre of independence' which forms 'the centre of the concept of *Gestalt* for the sake of the "precise, scientific" measurability' of the *Gestalt*' as 'the "correlative unity" of "elementary functions" of the soul'.[39] Furthermore, he emphasizes the impossibility of making a 'univocal use and application' of the transcendental depth effect, which is manifested in the pleasure generated by the 'beautiful' Gestalt, to the 'content of Christian theology', 'because the living God is neither a "being" ... nor "being" itself as this shows and reveals itself according to its nature in everything that appears and that has a *Gestalt*' (Balthasar, 1965, p.112). According to him, it is only by an excessive analogy that we can express the idea that the 'creation, reconciliation and redemption of the triune God' presents 'a genuine self-presentation and self-interpretation in the worldly substance of nature, man, and history' (ibid.).

Faith and rationality coincide in this 'excessive analogy' insofar as Balthasar extends the connection between the natural and the supernatural (nature and grace) within the dimension of time, and understands faith as an anticipation of an eschatological view of the whole. Faith grasps the point of unity sought in vain 'by the mind whose researches are guided by the meaning of the signs' in the 'realm of the natural' (ibid., p.169) and thereby takes part itself in Christ's coming to be a Gestalt in the space of the Church (cf. ibid., pp.506ff). This 'dynamic' extension of the Gestalt of revelation also explains why the determinacy and the semantic plurality of the biblical texts can converge on the concept of Gestalt: 'The *Gestalt* of Scripture,' writes Balthasar, 'is intentionally loose and dependent on perspective, to prevent us from attaching ourselves to it and taking the clothes for the body' (ibid., p.520):[40]

> The canonical picture of revelation is 'closed' because any intensification of God's gift of himself to the world in Jesus Christ is in itself impossible. But for

> the same reason, its divine insurpassibility, the picture of this content remains open for the whole of historical time, to be ever more deeply grasped and penetrated. (Ibid., p.530)

Progress in knowledge can, indeed, never build a bridge between God and the world through thought. Balthasar warns against such a misunderstanding of the *analogia entis*: it does not mean 'identity'; the human spirit and the Holy Spirit are not to be equated (ibid., p.305); *analogia entis* is concerned rather with God's revelation through creation as an unveiling leading to 'an ever greater veiling' (ibid., p.433). Consequently, there can be a point of intersection between secular and divine aesthetics only where the 'theological dialectic between veiling and unveiling', God's '*Übergestalt*' in the '*Ungestalt*' – that is, his glory *sub contrario* – comes to light: in the cross of Jesus Christ (ibid., p.442). This point of intersection between a natural and a theological aesthetic is however also the critical point at which Balthasar's perception of God threatens to pass over from incessant listening to a 'quietened vision'.[41]

Thus he transfers the principle of the holistic perception of the Gestalt from its original context in natural philosophy (Herder, Goethe), or in Gestalt psychology, to a theological (Christological) setting, and thus understands 'splendour' (*doxa*) or radiance as a substantial and, at the same time, transcending component of the Gestalt. And this moves the '*Übergestalt*' of the risen Christ into the centre of theological aesthetics, as the completion of every secular Gestalt and thus at the same time as the presupposition of a spiritual–physical overview. Thereby the '*Ungestalt*' of the crucified Christ, all the 'unconforming, unpleasant, unbeautiful, inappropriate, unreasonable aspects of the *Gestalt* of Jesus',[42] risk becoming no more than a stage on the route of theological aesthetics. The *theologia crucis* of broken Gestalthood threatens to be driven out by the *theologia gloriae* of perfect wholeness.[43]

Gisbert Greshake complained of this danger in an early review of Balthasar's theological aesthetics: 'Not even the words of the Scripture of the one Logos' could produce the 'harmony' of a *theologia gloriae*:

> As long as we live and are *in via*, we participate in the cross *and* the glorious resurrection of our Lord. In both cases a real participation; a real participation in the cross, too (in the dimension of the broken, the failed, the unaesthetic). Therefore any theology of aesthetics (of *gloria*) is always bound to bear the sting of being questionable.

'With the greatest respect,' he says, he does not know 'whether the writer is always aware of this,' since the 'elan of the beautiful often drives him beyond the measure he himself has set and into a possession and vision of *gloria* which really exists only in hope.'[44]

Admittedly, Balthasar does not overlook the fragmentary, but he subsumes it under an overall theological view by theologically extrapolating splendour – the radiance of every Gestalt that exceeds human comprehension – with the aid of a way of thinking based on analogy; and this he justifies by drawing in advance on the resources of trust. Even the collapse and shattering of this-worldly Gestalt (which finds its highest theological expression in what happened on the cross) does not throw the view of splendour into question or even into doubt, but on the contrary confirms it, since Balthasar interprets the 'breaks' in reality in the sense of an openness through which natural being becomes as it were transparent to God's appearing.[45]

Balthasar is trapped in the thinking in terms of *ordo* that comes from a theology of creation, and caught up in a 'fundamental opposition' to Enlightenment thought;[46] consequently in his decision that transcendent splendour is the defining characteristic of all beauty he leaves out of account that brokenness in which the 'beautiful appearance' has been seen in modern times from the point of view of truth.[47] Talk of the 'glory' of God thus comes under the suspicion of being a false appearance which is 'too beautiful to be true'. At the same time it threatens not to let the individual Gestalt be: in its efforts to guard the Gestalt against being dissected and overpowered by rationality, Balthasar's aesthetic succumbs to the opposite danger of overlaying the particular individuality of the Gestalt with the pre-appearance of the '*Übergestalt*'. Perceiving more in a Gestalt than it represents at first sight can, as a contemplative experience, lead to the discovery of multifarious examples of theological transparency in the Bible, but as the discursive mode of cognition in a theological aesthetics it can also lead one to reduce the present form of the text to the pieces of a jigsaw puzzle representing a pre-drawn theological *Gesamtgestalt* (total Gestalt).

4 The Perception of the Bible through the Formation of Gestalten: Mimesis and Metamorphosis

The concept of Gestalt has proved itself (in Balthasar's theological aesthetic by way of example) to be the nodal point for the perception of the Bible, since it unites determinacy and yet a range of meanings within itself, makes it possible to describe the effect of texts together with their reception as a coherent event, and is capable of embracing the transition from a perception (in principle) of the whole to the perception of a personal self-proclamation by God.

Is it possible to describe a biblical Gestalt of revelation without going down the road to Balthasar's problematic prolepsis and prematurely fusing the holistic tendency with which the perception of a Gestalt begins with an eschatological overview of everything? Can the biblical texts be understood in their transparency to God's self-disclosure without suppressing experiences of brokenness, failure and contrariety in an aesthetic of transcendence? To find an answer to this we shall recall in what follows some important details of the process of Gestalt formation in the perception of the Bible. Even readers who are not Lutheran in their bones may find here heuristic aids and suggestive stimuli in Luther.

The first thing to notice is that Luther does not simply identify the Gestalt of revelation in the Bible with 'what is there'. By the Gospel (as the epitome of the Bible's Gestalt of revelation) he understood 'not what stands in books and is composed of letters, but rather an oral preaching and a living word which resounds in all the world and is openly proclaimed, which can be heard everywhere'.[48] To put it generally, *the Gestalt of a biblical text is perceived in the first instance as a 'wording'* (*Wort-Laut*). Here Luther is swimming against the tide of historical development. The increasing transformation of speech into writing, promoted particularly by the advent of printing, was leading to a changed perception of texts, with a decline in reading aloud either to others or to oneself (*meditatio*) and its replacement by individual use of a visual text.[49] But Luther held fast to 'orality in writtenness'.[50]

Thus he understands the appropriation of biblical texts as a communication event (whereas Balthasar's view of the biblical Gestalt of revelation assumes that the ontological givenness of a transcendent splendour is appropriate to any and every Gestalt). By recognizing the claim of the texts to have 'something to say' and allowing them the first word, Luther relativizes the individual time-bound character of each successive edition of the text and transfers the emphasis onto an encounter with the Gestalt of the text as it comes to meet us as a whole in its 'literal meaning', which is more than just the sum of its letters.[51]

Beyond the general hermeneutical experience that a text 'says something' to me there is here also an expectation that God's speech is there to be apprehended in the biblical texts. In this respect the wording (*Wort-Laut*) of the Bible represents a 'mediating' kind of language; that is, it mediates linguistically a possibility for 'making sense' in which what is questionable is not the meaning of an individual in the context of a fixed order, but this order itself[52] – because God, as we have already noted, cannot be classified as one object alongside others within the catchment area of human cognition. As a 'language of faith' this mediating language is characterized by the 'unrest of questioning'; it 'forbids us to linger on what seems to us certain'.[53] Thereby those who apprehend the wording of the Bible are drawn into the theological creation of Gestalt. The perceptions of the Gestalt of the biblical revelation and the Gestalt of our own life are mutually illuminating; and by this the concept of Gestalt teaches us to look for the transposability of the characteristics we have apprehended, and in this way to unite specificity with multiplicity of meaning. For this a particular type of cognition is needed which can be described (in dependence on Luther) as the *vita passiva.*

If human cognition in general is for Luther not a 'work', 'something we do', but something 'that we receive and take',[54] then this is especially true of coming to know the word of God: 'it desires only to be well regarded, gazed upon, and taken deep into the heart'.[55] Accordingly, the *vita passiva* does not imply passivity in the sense of a dismal state in which one has no ability to influence what happens, but a sense of being addressed by the biblical texts, a perception and experience which knows how to let what has been apprehended be as it is. On the basis of Psalm 119, Luther established for this the threefold rule of *oratio*, *meditatio*, *tentatio*.[56]

With this trio he is opposing a treatment of the Bible that understands it in a double sense of the expression *zu grund.*[57] Anyone who thinks he has got to the bottom of the Bible after reading it once or twice has really reached rock-bottom with it, because the Gestalt of its text seems dispensable to him once he has grasped its supposed contents (a particular moral or doctrine). By contrast, the *vita passiva*, which includes a sensuous as well as a rational dimension,[58] is not closed: its openness, as Oswald Bayer comments, excludes the 'fixing' of a universally valid meaning 'by one's own authority', and teaches us 'to attain new experiences in meditation, in our dealings with the inexhaustible Bible'.[59]

How does the Gestalt of the biblical revelation look if in the fullness of possible relations to experience it retains its openness, as against being fixed in a 'closed picture', yet at the same time makes possible a certain apprehension of the word of God, an apprehension that remains recognizable in many different configurations? To answer this question we must first pose another: how can a theoretical 'orality in writtenness' take on the personal Gestalt of God's self-proclamation? The answer, as simple as it is full of problems, is: it can happen when we come to an existential encounter which decides matters of life and death. 'For a long time I regarded the Bible as a book that had been completely overtaken,' a therapist said to me recently, 'until I realized that when the Bible speaks of God, it speaks at the same time of the decisive themes of human nature: love and hate, despair and hope; real life, and the meaning of death.'

'The Lord kills, and makes alive' (1 Sam. 2:6); for Luther this saying (which he sharpened into 'God makes alive by killing'[60]) wraps up in itself the action of God as attested in the Bible. Only for the person who sets himself against the self-knowledge which destroys, in confrontation with what is prescribed in the Bible, can experience the literal sense of Scripture as transparent, producing a liberating encounter with God's word of grace. It is in the paradoxical realization – which runs counter to our usual expectations – *that God makes alive by killing*, that his self-proclamation achieves its peculiar Gestalt in the biblical texts.

Luther grasped this Gestalt in the distinction between law and grace. The inner tension in this distinction results from the fact that God's paradoxical self-proclamation, which acts in an unexpected and hence free manner, cannot be reduced to a common denominator. Hence Luther spoke repeatedly of the antithetical structure of the biblical message.[61] The tendency of Gestalt perception to be pregnant with meaning here runs against a boundary, for this antithetical structure cannot be evened out to make a unified 'good' Gestalt, even though there have always been attempts to do so. These range from the distribution of opposites to distinct bodies of text, so that the Old Testament is supposed to be identified with law and the New Testament with grace or gospel (this proposal is falsely attributed to Luther himself), through the didactic arrangement of law and gospel as successive stages in the experience of conscience, to the explanation found in popular piety according to which the antithetical gospel and law are seen as 'gift' (*Gabe*) and 'task' (*Aufgabe*), thus finally converting the antithesis into a *tertius usus legis*.

Yet the really problematic aspect of linking the Gestalt of biblical revelation with the experience of life and death does not lie in such attempts at smoothing it out, but in reinterpreting the antithesis of law and gospel as a method for overcoming the contingency of human experiences.[62] But the attempt to master existential contradictions by tracing them back to God's action as the greatest common denominator fails to recognize that the antithetical opening of the Gestalt of the Bible on to God's self-proclamation cannot of itself claim any plausibility in principle. How can the biblical message nevertheless be apprehended as a definite Gestalt of revelation, without making God's free self-proclamation turn into something obvious, or extending certain marks of the Gestalt to form a transcendent overview, thus eliding the breaks in this Gestalt?

Once again, it is illuminating to look at Luther's understanding of the Bible. It was possible for Luther to avoid smoothing out the tension between law and gospel because he saw them as joined together by being focused together on the Gestalt of Jesus Christ: in the crucified one who has risen again we see that God makes alive by killing. That God veils himself even as he reveals himself is not grounded in the immense fullness of meaning in events, but in the fact that it is he who acts just as much in the crucifixion as in the resurrection of Jesus Christ. Instead of bypassing this scandal of the cross through the synthesis of a *theologia gloriae*, we ought to endure the stark antithesis of God's action – as the deepest *tentatio* of faith, which keeps alive the sense of that which runs counter to us, that which is broken and that which fails!

Against the expectation that God's revelation similarly resolves into an intelligible whole, at least incipiently and proleptically, the linking of cross and resurrection transfers us to a movement characterized by a healthy insecurity. God appears in the biblical texts in the broken Gestalt of Jesus Christ. The metamorphosis (*Umgestaltung*) of the one who was crucified in his resurrection becomes the fulcrum and hinge of a perception which transforms the one who experiences it (cf. 2 Cor. 3:18). This definiteness of the Gestalt of revelation does not mean a 'canon within the canon', in the sense of a restriction in the choice of texts or their reduction to a specific theologoumenon. Rather, it means an 'abstraction' in Arnheim's sense (see section 1, above), a sharpening of perception which is essential if any coherent profile of the Bible is to emerge: 'to have Scripture without the knowledge of Christ is to have no Scripture'.[63] The *human picture of the king* (Irenaeus) appears, paradoxically, in the mosaic of the biblical texts (as in a jigsaw puzzle) only in the appearance of the one who had 'no form nor comeliness' (Isa. 53:2).

Translated from the German by John Barton.

Notes

1 *Adversus haereses* I:8:1 (*SC* 264, 112:9–12).
2 Ibid. (*SC* 264, 114:14–20).
3 Cf. Paul Ricoeur, *The Conflict of Interpretations: Essays in Hermeneutics*, Evanston: Northwestern University Press, 1974, pp.49–50.
4 Ibid., part II, pp.99–208.
5 Ibid., pp.49–50.
6 Paul Ricoeur, *Time and Narrative*, Chicago and London: University of Chicago Press, 1984, pp.52–87.
7 *Wahrnehmen* has connotations in German of an overwhelmingly passive kind – simply 'picking up' what is already there. In what follows it is also used to refer to a comprehension which gives shape (Gestalt) to what is appropriated, in the sense of Latin *percipere* (cf. English 'perceive', used to translate *wahrnehmen* here).
8 Wolfgang Metzger, 'Gestalt', in *Historisches Wörterbuch der Philosophie* (HWP), Basel: Schwabe, 1971–, 3, ed. Joachim Ritter, cols 540–48. The quotation is from col. 540.
9 Cf. Herbert Fitzek and Wilhelm Salber, *Gestaltpsychologie. Geschichte und Praxis* (Darmstadt, 1996), pp.17ff.
10 Ibid., pp.26ff.
11 Ibid., pp.49ff. See also Wolfgang Metzger, *Gestalt-Psychologie. Ausgewählte Werke aus den Jahren 1950 bis 1982*, ed. Michael Stadler and Heinrich Crabus (Frankfurt a.M., 1986), p.160. The tendency to pregnant meaning was first recognized and studied

in the realm of the way we see objects, but it can also be demonstrated, for example, in the functioning of human memory: see pp.185ff. Something that might be of particular interest to the biblical critic is the phenomenon of so-called 'mixed stories', in which the hearer or reader notices inconsistencies in the text, but the tendency to pregnant meaning does not allow him to hold the interwoven stories apart in his mind.

12 Cf. Fitzek and Salber, *supra*, n.9, p.70.

13 Cf. Metzger, *Gestalt-Psychologie*, p.103.

14 See Wolfhart Henckmann, 'Gestalttheorie', in Wolfhart Henckmann and Konrad Lotter (eds), *Lexikon der Aesthetik* (Munich: Chr. Kaiser, 1992), pp.92f; the quotation is from p.92.

15 Cf. Wolfgang Welsch, *Ästhetisches Denken*, 2nd edn (Stuttgart: Reclam, 1991), p.31: 'Gestalt psychology has taught us not only that there is a non-perception corresponding to each perception, but that such exclusion, such selectivity is constitutive of our ability to perceive.' Cf. also Johannes B. Lotz, *Ästhetik aus der ontologischen Differenz. Das Anwesen des Unsichtbaren im Sichtbaren* (Munich: J. Berchmann, 1984), p.43.

16 Rudolf Arnheim, *Visual Thinking*, London: Faber, 1970; German translation by the author, *Anschauliches Denken. Zur Einheit von Bild und Begriff*, Cologne, 1972, pp.150ff., 181.

17 Thomas Söding, 'Geschichtlicher Text und Heilige Schrift – Fragen zur theologischen Legitimität', in Christoph Dohmen, Christoph Jacob and Thomas Söding (eds), *Neue Formen der Schriftauslegung* (Quaestiones Disputatae, 140) (Freiburg i. B., Basle and Vienna: Herder, 1992), pp.75–130; the quotation is on p.78.

18 Cf. Ernstpeter Maurer, section 1, Chapter 4 of the present volume.

19 Metzger, *Gestalt-Psychologie*, p.388.

20 In addition, the connection between wording and reality is also fluid, because texts enshrine a poetic as well as a mimetic quality: see Paul Fiddes, Chapter 2 of the present volume.

21 'Abstracta initiis occultis; concrèta maturitati conveniunt.' J.G. Hamann, *Aesthetica in nuce* (1762) in *Sokratische Denkwürdigkeiten. Aesthetica in nuce, hg. von Sven-Aage Jørgensen* (Stuttgart: Theologische Bücherei (ThB), 1988), 107:27f. (Hamann is drawing on a saying of Johann Albrecht Bengel.)

22 Cf. ibid., 105:34ff. or 105:9.

23 Martin Kähler, 'Unser Streit um die Bibel' (1895), reprinted in M. Kähler, *Aufsätze zur Bibelfrage, hg. von Ernst Kähler* (Munich: Chr. Kaiser, 1967 (*ThB*, 37), pp.17–83). The reference here is to p.47: 'it is understandable enough to think that, where the main thing is present, things will be all right with the side issues, so far as that is necessary'.

24 Cf. for example Karl Barth, *Church Dogmatics*, I/1 (in German, *Kirchliche Dogmatik*, 11th edn, *I/1* (Zurich: Zollikon: Verlag der evangelischen Buchhandlung, 1985), p.333), Edinburgh: T.&T. Clark, 1961, who speaks of revelation, that is the 'self-unveiling', of God to human beings as a 'particular *Gestalt*'. In describing the concrete being (*Da-Sein*) of revelation he attributes a decisive meaning to the term 'Gestalt'. Barth does, it is true, base his dogmatic prolegomena on discussions of 'the Word of God in its threefold form (*Gestalt*)' (section 4), but the concept of 'form' remains strangely pale. We learn only that it is motivated by a concern for the Trinity (pp.124f.) and that the emphasis lies on the event of metamorphosis, the way the Gestalt becomes new (p.90).

25 Michael Albus, 'Geist und Feuer. Ein Gespräch mit Hans Urs von Balthasar', *HerKorr*, 30 (1976), 72–82; the quotation is from p.76. Cf. Manfred Lochbrunner, *Analogia Caritatis. Darstellung und Deutung der Theologie Hans Urs von Balthasars* (Freiburg i.B., Basle and Vienna, 1981), p.166.

26 Hans Urs von Balthasar, *Herrlichkeit. Eine theologische Aesthetik. Bd. I: Schau der Gestalt* (Einsiedeln: Johannes Verlag, 1961), p.634.
27 For the term 'whole' (*Ganzheit*) as a 'synonym for the term *Gestalt*', see Lochbrunner, *supra*, n.25, p.173.
28 For the context of Balthasar's dispute with historical–critical method, cf. Hanspeter Heinz, *Der Gott des Je-mehr. Der christologischer Ansatz Hans Urs von Balthasars* (Berne and Frankfurt a.M.: H. Lang, 1975), pp.63ff.
29 'Every theological Gestalt comes down ..., when it is mediated by the canonical picture of Scripture, to the Gestalt of the Lord' (535).
30 According to Jacob and Wilhelm Grimm, *Deutsches Wörterbuch*, vol. IV, div. 1, pt 2, Leipzig, 1897, the semantic range of the term '*Gestalt*' stretches from 'the way in which some *Gestalt* is placed [*gestellt*], made; what state it is in' (col. 4179), through 'the way something looks; appearance, exterior' (col. 4183) and 'the way something presents itself as sharply delineated, with distinctive characteristics' (col. 4184), to 'bearer of a *Gestalt*, person, being' (col. 4189).
31 Cf. Lochbrunner, *supra*, n.25, p.163.
32 In Thomas the term *lumen* is reserved for the designation of the power of cognition (*lumen naturale nostri intellectus* or *lumen supernaturale homini datum*); cf. *S. Th.* II-II q.8 a.1; *DThA* 15:154.
33 Cf. *S.Th.* I q.39 a.8; *DThA* 3:236f.
34 'He is what he is only by fulfilling, on the one hand, the promises that point to him, and, on the other, by himself promising what he will in due course fulfil' (191).
35 Cf. Lochbrunner, *supra*, n.25, pp.168–9.
36 Cf. ibid., p.171.
37 Cf. *S.Th.* I q.1 a.8; *DThA* 1:25 ('*gratia non tollat naturam, sed perficiat*').
38 'The perception of the spiritual *Gestalt* within the world offers an important analogy, the more so because the transcendence of the human being which takes place in it must always be secretly accomplished by a religious, indeed a theological *a priori*, and accordingly is not wholly unknown to us' (175).
39 Hans Urs von Balthasar, *Herrlichkeit. Eine theologische Ästhetik*, vol. III/1, *Im Raum der Metaphysik* (Einsiedeln: Johannes Verlag, 1965), p.33. English translation *The Glory of the Lord: A Theological Aesthetics*, Edinburgh: T.&T. Clark, 1982–.
40 In this context Balthasar does at least credit the historical–critical method with having contributed to a 'raised perspectivity' by 'loosening the texts', and to that extent 'having opened up quite new dimensions for the theological understanding of its object' (520f).
41 The 'best contemplative tradition', according to Balthasar's summary of a specially 'Catholic' danger in theological aesthetics (*Das betrachtende Gebet*, 2nd edn (Einsiedeln: Johannes Verlag, 1959), p.23), 'often tends to pass from listening to a quietened seeing'. ('Hearing' here stands as a synonym for 'faith'; cf. 26: 'Faith and hearing the word of God are one and the same thing.')
42 Cf. Michael Hartmann, *Ästhetik als ein Grundbegriff fundamentaler Theologie. Eine Untersuchung zu Hans Urs von Balthasar* (St. Ottilien: EOS Verlag, 1985), p.79.
43 Typical of this is a passage in Balthasar's summarizing essay 'Die christliche Gestalt' from 1970. Here he certainly maintains that the 'claim', the 'cross' and the 'resurrection' of Jesus Christ are an 'articulation' of his Gestalt, and that they 'reciprocally require and demonstrate each other in a flowing cycle'; but he also emphasizes that the resurrection 'overtakes' the 'tragedy' of the cross and so justifies it. (See Hans Urs von Balthasar, *Pneuma und Institution. Skizzen zur Theologie*, IV (Einsiedeln, 1974), pp.38–60; the words quoted are on pp.50f.)

44 Gisbert Greshake, 'Review of H.U. von Balthasar, *Herrlichkeit*, vols 1 and 2', in Una Sancta, Rundbriefe für interkonfessionelle Begegnung (US), 19 (1964), 370–73; the quotation is on p.373.

45 In this sense 'the outer manifestation or expression of an inner-depth' may be seen as the real identity marker that gives something perceived its Gestalt; cf. Brendán Leahy, 'Theological Aesthetics', in Bede McGregor and Thomas Norris (eds), *The Beauty of Christ: An Introduction to the Theology of Hans Urs von Balthasar* (Edinburgh: T.&T. Clark, 1994), pp.23–55; quotation from p.31.

46 Cf. Reinhard Hoeps, 'Das Gefühl des Erhabenen und die Herrlichkeit Gottes. Studien zur Beziehung von philosophischer und theologischer Ästhetik' (Bonn: Habilitationsschrift, 1988), pp.219f.

47 On this, cf. Willi Oelmüller (ed.), *Kolloquium Kunst und Philosophie*, vol. 2, *Ästhetischer Schein* (Paderborn, Munich, Vienna and Zurich: Schoningh, 1982), esp. pp.44f., 275, 280 and 318f (where there is explicit reference to Balthasar's 'Theology of Glory').

48 Martin Luther, *Epistel S. Pauli gepredigt und ausgelegt* (1523), in *WA*, 12, 259–399; quotation from p.259:10–13. This assertion can be applied not only to the Gospel in the narrower (New Testament) sense, but to the whole Bible. Martin Buber says, for example, in *Die Schrift und ihre Verdeutschung*, that in Scripture everything is 'genuine spokenness'; the translator's task is 'to experience the writtenness of the greater part of "Scripture" as a recording of its spokenness: a spokenness which, as the true reality of the Bible, everywhere reawakens people, wherever an ear hears the word biblically and a mouth speaks it biblically' (in *Werke*, vol. 2, *Schriften zur Bibel* (Munich and Heidelberg: Kösel-Verlag, 1964), pp.1093–1186; the reference here is to pp.1096 and 1114).

49 Cf. Sabine Gross, *Lese-Zeichen. Kognition, Medium und Materialität im Leseprozess* (Darmstadt: Wissenschaftliche Buchgesellschaft, 1994), pp.52f., 62 and 117.

50 Cf. Bernhard Waldenfels, 'Die Fremdheit der Schrift', in Marco M. Olivetti (ed.), *Religione, Parola, Scrittura* (Milan and Padua, 1992), pp.49–59; the quotation is from p.50.

51 One should not, however, exaggerate this emphasis to the point of playing off a 'synchronic' against a 'diachronic' reading of the Bible. Rowan Williams, 'Der Literalsinn der Heiligen Schrift', Evangelische Theologie (EvTh), 50 (1990), draws attention to the fact that the 'diachronic' reading of the Bible (corresponding to establishing its 'literal' sense) 'moves towards, or around, the element that gives unity: the history of the work of Jesus' (p.69), and so is a reading in faith.

52 Cf. Johannes Anderegg, *Sprache und Verwandlung. Zur literarischen Ästhetik* (Göttingen: Vandenhoek & Ruprecht, 1985), pp.49ff.

53 Ibid., p.90 (in the context of remarks on Luther).

54 Martin Luther, *Sermon on John 16–20*; *WA* 28, 43–479; quotation from 100:25f.

55 M. Luther, *Kirchenpostille*, 1522; *WA* 10 I 1:62:6.

56 Cf. Martin Luther, 'Preface to the first volume of the Wittenberg edition' (1539), *WA* 50, 657–61; the quotation is from pp.659f.

57 Cf. ibid., 659:25–7: 'take care that you do not grow weary, or think that in reading it once or twice you have done enough, heard, said and understood everything completely (*zu grund*)'.

58 Martin Luther, *Randbemerkungen zu Taulers Predigten* (*c.* 1516), *WA* 9:95–104: the quotation is from 97:12: '*nota, quod divina pati magis quam agere oportet, immo et sensus et intellectus est naturaliter etiam virtus passiva.*'

59 Oswald Bayer, 'Oratio, Meditatio, Tentatio. Eine Besinnung auf Luthers

Theologieverständnis', in *Luther Jahrbuch*, Jahrbuch der Luther-Gesellschaft (LuJ), 55 (1988), 7–59; the quotation is from p.10.

60 Martin Luther, *De servo arbitrio* (1525), reprinted in Luther, *Studienausgabe*, ed. Hans-Ulrich Delius, vol. 3 (Berlin: Evangelische Verlagsanstalt, 1983), pp.177–356. One p.206:16–19, we read '*Sic Deus dum vivificat, facit illud occidendo, dum iustificat, facit illud reos faciendo, dum in coelum vehit, facit id ad infernum ducendo, ut dicit scriptura, Dominus mortificat (et) vivificat, deducit ad inferos et reducit.*'

61 Cf., inter alia, Martin Luther, *Vorlesung über Jesaja. Scholien* (1532–4), in *WA* 25:87–401, esp. 337:21f: '*Sic enim solet scriptura: fere semper ad antitheses respicit*'; *In epistolam S. Pauli ad Galatas Commentarius* (Lecture, 1531), *WA* 40 I:391:3–5: '*scriptura habet modum, quod plena antithesibus; et est quoddam genus fecundum, interpretari scripturam per Antitheses et eas videre.*'

62 The first signs of such a development can be found in Gerhard Ebeling, who understands Luther's antithetical perception as 'an instruction to be open to life', and thus harnesses it to the contradictions of the world of our experiences. ('Einfalt des Glaubens und Vielfalt der Liebe. Das Herz von Luther's Theologie', in Gerhard Ebeling, *Lutherstudien*, vol. III (Tübingen: J.C.B. Mohr, 1985), pp.126–53; the reference here is to p.144.)

63 Martin Luther, *Kirchenpostille*, 1522: *WA* I 1:628:6f.

Six

Allegoria: Reading as a Spiritual Exercise

Graham Ward

Wim Wender's film *In weiter Ferne, so nah!*, which won the Grand Prix du Jury at Cannes in 1993, opens with a quotation from Matthew's Gospel: 'if your eye is healthy, your whole body will be full of light; but if your eye is unhealthy, your whole body will be full of darkness' (6:22). The film narrates the story of one angel's experience, Cassiel's. So concerned is he with humankind that he asks to become human and his wish is granted. Separated from his angelic state and angelic company he experiences the nature of being human. He sinks into drink and despair. He prays to his angelic friend Raphaela: 'We humans are confined by what is visible, Raphaela! Only what we can see matters. It is all we believe in. Invisible things don't count. Only the things we touch truly exist for us.' The film offers a beautiful and imaginative critique of materialism along the lines of Walter Benjamin's belief that 'Materiality – but here soulless materiality' is the home of the satanic.[1] Benjamin calls for a reassessment of allegory as a form of cultural critique countering that materiality which is 'emancipation from what is sacred'.[2] Wim Wender suggests something similar: we have to learn to see things otherwise.

The title chosen for this chapter bears the traces of its genealogy. With the association of allegory and spiritual reading I am interweaving my text with those mediaeval forms of interpretation which, drawing upon the exegetical methods of the Alexandrine School, systematized a fourfold reading of Scripture: the historical, the allegorical, the tropological and the anagogical. The central division was between the literal and the spiritual senses. As Aquinas notes, and here he is only following in the wake of a pronounced tradition, 'Of these four, allegory alone stands for the three spiritual senses' (*Summa Theologica*, I.Q.1 Art 10). It is important for what I wish to argue for here – a theological understanding of materiality or phenomena – that allegory as such was intimately connected in the mediaeval mind with a doctrine of creation. The second discourse my title is associated with is the set of meditations composed for the training of the Jesuits by their sixteenth-century founder St. Ignatius Loyola. These meditations, entitled *The Spiritual Exercises*,[3] employ imagination as a methodical principle. The

Scriptures are not simply read, they are internalized as prayer. Reading here is not a process of decipherment and the biblical text does not stand as an object before a subject. Reading here is a spiritual exercise; it is a form of 'touching, as being touched', to cite the French philosopher Jean-Luc Nancy.[4] Subject and object both possess permeable membranes and the reading effects a transpositioning (in the full, rich meaning of that word). The third discourse my own text is in dialogue with is the work of the Dutch–American literary critic and theorist Paul de Man. De Man, in 1979, published an influential volume on the work of Rousseau, Nietzsche, Rilke and Proust, entitled *Allegories of Reading*.[5] With the work of Paul de Man we move towards postmodern understandings of *allegoria*: an *allegoria* which returns to a reappraisal of the ancient and mediaeval practices of allegorical composition and interpretation after the Enlightenment and Romantic denunciation of allegory in favour of the symbolic. What I wish to argue for in this chapter is a turn from the stasis of analogy and symbol (important categories for modernity) to the dynamism and semiosis of allegory. But, importantly, the semiosis of allegory is read theologically as a concomitant with a doctrine of creation. For, outside of such a theological reading, semiosis in itself simply announces an aesthetics of nihilism – an annoucement encountered many times with poststructural accounts of the free-floating sign. But the move from static atemporal discussions of analogy and symbol to allegory will lend itself to a rather different model for the hermeneutical task: one that is founded upon narrative, mimesis and participation and one which presents a more dynamic view of the relationship between revelation (the event of Christ), disclosure (a participation in that event), representation and knowledge.

Introducing the Theme

If revelation is understood as the self-giving of God in Christ such that we have knowledge of Him, then our truth claims concerning God must have their origin in an event God Himself executes. The structure of revelation is therefore trinitarian, though whether the event of Christ is an open one (a present continuous action) or a closed one (a punctiliar aorist action) we leave undecided as yet. If hermeneutics is concerned with interpreting the testimonies to that event – insofar as any experience of God has to be mediated, that is attested to, in some discursive form – then Christian hermeneutics must begin with the biblical forms of such testimony: the Gospels.[6] Though whether hermeneutics is integral to that continuing event (a theological hermeneutics) or treats the mediation of that event as its object (a universal hermeneutics), we leave undecided as yet. The Preface to

Luke's Gospel expresses the need to build upon the testimonies of those who experienced the events.

> Inasmuch as many have undertaken to compile a narrative [*diegesin*] of the things which have been accomplished [*peplerophoremenon*] among [*en*] us, just as they were delivered [*paredosan*] to us by those who from the beginning were eyewitnesses [*autoptai*] and ministers [*huperetai genomenoi*] of the word, it seemed good to me also, having followed [*parekolouthekoti anothen*] all things closely [*akribos*] for some time past, to write an orderly [*kathexes*] account for you, most excellent Theophilus, that you may know [*epignos*] the truth [*asphaleian*] concerning the things of which you have been informed [*katechethes*].

What Luke's Preface also proclaims is something of the complex nature of that testimony. The RSV translation portrays Luke's Gospel as a modern form of historiography. It is concerned with the sacrosanct hallmarks of such historiography: empirical evidence gathered from first-hand sources or the archives they left behind them, the correct ordering of this evidence, its careful researching, its verification and its reliability. A positivism remains paramount and it is the positivism which is to persuade the contemporary reader that these were and are indeed the facts of the case. A certain employment of technical or official terms and a certain appeal to the Hellenistic genre of scientific prefaces appears to be there in the Greek, but not unambiguously. In a recent appraisal of Luke's Preface[7] aporias are emphasized: 'the effect of the long words is to obscure the thought Luke is trying to convey. Obscurity is deepened by the amphibolous position of several words' (Alexander, 1993, pp.104–5). Other scholars have attested the seemingly pretentious, over-inflated style, the ambiguities of diction and syntax, the allusiveness of meaning and the 'double focus in assessing the significance of Luke's words' (ibid., 123). It is easy to pass this off as Luke's white-collar worker Greek education – shorthand for bad writing (ibid., pp.105, 168–86). But what is evident is that the scientism of modern historiography is not present in the Greek: 'most of the varied approaches to reading Luke–Acts as "history" in the Greco-Roman tradition are based on a misreading of the preface … Luke promises not independent "investigation" but faithful recording of received tradition (verse 2); he does not challenge his predecessors but ranges his own work alongside theirs' (ibid., pp.200–202).

Luke emphasizes, then, that what is to follow is a narrative within which events will be arranged. The conditions governing the arrangement are not divulged. Representations of time play an important function in Luke, as the dating and paralleling of John's birth and Jesus' indicate, but 'the "order" that he promises is probably no more than the inevitable concomitant of the move from oral storytelling to written narrative' (ibid., p.202). Even so, this narrative is not composed of just any set of events, they are events which have come to full measure: *plerophoreo* is linked to that favourite Pauline verb *pleroo*; it carries the associations of to pervade, to perfect, to consummate. If Luke is the author of Acts then he had close contact with the Pauline community and Paul himself. Christ is the fullness of God towards the salvation of the world. These events announce a spiritual, soteriological fruition; they have borne (*phoreo*) or conveyed a fullness within which we have participated (*en hemin*). 'The phraseology of verses 1 and 2 clearly implies two groups of people, those among whom the events were "accomplished" and those to whom the tradition was handed down, and the same pronoun is used of both. There must therefore be a reference to the *corpus christianorum*' (ibid., p.112). The verb is passive, the community (we) have received these things and been consumed by them. Furthermore, Luke makes plain that, as he is communicating these events through his narration to Theophilus, so these events were communicated (orally?) to those like Luke. The verb *parodidomi*, while certainly meaning 'to hand down' (Mk 7:13. Acts 6:14) and suggesting a teaching (and charism?) passed on in a fashion similar to the doctrine of apostolic tradition, also suggests placing in the hands of a higher power. It is not simply a delivery, but also a delivering up. The verb is used in all four Gospels to talk about the handing over of Jesus to the Roman and Jewish authorities. Is there also a hint of betrayal or the recognition of a potential betrayal? That is, as Christ is delivered 'into the hands of sinful men' (Luke 24:7), is the narration of the events of Christ's life, events which communicate because they disclose a salvific effect, also being handed on to those who may treat these things disrespectfully? Paul will talk of not discerning the body of Christ and consuming the eucharist unworthily. Is there a betrayal also possible here in hardening one's heart to the power of God as it is disseminated in the telling of these events; a telling by *autoptai* (not eye-witnesses so much as those with first-hand experience of the facts – (Alexander, 1993, pp.120–23)) and ministers of the Word? These witnesses subordinate themselves to the Word. Their testimonies are such that the Word speaks through their words; their creation becomes creative. They attest the message Jesus himself proclaimed (the Word is also used to describe Jesus' own message in Luke 8:11–21); they retell a telling. This is discipleship, the following in the wake of and the passing on of that which we have received. Luke announces his own participation in this (and therefore the participation of his narrative?) when he uses the verb *parakoloutheo*: 'to follow after' or 'to follow faithfully'.[8] H.J. Cadbury, back in 1922, suggested translating this (and the following word, *pasin*) as 'having participated in [them] all' (p. 502). 'Following' is a synonym for discipleship, obedience, subordination to the Word (Luke 5:27). There has been some discussion here of whether Luke is falsely claiming that he too is one of the eyewitnesses. Those opposed to this idea wish to translate his use of the verb as 'to investigate'. But there is no need for such contortions. Luke stands in the line of those whose lives have been caught up with the salvific events that are being spoken of and written about. His 'following' is a writing or a rewriting of the original Word, writing of the living out of the faith. This writing as praxis demands for Luke a written account, just as the 'following' of the witnesses demanded an oral account. The event of revelation enjoins a dissemination. Both tellings are related to the advent, the giving of the Word. Both tellings disseminate the salvific fullness of that Word. *Akribos*, then, might also carry the sense of 'diligently': that is, it might describe a moral and behavioural disposition akin to servant and follower, as well as an evaluation of the precision of the research (or the account, if 'accurately' is a description of the writing).

The emphasis of this whole sentence devolves upon the final *hina* clause and the knowledge that Theophilus will attain through this telling. It is a knowledge distinct from that gained through oral teaching (*katecheo*).[9] There is something certain and established by this knowledge. But what? The events or the account of the events? *Asphaleian* is 'assurance' or 'security' about this truth which is not taught. The assurance here need not be that concerning simply the contents of the account or that concerning the writing of the account as superior to its oral narration (Alexander, 1993, p.192). What may be assured is not an intellectual understanding, but a salvific communication, a disclosure of or participation in the revelation. There is a knowledge of God, a disclosure, and it pertains to the telling of the story, the narrative, the writing which is also an obedient following after. The writing itself may have a power because it participates in the truth it announces. As such, knowledge is not a seizing and possessing, but a following in the wake of, a continuing activity, a lifestyle.

Development of the Theme: Aristotle, Mimesis and Knowledge

It is this kind of knowledge, a practical knowledge in the Aristotelian sense of *phronesis* that will direct the thinking of this chapter. For Aristotle, there is a clear link between knowledge, *mimesis* and the nature of analogy. This interassociation connects his eudaemonistic ethics to *therapeia*, rhetoric to catharsis, logic to stylistics, as we shall see. And, by extension, this cluster of notions has political consequences. Hence, of tragedy, Aristotle writes that 'by means of language enriched with all kinds of ornament ... it represents men in action ... and through pity and fear it effects relief to these and similar emotions' (*Poetics*, 1449b21–8). If we work backwards from the sequence here announced, knowledge begins with experience, the excitation of the passions common to all, and is expressed through the symbolic form of utterance. In *De Interpretatione*, Aristotle elaborates by emphasizing that spoken words are symbols and written words are symbols of those symbols (16a3–7). The exchange value of these symbols is established by convention: their meaning is defined and confirmed within social practices. There is no natural relation between names and things in themselves.

Where a gap opens between our naming and our experience of the world, the communication of meaning is paramount and therefore Aristotle calls for a style which is proper for the subject matter to be conveyed. Analogy, a subset of metaphor (being a metaphor of proportion) in *Poetics*, is viewed as the most important kind of figure in Book III of *Rhetoric* because of its facility to communicate a subject vividly and actively: 'expressions represent a thing to an eye when they show it in a state of activity' (*Rhet.*, 1411b2). The point of communication is impact and event: 'such expressions arrest the hearer's mind, and fix his attention' (*De Interpretatione*, 16b19–22). So the rhetorician aims at *pathos*, the dialectician aims at *pistis* (conviction) and the syllogist aims at *episteme* (knowledge) and scientific demonstration. In *Poetics*, 'under the head of Thought' each of these aims Aristotle conceives in terms of a specific linguistic effectivity, as 'all the effects to be produced by language' (1456a38–b1). If 'purity of style consists in calling things by their own proper names' *(Rhet.*, 1407a3) this is not because things have a direct correspondence to their proper names, but a style of communication is advocated which is appropriate to the experience and communication of those things. *Mimesis* is effective, imitating and conveying an action, to the extent that its metaphors are proportional (analogical). This connection between language, meaning and action can be seen as a development of Aristotle's argument in *De Interpretatione* that neither a noun nor a verb independently has meaning (16a19–27 and 16b6–8, 19–22). Communication arises only in their association as name (*onoma*) and expression (*rhema*); only as such is there *logos* (significant meaning).

There is no absolute distinction that can be made, then, between analogy as a mode of argumentation (what Aristotle terms an 'enthymeme') and analogy as a mode of metaphorical expression. Logic and rhetoric are inseparable from the appropriate style necessary for the communication of meaning; just as a virtuous act is one done appropriate to the situation. In fact, 'It is the logician, capable of examining the matter and forms of a syllogism, who will be in the highest degree a master of rhetorical argumentation.'[10] Thus even in speculative philosophy where the definition of words is essential to clarity of demonstration, concern is expressed for 'those unacquainted with the power of names' (*de sophisticis elenchis*, I, 165a1–18), 'actual definitions [where] equivocation slips in unnoticed' (*Top.*,

I,100b6) and the ineradicable use of words whose meanings are neither univocal nor equivocal. These words Boethius called modes of equivocation *a consilio*; more recent scholars have called them *pros hen* equivocals.[11] A metaphoricity remains constitutive of all communication; what is to be discerned is the proportionality in the metaphoric, the approriateness of the style to the contents of the communication. The distinction between speculative and poetic discourse, for Aristotle, is more a matter of the relationship of function to ends, *ergon* to *telos* or, as Wittgenstein might put it, language games.[12]

The point at issue here is that, for Aristotle, analogy is part of a larger symbolics of action and effective communication. It is both a rhetorical and logical tool, though as a logical tool it is less effective for strict demonstration of the truth because as an enthymeme it lacks or presupposes a fundamental premise. As one scholar puts it: 'an argument from analogy assum[es] the validity of a regular induction and demonstrat[es] a mere probability'.[13] The aim of effective communication is wisdom and the wholeness which acts as the goal in the pursuit of the good. Communication is a continuing work within the symbolic, a work corresponding to Aristotle's conception of the material world as a world in motion; a work corresponding to Aristotle's *ergon* argument.[14] As Ricoeur puts it, 'Wherever something is in a state of becoming, predication is possible: predication is based on physical dissociation introduced by motion.'[15] The question is, in order for us to have true knowledge of our experience of the world, what gives the endlessly conceptual labour a direction and a structure? Or, put in another way, what acts as non-discursive interpretants for this chain of symbolic, arbitrary (in the Saussurean sense) substitutions? There are two answers: a semantic hierarchy (related to the categories and Aristotle's twin concerns for logical coherence and clarity of definition) and a moral teleology. These provide the vertical and horizontal axes which, it is hoped, contain the slipping, the ambiguity, the equivocation of meaning.

We can approach the spinal cord of semantic hierarchy through Aristotle's discussion at the beginning of *Categories* of paronyms: 'When things get their name from something, with a difference of ending, they are called *paronymous*. Thus, for example, the grammarian gets his name from grammar, the brave get theirs from bravery' (1a12–15). There are primary and derivative meanings. If there is to be a distinction drawn between paronymy and analogy then this semantic hierarchy appears to offer it. Paronymy relates a series of different relationships to the same thing. Analogy, it might be said, discovers comparative identities between different things. This distinction corresponds closely to the mediaeval distinction between *analogia proportionalis* (where comparative terms share proportionally the same predicate) and *analogia attributionis* (where one term possesses the predicate properly and the other only by extension). But this is not a distinction Aristotle himself drew and his definition of analogy as proportional metaphor confounds the scholastic distinction.[16]

Most notably for Aristotle, 'being' itself is paronymous. 'There are several senses in which a thing may be said to be, as we pointed out previously in our book on the various senses of words; for in one sense it means what a thing is or a "this", and in another sense it means that a thing is of a certain quality or quantity or has some such predicate asserted of it. While "being" has all these senses, obviously that which is primary is the "what", which indicates the substance of a thing' (*Metaphysics*, 1028a10–15). The burden of *Metaphysics* is the elucidation of the relationship between the many and the primary with respect to the first philosophy, an examination of being *qua* being. For each substance is individual and Aristotle writes that 'we seem to be seeking another kind of substance, and this is our problem, i.e., to see if there is something which can exist apart by itself and belongs to no sensible thing' (1060a10–12). Through the paronymy of 'being' Aristotle attempts to correlate the semantic hierarchy with an ontological hierarchy, 'the most unchangeable principles, being and unity' (1060a37–8), and there is a recognition that, if this cannot be done, if this ordering cannot be established, then nothing can be known in anything but a particular and limited way. 'A further difficulty is raised by the fact that all knowledge is of the universal and of the "such", but substance does not belong to the universals, but it is rather a "this" and separable' (1060b20–2). The intellectual wrestling is explicit. Aristotle will advert to his difficulties and, while advocating that there 'is a principle in things' admit that 'About such matters there is no proof in the full sense ... For it is not possible to infer this truth itself from a more certain principle' (1062a2–5).

Several aporias reveal themselves: the aporia of the individual substance and the universal presents an aporia of the noetic and the ontological. Both these are further related to 'Another aporetic [which] exists between signification (with real reference) and predication (which tends to leave it behind)'[17] – between symbols and the things they symbolize. What does this add up to? One recent scholar concludes, 'Aristotle's reflections on substances promised that the aporia would be finally resolved, if only language could be made to circumvent its own disutilities.'[18] But language cannot circumvent its own disutilities, it seems, despite Aristotle's constant return to signification and definition (1062a14–16). In fact, aporias are 'impressionistically linked through the facilities of language'.[19] Analogies drawn from colour, letters of the alphabet, ensoulment of the body, medicine and mathematics replace demonstration. We find the same method employed earlier in *Metaphysics* when Aristotle attempts to distinguish between 'actuality' and 'potentiality', only to conclude that 'we must not seek a definition of everything but be content to grasp the analogy' (1048a36–7). It now transpires that what began as an examination of the ontological order in order to stabilize the logic of paronymy suffers inversion. As one scholar notes: 'the logic of paronymy becomes indispensable; it is the clamp that prevents ontology from disintegrating'.[20] And ultimately, this paradox is only resolved in the turn towards God as the principle of that 'which can exist apart and is immoveable' (1064a29–1064b14), as the primary and prior source of all derivation.

The necessary relation between the noetic and the ontological, the solution to the universal knowability of the individual substance, rests, finally, upon the rhetorical and the theological. But the turn to God only opens the old debate between whether 'first philosophy' is ontology or theology. Because unless it can be demonstrated that ontology is theological for Aristotle – that God is the primary substance from which all other substances are derived – then a further aporia opens between being *qua* being and the divine. Earlier in *Metaphysics* (books VII–IX) it is unclear whether God as prime mover is also creator and cause of all that is: 'the connection between theology and ontology was abandoned'.[21] On the other hand, *Metaphysics*, XII 6–7 suggests an eternal unchanging substance different from the two natural substances. And the relationship between the two natural substances and the third unchanging one is paronymous. 1072b13–15 famously states, 'On such a principle, then, depends the heavens, and nature.' No doubt the debate on the relation of theology to ontology in Aristotle's thinking and whether this relation changed over the writing of the different sections of *Metaphysics* will continue. Ironically, if Aristotle systematically followed through a hierarchical relationship between primary, secondary (the terms are found in *Categories*, where Aristotle also denies that there are degrees of substance – 3b33f) and even tertiary substances, he would be affirming rather than rejecting the Platonic relationship between Matter and Form. For us the question of resolving the relationship between theology and ontology in Aristotle is significant, but not essential. What is essential is the extent to which substance can be substantial when so much depends upon the distinction between primary, secondary and tertiary, and yet, as Alexander of Aphrodisia (one of Aristotle's first commentators) notes, 'the principles [of substance] are not made known through axioms, as they are not demonstratable'.[22] What remains when logic and the categories fail to produce knowledge (*episteme*)? Only, I suggest, the unstable nature of analogy itself, hovering between being a mode of argumentation that cannot, finally, be given ontological validation (and therefore constitute a form of knowledge as Aristotle understood knowledge) and a mode of rhetoric. Furthermore, analogy is located within a wider symbolics which responds via social consensus, use and convention to the larger temporal movements and *erga* which characterize the physical world as Aristotle conceives it. What remains is allegory.

In the light of this, what, then, is philosophy for Aristotle but a way of living among the names and things which constitute the world, ever evaluating, defining and interpreting them? This is the human *ergon* as a language animal contextualized by a world governed by a principle of movement (*Met.* 1075b37), situated within time. This *ergon* marks out the path of purposeful pedagogy. Analogy is part of this wider and continuing pedagogical scheme in which identities can never be fixed and definitions only approximated. I use the word 'allegory' with relation to this pedagogical path because specifically, as Paul de Man has pointed out, allegory constitutes a rhetoric of temporality. Allegory 'always corresponds to the unveiling of an authentically temporal destiny'.[23] The moral philosopher and classicist, Martha Nussbaum, points up the ethics of this Aristotlian notion of dialectic as continuing clarification within a 'therapeutic community', linking it quite specifically to the relationship between rhetoric and emotion. Emphasizing that Aristotle's lectures 'do not claim finality'[24] and that emotions have an intimate relation both to belief and to judgment,[25] Nussbaum argues that the purpose of rhetoric is to create, take away and modify emotions 'by discourse and argument'.[26] In this way emotions, closely bound to judgment and therefore effected by modifications of judgment, are educated and 'brought into harmony with a correct view of the good human life'.[27] Hence literature has an important part to play in providing examples in the *Nicomachean Ethics* and Aristotlian *mimesis* concerns itself with the creation of dramatic unity (of action, time and place) and presenting universals as particulars (*Poet.*, 51a36–51b10). Thus the discourse of poets attempts a task Aristotle set himself to accomplish as a philosopher in *Metaphysics* – and possibly Sophocles fulfils the task much better.[28] *Praxis* and *poiesis* draw close to one another. The latter can effect the former and the former is that which is imitated by the latter. They are not the same, but only to the extent that doing-as-becoming and making are distinct activities. They are the same as two dynamic responses to and participations within the cosmic movement. They are both expressions by which the soul may arrive at truth (*Nicomachean Ethics*, VI, 3).

By viewing the human being's work as a journey through a conceptual allegory that requires judgment and clarification (providing a role for philosophy as a critical discourse) I am not suggesting the world is appearance. We will leave that to Platonists. The world is not appearance for Aristotle; the world is substance, we can trust our perceptions of this world and we develop notions of experience from repeated familiar perceptions of the sensuous and emotional. Intellectual activity abstracts from sensation, but the concrete particular which gives rise to sensation remains. The intellectual abstraction aims at grasping the universal in the concrete particular and, however aporetic Aristotelian ontology and epistemology is at this very point, nevertheless with Aristotle there is an intense concentration upon the embodied. The embodied is transfigured when its universal form is understood. It is taken up into and receives its full significance through the universal. As such, substance always retains a certain permeability. Linguistic symbols are always symbols of this sensible permeability. Furthermore, as symbols they are interpretations of experience, 'symbols of affections' (*De. Int.*, 16a3). Wisdom and the pursuit of the good life effect a process of rational discrimination which structures, clarifies, interprets and evaluates these symbols, these interpretations of this permeable substance. Aristotle listens through the language to what the world announces about its structures, its balances, its movements and the divinity of its end. Matter finds its fulfilment in receiving form and 'The Ultimate form it "hopes" to receive … is the divine life of the Prime … and it is in so far as we too receive that form that we can understand the world.'[29] Both creation and creature have a vocation within the purview of this dynamic.

Development of a Second Theme: Gregory of Nyssa, Allegoria and the Spiritual Sense

Having examined the association of *mimesis*, *praxis* and knowledge, we return to the original focus of this study, the reading of Scripture and the nature of God's revelation attested there. In introducing Gregory of Nyssa's work at this point, the intention is not to establish a comparison and contrast between Aristotle and Gregory. It would be important to do such work: examining the similarities and differences of their thinking on the pursuit of the good life, their anthropologies, ontologies and epistemologies; others have demonstrated how profoundly Gregory has been influenced by Aristotle and how unplatonic is the general character of his thought despite several critiques of Aristotelian *technologia* in *Contra Eunomium*.[30] The intention here is to develop Aristotle's appreciation of the inseparability of *mimesis* and *phronesis*, rhetoric and logic, the temporality and movement of matter and the universal speculation of *theoria* in terms of an allegorical reading of the Scriptures. This reading will, in turn, imply and issue from a theology of representation and reading, as we will see. From analysis of the metaphysics, ethics and aesthetics of representation we move to the practice of reading, the inner dynamics of reader–author–text installed by narrative. We will proceed through an examination of that classic spiritual interpretation of the Scriptures found in *The Life of Moses*.[31]

In Book I of that study, Gregory retells the story of Moses as it can be pieced together from the Books of Deuteronomy and Numbers, the Letter to the Hebrews and Jewish Midrashim. The emphasis is upon the historical and the psychological. Where he deviates from the Scriptures he is concerned with painting a certain realism, a concreteness, about this figure and a plausibility about the events within which he participates. Before the smoking mount Sinai, Moses' 'whole being so trembled with fright that his faintness of soul was not concealed from the Israelites, but he was as terrified as they were at what he saw and his body shook violently' (I:43). Corporeality may exist without appetitive passion, sustained without food or drink, for 40 days and nights while Moses was wrapped in the darkness of God on the summit of Sinai (I:58, 60), but Gregory nevertheless wishes to affirm the historical particularity of this man and his actions. It is only on the basis of such that he can move from the material and mutable to the practical wisdom, the general outline of the perfect life. As with Aristotle, it is the particular which must embody the universal. 'Always remaining the same, [Moses] preserved in the changeableness of nature an unchangeable beauty' (I:76).

It is in Book II that 'a more figurative spiritual sense' (literally 'a more tropical theoria') (II:43) is worked out. The soul is to be trained in an ascent towards divine illumination just as in Plato's Cave allegory the philosopher king is to be trained. Once Moses has been illuminated at the burning bush, he is to liberate the Hebrews from Egypt in the same way as the philosopher king is to return to the Cave to release the prisoners. The move from bestiality to enlightenment is mapped out metaphorically in terms of being released not from the mud, clay and chaff of the sensual in themselves. This is where Gregory does not follow Plato. In itself this materiality is good. But we must be released from our dependence upon materiality in and for itself: Benjamin's 'soulless materiality'. What affects the transformation is being able to see the invisible as it pertains to the visible creation, to read the Logos in human beings and the wider world. Creation has to be reread, theologically. We need instruction for this, hence the important role of the teacher and the mode of the teaching (of which we will say more later). For the soul is to be trained in its reading of the world, trained in understanding the perceptions and experiences which inscribe themselves upon that soul. The dynamic of this training is twofold, the soul's desire for God who is alone desirable' (II:25) and the operation of the Spirit in creation. This philosophy of desire is theologically dependent upon the divine Personhood of the Spirit, which Gregory insisted was necessary for a coherent understanding of the Trinity. Through the Spirit the soul is led to a knowledge of that which subtends all other knowledges and understandings of what is, the Logos: 'It seems to me that at the time the great Moses was instructed in the theophany he came to know that none of those things which are apprehended by sense perception and contemplated by the understanding really subsists, but that the transcendent essence and cause of the universe, on which everything depends, alone subsists' (II:24). The condition for ontological and noetic possibility is theological. The recognition of this is both given, via revelation, and earned, by the employment of the intellect. We are enslaved to the material and sensual without the exercise of our rationality (II:46) and without our participation in the eschatological economy of the Spirit. The recognition of the universal and immutable in and through the particular and mutable is cashed out in terms of the virtuous life; a life now ordered, oriented and interpreted by that which has been revealed.

The narrative of Moses's life becomes, when interpreted allegorically, a model for our imitation; a paradigmatic form is discerned within the material details. The allegorical text, then, parallels (and it is the nature, operation and significance of that parallel which interests us) the historical people, circumstances and events themselves. Just as these details compose a reality (for Gregory would not have doubted that these things occurred as they were transcribed) which is poised between what Aristotle would call matter and form, so too is the text, as it composes the narrated world, poised between *historia* and *theoria*. Both realities – the concrete universal and the narrative – provide spaces for the operation of what David Tracy terms 'the analogical imagination'. Both in the *actual experience* of Moses before the burning bush, for example, and in the *narrated account* of Moses before the burning bush a space is opened between sign (or what Aristotle would call symbol) and meaning. Within this space lies what Gregory frequently will term 'a hidden doctrine' ready for disclosure by the reader.

Paul de Man, commenting upon the structure of allegory, states that 'the relationship between the sign and meaning is discontinuous, involving an extraneous principle that determines the point and manner at which the relationship is articulated ... [T]he sign points to something that differs from its literal meaning and has for its function the thematization of this difference'.[32] De Man reappraises and understands *allegoria* within a poststructural view of the construction of all worlds of meaning from the free-floating and endless dance of signs. And this is evidently neither Gregory's cultural context nor anything he would understand by an allegorical appreciation of the world. For Gregory, what is allegorical primarily is creation; it is a description of the created order as the invisible is apprehended within the visible. His allegorical readings are readings of the world, but they are also readings of scriptural texts. The scriptural texts disclose the nature of the world. Creation is represented in these texts in a way which instructs the soul in the things which are hidden. Scripture is a reading of creation. As such, the discontinuities between sign and meaning in allegory, which de Man alerts us to, are not only evident, they are more complex. Because the sign is not simply the literary sign in the scriptural text, it is also the body out there in the world which points towards other possible disclosures. So, for example, there is no evident connection between a burning bush and the immaculate conception (II:21), the staff of Moses and the incarnation (II:26, 27), Aaron and the angels (II:51). Yet Gregory insists there is a theological, a hidden, connection. Furthermore, each of these signs can change their meaning as the narrative and interpretation unfolds: the burning bush becomes a picture of the incarnation, the rod becomes 'the word of faith' (II:36) and then the cross, Aaron is a sign of an angel while he stands alongside Moses before the Pharaoh and a sign of a demon when he leads the Israelites in the worship of idols. Gregory emphasizes this discontinuity between object and name, sign and meaning, perception and knowledge: 'The whole creature cannot go outside itself by means of a comprehensive knowledge. It always remains in itself. And whatever it perceives, it forms a perception of by itself. It is incapable of seeing a thing outside its own nature, even if it thinks it is glimpsing an object that goes beyond it' (*C.Eunom.*, 12; II 1064 BC). He associates this with his theology of *diastasis* – the separation between God as uncreated and created human beings.

Let me draw out two consequences of this dislocation between sign and meaning, imaged perception and knowledge, and the allegorical procedure which both creates and perpetuates while seeking to resolve this dislocation. First, with reference to Paul de Man's analysis of allegory, it is the 'extraneous principle' imposing itself upon the object perceived (in Moses' case, the burning bush) or the object depicted which disrupts identification. A is no longer A, A is also B (and C and D). It does not just disrupt once, but, having disrupted, it continually disrupts. As the narrative continues the reidentifications, A as B, are not standardized. Shoes with reference to Moses before the burning bush are identified as dead, earthy things which have to be stripped away before illumination is possible. 'Sandalled feet cannot ascend' (II:22). Shoes with reference to the eating of the passover are identified as forms of necessary protection against the 'thorns of life'. 'Shoes are the self-controlled and austere life' (II:107). In this processive reidentification, nakedness also undergoes a semantic shift. What this effects is an inability to grasp any object as a self-subsisting entity, a body to be owned. There is no stability of the identification. All possession and understanding is provisional for, as Dorrie points out, '*Nun ist der Logos keineswegs das als solches passive Objekt des Forschens und Suchens*.'[33] Allegory as such forestalls what otherwise would be idolatry. We are pushed beyond the symbiotic equation of knowledge and perception, because what is seen 'kindles the desire for the hidden through what is constantly perceived' (II:231). If the play of the invisible within the visible, the incorporeal within the corporeal is not perceived there is no perception. There is blindness. Such uninformed perception, such grasping of objects and bodies as if they were self-subsistent entities, leads to lust, the misdirection of desire. Gregory speaks of 'the very root of evil – namely, the desire which arises through sight' (II:304). He follows here a line of theological thinking which has consistently offered a critique against what has come to be called, by Jacques Derrida and Luce Irigaray, 'occularcentrism', the ideology and pornography of visibility. Seeing belongs to God alone: *theoria* is associated with *theos*.

Secondly, what determines the multiple reidentifications in Gregory of Nyssa's text is threefold. There is (a) the iteration of the object elsewhere in the Scriptures – for example, the various employments of 'serpent' in the books of Genesis and Exodus and the Gospel of John redefine each other and 'you of course understand the "cross" when you hear "wood"' (II:132). We might term this the scriptural principle of intratextuality. Augustine, in *De doctrina Christiana*, expounds the principle (and its theology): 'the Holy Spirit has magnificently and wholesomely modulated the Holy Scriptures so that the more open places present themselves to hunger and the more obscure places may deter a disdainful attitude. Hardly anything may be found in these obscure passages which is not found plainly said elsewhere' (II:6). This principle blurs distinctions between primary text and secondary interpretation and the hierarchy which privileges one text above another. Intratextuality presents a flat field of signs and displays a constant trafficking between one text and another through the processes of allusion, citation, iteration, reinscription and rewriting, examples of all of which Gregory of Nyssa's text provides.

Then there is (b) the tradition of the Church fathers or the rule of faith. For the staff's transformation into a snake as a sign of the incarnation appears in Irenaeus, *Adversus haereses* 3.28 and it will appear later in Cyril of Alexandria, *Glaph. in Ex.* 2.299. We can include here Gregory's appeal to Jewish Midrashim and his indebtedness to the allegorical reading of Philo. We might, following the work on reader response theory by Stanley Fish, term this an appeal to the interpretive community, if Fish's understanding of this operation was not in fact a secularized notion of *ecclesia* and *paradosis*. Such communities stabilize, by authorizing, certain meanings; they create certain ideological readings and in shaping these readings they shape, at the same time, the readers.[34] We will return to the politics of this 'readings shaping readers' and the relationship between the operation of the analogical imagination and ideology later.

Gregory also (c) employs theophany itself as determining reidentifications, just as in his telling of Moses' life there are three moments of revelation: the light of the burning bush, the darkness on Mount Sinai and the view of God's back as He passes by. As a theophany this last episode, which is

God's response to Moses' desire to see Him, is most significant. The first theophany is mediated (through the bush). The second on mount Sinai is an entry into darkness and incomprehensibility. This third theophany is the only one where Moses 'sees' God, but not face to face. Throughout his work Gregory emphasizes that God is 'The-Always-Greater' (*In Canticum Canticorum*, 8; I, 941 B σε τρεχων ἑαυτου μειζων παντοτε) and the soul will never reach its final perfection (*C.Eunom.* 1, II, 340 D). Only a spiritual rewriting of 'God's back' as the traces of God's activity in the world restores the narrative's intention. The revelation, then, turns out to be a figure for God's mediated presence, a representation of a representation. As theophanies the three events do not suggest the immediacy of knowing God. There is always a distance, a *diastasis*, traversed by representation and desire. Moses' final contact with God is his subsumption into heaven 'leaving behind no sign on earth nor any grave as a memorial' (I:75). These theophanies, then, are emphatically moments of negative knowledge, knowledge beyond intelligible knowing, knowledge only *that* God is and not *what* God is. Nevertheless, the theophanies are disclosures of ultimate truth, moments of authorization which hold the whole narrative progress in order. The meaning and unfolding structure of the action (the history) and the contemplation (the spiritual interpretation) circulate about these moments; moments when the narrative is suspended, frozen in light or darkness. This suspension of the narrative is not, though, accompanied by lacunae in the telling, the writing itself. However filled with light or consumed by darkness, however ineffable, Gregory's language still proceeds. Theology, attestation, requires its rhetoric: oxymoron, paradox and analogy take over. The writing is necessary 'to signify our reasoning' (*De hominis opificio*, VIII:2), to trace the allegorical in both the scriptural text and Moses' experience. We write as we reason and this is our teaching. The presence of God is staged; His passing is performed.

Where knowledge, perception, representation and true presence coincide is in the Logos. Heinrich Dorrie notes: '*Folgerichtig fordert Gregor, das Bild Christi in der eigenen Seele aufzusuchen and es von aller Verdunklung und Verunklarung zu reinigen und zu befreien.*'[35] 'The senses of the soul' (γλυκαινεται τα της φυχης αισθητρια) are sweetened by the charm of the apple tree of the Word (*In Cant.*, 4; I, 844 B). What is finally revealed to Moses, having been led towards it by trumpets which signified preaching and prophecy, 'the Spirit through his instruments' (II:159), is the Word itself. The Word is a twofold divine form of writing. First, there is the Logos presented through the representation, the analogy, of the heavenly tabernacle. The divisions within the tabernacles correspond to Christ's human and Christ's resurrected body (II:174). In II:216 the incarnation is pictured as God writing upon human material. Again the presentation is not finally perspicacious; the rhetoric slides: as the narrative and the exegesis follow each other, the tabernacle is also the celestial world (II:179), the Church (II:184) and the human body (II:245). Perhaps this semantic slipping is why prayer and praise even in the tabernacle is described as 'a verbal sacrifice' (II:182) – the meaning of the words is handed over, abandoned, from the moment of their utterance. Words, like the Word, experience a kenosis.[36] Secondly, there are the tablets of stone written by God which are also a picture of the soul. These are first written upon by the hand of God and subsequently rewritten upon by the action of the Word (II:316). At the pinnacle, holding the rest in order, the form to which all aspires is writing itself, divine and human interwoven, one providing the conditions, even necessitating, the other: *Scriptura, écriture*. 'The Holy Spirit is called "finger" in many places in Scripture' (II:216).[37]

Despite the Platonic/neoplatonic motif of ascent and the disciplining of the senses through *eros*, there are sufficient parallels here with Aristotle's understanding of the relationship between *mimesis*, *theoria*, metaphysics and theology. Not least is the concern to affirm the corporeal, not disregard it. The aporetics of ontology and epistemology are also evident in Gregory's allegorical reading of the pursuit of truth and the virtuous life. We will develop this. These aporetics follow, as I said, from the ultimate *diastema* between creator and creation. They lead to a process of coming to know, not a knowledge. They announce a new kind of space for reflection. Allegory, by opening the semiotic can of worms, disassociating sign from meaning, installing an ontological and noetic aporia, and indeterminancy, both creates this space and seeks to work productively within it, containing the arbitrary. The opening of this new spatiality through allegory is clearly presented in Gregory's interpretation of the ascent of Moses up the mountain and into the darkness of God (II:152–69). For, as the narrative proceeds upwards, so the allegorical interpretation, which views this ascent as an interiorized event of illumination beyond sense impressions and reasoning, speaks of penetrating depths and elevation of the mind. If allegory always operates beyond real time (see de Man), transposing and disrupting the historical, it is also a strategy for the disruption of geographical space, installing a deliberate obfuscation of spatial dimensions. A sacred space is opened, what Gillian Rose has called the 'broken middle'.[38] This is a space which is constantly transgressing its own dimensions, a space which cannot be located 'here' or 'there' because it is a space which cannot be contained, a space which deconstructs its boundaries: 'in speaking of "place" [Moses] does not limit the place indicated by anything quantitative (for to something unquantitative there is no measure)' (II:242).[39] This space can be neither limited nor defined. It is a space for dispossession. Read in terms of ecclesiology, this is a liturgical space.[40] Read theologically in terms of contemplation, this is a place for the interpretative play within representation itself. As such, *allegoria* is like the convexed mirror at the centre of Jan Van Eyck's famous painting, *The Arnolfini Marriage*. It announces a certain reflexivity about representation and interpretation itself; a self-consciousness, within *mimesis*, of the dialectic between semiosis and interpretation; a self-consciousness about the way representation constructs our worlds, our notions of identity and reality and how that linguistic construction remains continually open to being rewritten, reinterpreted. The allegory, the hidden doctrine, of the created orders themselves and the allegory of the representation of those orders draws attention to the rhetoric of our knowledge of God's world, its metaphoricity. Furthermore, *allegoria* offers a reflection upon reading itself, the reading which always rewrites, performs the textual score in its own key, according it its own rhythm, with its own attention to certain details and blindness to others. It is in this sense that Paul de Man calls allegory 'metafigural'[41] – it is both a strategy of reading and writing and a reflection upon the act of representation itself with respect to reading and writing. *Allegoria* provides Hermes with a mirror in which to contemplate his own character as messenger of the gods, diplomat, trickster and thief.

What then of the reader, who is also pupil, the one under instruction, both for Aristotle and for Gregory of Nyssa? Daniélou notes how Gregory's concept of *akolouthia* depends upon Aristotle's.[42] It is important to point out that allegory never speaks in its own name. The principles of intratextuality and interpretive communities, and the advent of the theophanous, are appeals by the exegete to symbolic fields larger than the single reader, other voices which keep a check upon the arbitrary. The self as author is authored and given authorization from elsewhere. Ethically, in destabilizing identity, allegory destabilizes selfhood. The 'I' dissolves into the others which speak in, through and for the I. Allegory creates not only reading but readers, it is a form of discursive power like prayer and confession,[43] rhetoric in the service of soul making. The 'I' is led on a narrative of purification; the reading is a spiritual exercise, for in the reading the 'I' enters this space of dispossession and is continually renamed – as Moses, as an Egyptian, as an Israelite, as a pillar, as a sanctuary light. 'For not everyone is named brother or friend or neighbour in a good sense by Scripture. It is possible to be both brother and foreigner, both friend and enemy ... Scripture ... gives indication of the double meaning of brotherhood, that the same word does not always signify the same thing but may be taken with opposite meanings' (II:208, 210). Reading as contemplation is a form of ethical praxis, integral with the pursuit of the virtuous life. The place and identity of the 'I' is ambivalent; it is an ambivalence which results from a disassociation of name and meaning. This engineers a space for the operation of the Spirit and what Balthasar, discussing the work of Gregory, terms a 'knowledge by desire' as distinct from a 'knowledge by image'.[44] Gregory names God as 'You whom my soul loves' and emphasizes that in desire alone do we see God, insofar as we can (see *In. Cant.*, 8; I, 941 AB and 12; I, 1024 BC). Not that representation can be transcended, as we have seen, only that representation can be transfigured through and in desire, through and in the Spirit.

It is at this point that we can only appreciate Gregory's concern with allegorical reading of creation and text, and the destabilization of identity, within wider systematic concerns in his theology. Primarily, there is his concern with the Trinity as the community of processive love. This is linked to his desire to establish the deity of the Holy Spirit, who, as union of Father and Son is Person, and who, as processing from the Son, also crosses the *diastema* of creator/creation. This leads Gregory to begin his theology from an existential philosophy of desire and a theological understanding of human being made in the image of God. We are created with passions that we might be drawn to love God (*In Cant.*, 4; I, 844 B). The operation of this desire will move us beyond the inertia and lust of 'soulless materialism' towards deification.

Where narrative, allegory, knowledge and virtue meet is in this theological understanding of personhood. Here what is 'I', what is identified, what is named, 'all names have equally fallen short of accurate description, both those recognized as insignificant as well as those by which some great concept originated in sense impression' (II:176), finds its place in 'the power which encompasses the universe, in which lives the fulness of the divinity, the common protector of all' (II:177). There is here a doctrine of participation, but to enter into the possibilities of that participation, to begin to ascend towards the truth and the good life, requires faith and free choosing. Symbiotic analogies of God and creation are not self-evident. An irreducible opposition between God and human beings prevents such a natural theology. A space remains, a distance, and it is this space which *allegoria* installs and works productively within that it might be resolved. The presence of God pervades creation, and our knowledge of that presence develops in, through and as the vocation to true personhood, the move towards becoming a person in Christ. All exists within the Word. The Word is unitary. All things find their definition then in and as the Word. Knowledge of God comes through illumination, the employment of one's reason towards that which is invisible and the necessary dispossession this precipitates. Revelation in all its forms is the continual perichoretic receiving and pouring out of love which is the Trinity and within which all things move, as such divine disclosure *occurs* only in and as time and narrative, *as* history, *as* metonymy or the continuing chain of signs.[45] Just as salvation is a matter of the body and the soul, so revelation *is* story, our story within God's own story. The metonymic and horizontal axis of movement into the future from out of the past has a vertical, metaphoric or analogical axis, a transcendent reference. Both are required. Analogy cannot present a frozen glimpse of the eternal truth. It is part of a larger and more dynamic symbolics. Knowledge of God can only issue from allegory, an allegory created as the invisible strikes through the visible, an allegory created by infinite love: God's love for us and our desire to close the space which separates our signs from their meaning, our desire for the first, last and only Word. Within a doctrine, then, which affirms that 'the word "Godhead" signifies an operation and not a nature' ('On "Not Three Gods"' [*Ex.commun.not.*]) narrative – the representation of an action – is not simply the vehicle for disclosure (that is, a divine disclosure is contained within it and extractable by some hermeneutic process), or the means for disclosure (that is, illumination uses the form of narrative as an instrument for its own purposes). Both these understandings of the relationship of divine communication to narrative are docetic: the body of the text is epiphenomenal. Rather, narrative as the allegorical representation of God and human salvific action in the world *is* disclosive – for the disclosure itself is not an event but an eventing, an always in the process of coming to be. The disclosure is the continuing outworking through the Spirit of God's revelation of Himself in Christ. The operation of the Logos is not yet complete; that is why allegory remains; the work of Christ is unfinished until human beings are deified: 'all will be one body and one spirit' (*In. Cant.* 15; I, 117A ἐν σωμα γενεσθαι τους παντας και ἑν).

Recapitulation

There is not an attempt in this chapter to harmonize Aristotle and Gregory of Nyssa, but there are links between Aristotelianism and neoplatonism.[46] Gregory was profoundly influenced by Aristotelian notions of the temporal, the dynamic, the universal and the corporeal. His was a doctrine of embodiment which took seriously the roots of Christian revelation in the historical and the concrete. Christianity needs, then, to read the spiritual, the universal in such a way as not to denigrate or dissolve the historical and concrete. Discovering the eternal and unchanging within the particular and temporal is the axiomatic concern of Christology, incarnation and sacramentalism. Aristotle provides us with a welcome metaphysics of embodiment. The aporetic character of that metaphysics is also significant, for Christianity cannot found a metaphysics on the equation of reason and being, as Gregory reminds us with his emphases on the *diastema* between the uncreated Creator and the orders created out of nothing. Ours has to be a metaphysics of the saints, not the metaphysics of secularity.[47] The incorporeal is always discovered in the corporeal, the invisible within the visible. Furthermore,

Aristotle's emphasis upon the dynamism of creation, on time, on becoming, or the teleology of the good life, could all find a place within Christianity's concern with history, the transience of all things, eschatology and redemption. But, more significantly, this chapter has been concerned to develop Aristotle's understanding of the relationship between *mimesis*, metaphysics, ethics and theology (a relationship which hinges on the nature of analogy) through Gregory of Nyssa's theological understanding of allegory as analogical discourse. On the basis of this development several observations can be made about the relationship of narrative both to revelation in the exclusive sense of God's revelation in Christ and to disclosure, the mediation of that revelation through the Spirit in creation.

What remains and is safeguarded in allegorical reading is textuality itself, writing, the body of the scriptural text. The letteral (though not the literal, which is already an interpretation), the written, in its materiality is affirmed. The allegorical simply extends the letteral, supplements it both in the sense of adding to it and altering it. It sucks as a child on the textual breast and as Gregory states, 'the Word ... changes His power in diverse ways to those who eat. He knows not only to be bread but also to become milk and meat and greens and whatever else might be appropriate to and desired by the one who receives him' (II:140). As such, interpretation cannot dissolve the letteral into the meaningful. As Augustine exclaims concerning the Scriptures, 'The surface meaning lies open before us and charms beginners. Yet the depth is amazing, my God, the depth is amazing. To concentrate on it is to experience awe.'[48] The reading shapes and reflects the reader, provoking the desire to understand, provoking the supplementation, the further writing. Language and the circulation of immanent and transcendent desires (human and divine eros), these remain central to appreciating the relation between narrative and revelation, time, becoming and personhood. That is why we need to explore the work of Lacan, Kristeva and Irigaray alongside the theologies of Barth and Balthasar. We get confused by our grammar, taking 'revelation' as a substantive. As such revelation becomes an event of making something known. We ask about the contents of such knowledge. This has led some to view revelation as propositional.[49] Theophanous events do occur in Scripture; Gregory is drawn towards them. But they occur within a temporal movement that is not, in itself, insignificant. The theophanous event is the result of all that has proceeded it and will in itself be partial for it will be followed by all that comes as a consequence of it. It is an event within a continuing chain of events. The creature 'never halts at what it has reached, but all that it has acquired becomes by participation a beginning of its ascent to something still greater' (*C. Eunom.* 3.6.74). Moses did not stop in his ascent. The theophanies were stages within revelation, not punctiliar moments of perfect realisation (II:227). Disclosure is an action, not an event –

the continuing, generative action of revelation in the temporal and material. It is an action we are a part of and therefore even our attempts to extract ourselves from time and space and examine the content of any experience, moments of self-reflection, are part of the revelatory dynamism. The contents are continually contextualized and, as such, the meaning we give to them shifts, changes. If God transcends our ability to know Him then divine revelation cannot be the communication of knowledge such as we are used to deducing and inferring from our experience. Illumination can only be the communication of the form, the mediation of God. What we see of this form and what we are to understand by it is akin to the division between sign and meaning in language, in *mimesis*, which allegory draws attention to. Any contents, any understanding of our experience, is provisional and reinscribed elsewhere, rewritten. Gregory writes, 'This truly is the vision of God: never to be satisfied in the desire to see him' (II:239). As such what is revealed in revelation is the nakedness of one's continual desire to see, to understand. What is revealed is an eros which transcends us and our grasp of the created order; and only insofar as desire is God Himself in His perichoretic triunity is this a disclosure of the form of God. Illumination as the *actio* of revelation continues towards a not-to-be-realized eschatological horizon; it is coextensive with vocation and discipleship. The ethics of such a following – and here again Gregory follows in the footsteps of Aristotle – is the ethics of moderation or the mean (II:288–90).[50] The teleology of all action is, for both philosopher and theologian, conformity to the Good (II:317–18; *Nicomachean Ethics*, Book X), though, of course, the nature of the Good is interpreted differently for philosopher and theologian. *Mimesis*, as Aristotle observed, is both the representation of action and a form of action itself, both a making (*poiesis*) and a doing (*praxis*). The dreams of speculative philosophy for a coherent epistemology are broken. A complete account of the conditions for the possibility of knowledge is aporetic. There is only *phronesis*, practical wisdom, the process of getting to know which is integral to the pursuit of the good life. We who live in the age of the Spirit of Christ, within the redemptive work of the Holy Spirit, must speak of, through and by revealedness. The language we employ, the stories we tell, must be allegorized in order to open up a space between what we think we know and what is true, between what Aristotle would call *deutera ousia*, and the socialized concepts which name our impressions of it, and the *prote ousia*, the substance beyond substance which is God. Allegory brings together rhetoric, aporetics, temporality and transcendence. It is a pedagogy, a teaching, a spiritual exercise. The reading which surrenders itself, its certainties, its grasp of things, is contemplation, is praying, as St Ignatius and, more recently, Hélène Cixous,[51] understood. The final responsibility belongs both to the reader and to the operation of grace which rends the equivalence of perception and understanding – that is what allegory pronounces. Gregory concludes his *Life of Moses* by turning to his reader: 'it is time for you, noble friend, to look to that example and, by transferring to your own life what is contemplated through spiritual interpretation of the things spoken literally, to be known by God and to become his friend' (II:320).

If we relate this conclusion to the vexed question which often dogs this story-revelation debate – is it just as theologically and spiritually valid to read Proust as to read the Gospel of St John? – I would have to answer in terms very close to those of Clement of Alexandria (terms evident in Augustine's *Confessions*): 'if Hellenistic philosophy comprehends not the whole extent of the truth, and besides, is destitute of strength to perform the commandments of the Lord, yet it prepares the way for the truly royal teaching, training in some way or other, and moulding the character, fitting him who believes in providence for the reception of the truth' *(Stromateis*, 1.16.80.6).

The project we set ourselves in the beginning was an examination of the relationship between story and revelation. What I am suggesting is that, though there may be a distinction drawn between them, there cannot be a polarity. My argument suggests that time, space and representation are products of a *diastema* established by God. Furthermore, my argument suggests that through the Spirit these become sacramentalized. It follows that it is in our experience of the world (which to be understood as experience must be represented), in our wording and our reading, in our storytelling, that we are redeemed.[52] The triune God, by His revelation in Christ and through His Spirit, moves within the processes of time and human desire itself. Because we are made in *the image of* then are we destined to be *homo symbolicus*. My argument presupposes that the Godhead is an activity, not an object and, therefore, that His revelation of himself is a continuously unfolding process, within an eschatological horizon, not an event. This unfolding process is the *dunamis* of love itself and therefore the content of such revelation is a getting to love, a pedagogy in adoration, a plotting of praise, a liturgy, not an intellectual property. As such our creative storytelling takes place within the operation of God's triune loving; we exist in God's endless impartation of Himself. Is hermeneutics as a *scientia*, then, simply a product of Protestantism's symbiosis with modernity, simply a development of the mediaeval concern with *grammatica*, a more systematic attempt to stabilize the sign?[53]

Coda

At the end of Wim Wender's film, Cassiel, having sacrificed himself for a little girl, returns to the angelic realm. The closing shots follow the main human characters as they sail towards new horizons, Cassiel and Raphaela conclude the film with a voice-over:

> You. You whom we love. You who do not see us. You who do not hear us. You imagine us in the far distance, yet we are so near. We are the messengers who bring closeness to those in the distance. We are not the message, we are the messengers. The message is love. We are nothing. You are everything to us. Let us dwell in your eyes. See your world through us. Recapture through us that loving look once again. Then we'll be close to you and you to Him.

This is the film's final and most poignant statement against 'soulless materialism'. Again it follows, albeit without any reference, Walter Benjamin's recognition that 'allegories fill out and deny the void in which they are represented, just as, ultimately, the intention does not faithfully rest in contemplation of the bodies, but faithlessly leaps forward to the idea of resurrection'.[54]

Notes

I would like to thank Professor Wolfram Kinzig of Bonn University for his careful reading of an earlier draft of this text, for his comments, his criticisms and his helpful suggestions on the German Nyssa scholarship. The faults and infelicities of the piece remain my own.

1 *The Origin of German Tragic Drama*, tr. John Osborne (London: New Left Books, 1977), p.230.
2 Ibid.
3 Tr. Thomas Corbishley SJ (Wheathampstead: Anthony Clarke, 1973).
4 *The Birth to Presence*, tr. Brian Holmes *et al.* (Stanford: Stanford University Press, 1993), p.198.
5 *Allegories of Reading: Figural Language in Rousseau, Nietzsche, Rilke and Proust* (New Haven: Yale University Press, 1979).
6 This raises a thorny though pertinent question, the question of the relationship between the Gospels and the Pauline epistles as testimonies to the event of Christ. I am suggesting here, counter to a Protestant emphasis on the priority of Paul, that the Gospel narratives, inasmuch as they represent the life and work of Christ, are disclosive. That is, they enable the reader as a practitioner of faith to participate in the ongoing Trinitarian outworking of the incarnation, death and resurrection of Christ. The question as to whether the Pauline epistles (or the Revelation of St. John) also facilitate such a participation immediately arises. I would answer 'no', insofar as these deal only indirectly with the event of revelation. They can be disclosive to the reader as a practitioner of faith, but the character of that disclosure has to be understood on the basis of the Gospels. In other words, and I am in no doubt that this is controversial, the Gospels have to interpret the rest of the Bible. In the Gospels the canon has a molten core from which it receives the light by which it can be read by faith. For the Gospels present us with Him with whom we have to do as creatures – the Christ.
7 My discussion of this Preface is heavily indebted to the two most thorough analyses of

Luke 1:1–4 in English: H.J. Cadbury, in *The Beginnings of Christianity*, vol.II, ed. F.J. Foakes-Jackson and K. Lake (London, 1922), pp.401–20; Loveday Alexander, *The Preface to Luke's Gospel* (Cambridge: Cambridge University Press, 1993). The interpretation of this passage is solely my responsibility.

8 Cf. Alexander, *supra*, n.7, pp.128–30 for the several interpretations of this word.

9 There is an interesting ambivalence which emerges through this word, which has also been understood as 'report', that is, evil reports about the Christian sect presented to the Roman official Theophilus. Whether Theophilus had such an official status is doubtful (Alexander, 1993, pp.187–200), but the semantic ambivalence of the word does relate to whether Theophilus is an insider (a Christian) or an outsider (someone to whom a Christian apologetic has to be made). This is not irrelevant to the doubleness of much of this Preface. While not employing explicit Christian terms (as if then the narrative was aimed at fostering relations with Hellenistic non-Christians) there are words which do have Christian connotations, as we have seen. It is as if, should Theophilus be a Christian, the Gospel is directed to someone over his shoulder who is not. If Theophilus is not a Christian then this is *apologia*, appealing to Hellenic officaldom by the employment of a neutral, even scientistic, rhetoric. Either way, the Gospel has another intention, an allegorical intention.

10 Sr. Miriam Theresa Larkin CS, *Language in the Philosophy of Aristotle* (The Hague: Mouton, 1971), p.51. On Aristotle's understanding of language and how it was received and understood by patristic, mediaeval and Enlightenment exegetes, see Hans Arens, *Aristotle's Theory of Language and its Tradition* (Amsterdam: John Benjamin, 1984).

11 Cf. Larkin, *supra*, n.10, p.75 and her conclusion: 'Aristotle uses the term "metaphor" in such a way that the term itself is a *pros hen* equivocal' (p.101). See also Ricoeur's analysis of paronyms in *The Rule of Metaphor*, tr. Robert Czerny (London: Routledge, 1978), pp.259–72.

12 For how this concept of *mimesis* relates to appropriate ethical action, *phronesis* and Aristotle's concept of the mean, see Stephen R.L. Clark, 'The Doctrine of the Mean', in *Aristotle's Man: Speculations upon Aristotelian Anthropology* (Oxford: Clarendon Press, 1975), pp.84–97.

13 Larkin, *supra*, n.10, p.52.

14 See Clark, *supra*, n.12, pp.14–27.

15 Ricoeur, *supra*, n.11, p.268.

16 Cf. G. Patiz's 'Theology and Ontology in Aristotle's Metaphysics', in Jonathan Barnes, Malcolm Schofield and Richard Sorabji (eds), *Articles on Aristotle*, vol 3 (London: Duckworth, 1979), pp.48–9.

17 Edward Booth, *Aristotelian Aporetic Ontology in Islamic and Christian Thinkers* (Cambridge: Cambridge University Press, 1983), p.17.

18 Ibid., p.8.

19 Ibid., p.17.

20 Patiz, *supra*, n.16, p.39.

21 Ibid., p.47.

22 Quoted by Booth, p.28. Abstracts from Alexander of Aphrodisia's *Commentary on Metaphysics* can be found in W.D. Ross, *Aristotelis Fragmenta Selecta* (Oxford: Oxford University Press, 1955).

23 *Blindness and Insight: Essays in the Rhetoric of Contemporary Criticism* (London: Methuen and Co., 1983), p.206.

24 *Therapy of Desire: Theory and Practice in Hellenistic Ethics* (Princeton: Princeton University Press, 1994), p.76.

25 Ibid., p.80. Cf. Clark on perception, *supra*, n.12, pp.69–83.
26 Ibid., p.83.
27 Ibid., p.96.
28 Cf. Gerald Else, *Plato and Aristotle on Poetry* (Chapel Hill: University of North Carolina Press, 1986), where he argues for the connections between poetic structure and the syllogistic form, pp.1110–12, 128–9.
29 Clark, *supra*, n.12, p.67.
30 See Hans Urs von Balthasar's study of Gregory of Nyssa's work, *Presence and Thought: An Essay on the Religious Philosophy of Gregory of Nyssa*, tr. Mark Sebane (San Francisco: Ignatius Press, 1995) (first published in 1942). Also E. von Ivanka, 'Vom Platonismus zur Theoriemystik. Zur Erkenntnislehre Gregors von Nyssa', *Scholastik*, 11 (1936), 163–95. D.L. Balas is right when he states that Gregory's knowledge of philosophy included middle Platonism, early Neoplatonism as well as strong Aristotelian and Stoic elements (*Theologische Realenzyklopädie*, Band XIV (Berlin: de Gruyter, 1985), p.177). The work of Heinrich Dorrie has emphasized the parallels with Plato's work: the *Phaedo* on Gregory's *De Anima* and *Timaeus* on Gregory's exegesis of *Genesis*. (See here also Monique Alexandre, '*L'exégèse de Gen. 1, 1–2a dans l'* In Hexaemeron de Grégoire de Nysse: deux approches du problème de la matière', who argues that Aristotle's concept of matter is thoroughly Aristotelian, in Heinrich Dorrie, Margarete Altenburger and Uta Schramm (eds) *Gregor von Nyssa und die Philosophie* (Leiden: Brill, 1976, pp.159–92).) Nevertheless, many other scholars have pointed out Gregory's indebtedness to Aristotlean vocabulary and concepts. From his work Werner Jaeger infers that 'Gregor hat die aristotelische Kategorienlehre offenbar gut studiert': *Gregor von Nyssa's Lehre vom Heiligen Geist* (Leiden: Brill, 1966). Jean Daniélou, examining Gregory's understanding of theoria 'comme méthode discursive pour arriver à une connaissance sure' points out that 'c'est à Aristote que se rattache la méthodologie de Grégoire': *L'Etre et le temps chez Grégoire de Nysse* (Leiden: Brill, 1970), p. 5.
31 Throughout this chapter I am making reference to the translation by Abraham J. Malherbe and Everett Ferguson (New York: Paulist Press, 1978).
32 *Blindness and Insight*, *supra*, n.23, p.209.
33 *Reallexikon für Antike und Christentum*, Band XII (Stuttgart: Anton Hiersemann, 1983), p.882.
34 *Is There a Text in This Class? The Authority of Interpretive Communities* (Cambridge, Mass.: Harvard University Press, 1980), p.336.
35 *supra*, n.33, p.882.
36 See here, II.247, where no fewer than 18 redefinitions are given for 'the opening in the rock' into which Moses retreated when God passed by.
37 Philo's work also stressed the written form of revelation, unlike Clement of Alexander who, later, drew attention to the voice as revelatory. Cf. David Dawson, *Allegorical Readers and Cultural Revision in Ancient Alexandria* (Berkeley: University of California Press, 1992), esp. pp.73–126, 183–234.
38 *The Broken Middle: Out of Our Ancient Society* (Oxford: Basil Blackwell, 1992). See especially pp.277–96.
39 See II:243 for a temporality which is eternal: 'how the same thing is both a standing still and a moving', like Aristotle's concept of God.
40 See Jean-Yves Lacoste, *Expérience et Absolu* (Paris: Presses Universitaires de France, 1994) for an exploration of how personhood experiences a dispossession and kenosis in and through liturgy.
41 *Allegories of Reading*, *supra*, n.5, p.275.
42 Daniélou, *supra*, n.30, pp.43–5.

43 Cf. Michel Foucault, *The History of Sexuality*, vol. 1, tr. Robert Hurley (London: Penguin Books, 1981) for a discussion of confession as social engineering (pp.18–21, 60–61); also Talal Asad, *The Genealogies of Religion: Discipline and Reasons of Power in Christianity and Islam* (Baltimore: Johns Hopkins University Press, 1993), pp.83–167.

44 Balthasar, *supra*, n.30, p.133.

45 For an examination of the structural linguistic axes of metaphor and metonymy as they relate to Scripture, see my 'Biblical Narrative and the Theology of Metonymy', *Modern Theology*, 7(4) (July 1991), 335–50.

46 See Booth, *supra*, n.17.

47 See Balthasar, *The Glory of The Lord*, vol. 5, tr. Oliver Davies *et al.* (Edinburgh: T.&T. Clark, 1991), pp.48–140.

48 *Confessions*, tr. Henry Chadwick (Oxford: Oxford University Press, 1992), p.254.

49 Most recently, Richard Swinburne, *Revelation: From Metaphor to Analogy* (Oxford: Clarendon Press, 1992).

50 On the theological importance of following in Gregory of Nyssa, see II.252 and *In. Cant*, 12.

51 Cf. *Reading with Clarice Lispector*, tr. Verene Andermatt Conley (Hemel Hempstead: Harvester Wheatsheaf, 1990).

52 There is a further implication here. We have frequently asked over these past years whether all stories can be redemptive, given that the Scripture's close correlation between the Christ event and representation is going to make Scripture the most redemptive form of *mimesis*. But there are, after all, narratives of evil. On this account of the relationship between story and revelation, the extent to which something is recognized as good or evil will depend upon spiritual discernment or theological perception: that is, whether the divine can be seen within the ordinary, the invisible in the visible. Nothing by necessity is evil either in creation, experience or representation.

53 Cf. Jesse M. Gellrich, *The Idea of the Book in the Middle Ages: Language, Theory, Mythology and Fiction* (New York: Cornell University Press, 1985), p.21.

54 *The Origin of German Tragic Drama*, *supra*, n.1, p.233.

Seven

'Revelation' and 'Story' in Jewish and Christian Apocalyptic

Michael Wolter

1 Apocalyptic as Revelation in Stories

1.1 In what follows 'revelation' is taken to be the leading term and 'story' related to that, so I will not go into what function revelations have within the temporal and causal sequences of stories. Rather, this study will use texts in which stories are the content of revelation. Relating the two concepts in this way has some heuristic value because it corresponds very closely to one of the specific characteristics of the literary phenomenon known since the nineteenth century as 'apocalyptic'.

This word is used here both as a noun and as an adjective in the restricted, technical sense, to refer broadly to the literary category. The term 'Apocalypse', or 'revelation', is the first word of the Revelation of St John, and is applied now to a series of writings from the Hellenistic Roman period which are comparable to the last book of the Bible with regard to form and content (Dan., 4 Ezra, Syr Baruch, Ethiopic Enoch and the like).[1] 'Apocalyptic' here means nothing more than revelation literature. All texts brought together under this collective term have, as their most important distinguishing feature, the course of historical events being revealed to and interpreted by a holy person and/or prophet chosen by God. This presupposes an understanding of history in which its course is established in advance by God and exists in Heaven before it is transformed into earthly events. During the esoteric revelation experience, the fictive visionary receives an insight into events, which from his standpoint have not yet occurred, and he records the vision and its interpretation in his writing. In this sense the Apocalypses are (from a form-critical point of view) framework genres, in which the widely divergent smaller genres that constitute them can be brought together.[2]

Not surprisingly, a large part of these forms of literature consists in smaller units which are to be fitted into the narrative types of texts. They find their concrete linguistic expression in texts, which we can designate by the neat and typically English word, 'story'.[3] So, as regards the relation between our framework genres and smaller units, the form of an Apocalypse is very largely intended to reveal or unveil stories. The title of the Greek Apocalypse of Baruch is therefore appropriate. It is Baruch's 'narrative[4] and revelation concerning the unspeakable things, which he saw at God's behest' (Greek Baruch, Prologue 1). That this connection is constitutive is also clear from several texts from St Paul. Wherever Paul elucidates his argument through the express communication of esoteric revelation, he tells stories. We see this in 1 Thessalonians 4:16–17: the *narratio* of the sequence of events is (i) The Lord's coming; (ii) Resurrection of the Dead; (iii) simultaneous pulling up into heaven of the living and the resurrected; (iv) everlasting fellowship with the Lord. This is intended to support the thesis that the dead too can be taken up (v.14). See also the communication of a mystery in 1 Corinthians 15:51f.: the resurrection of the dead as incorruptible, and the transformation of the living; also Romans 11:25b–27, which presents the story of Israel from the present partial hardening up to the future salvation by the deliverer who is coming from Zion.

1.2 First we will mention a few types of stories (not a complete inventory) which might be the content of esoteric revelation.

1.2.1 Stories of universal history. An example of this is the so-called 'animal vision' in Ethiopic Enoch (85–90). It provides 'a thought out sketch of history'[5] from human beginnings through to the establishing of the messianic kingdom.

1.2.2 Stories of contemporary history. The revealed story consists in this case in a historical snippet. Daniel 7 is an example and will be discussed in more detail in section 3.

1.2.3 Story outcomes. This heading groups together a number of visionary texts which at first glance do not reveal stories, because they do not narrate, but rather describe: in particular the eschatological salvation and damnation of the righteous and sinners. Two examples follow.[6] The first is from The Apocalypse of Peter (Akhmim) 15–20:

> 15 And the Lord showed me a vast place away from this world, gleaming in light, where beams of sunlight shone through the air. The earth itself was strewn with never-fading flowers, and was full of edible vegetables and plants which bloomed splendidly and bore ever-ripe, enjoyable fruit. 16 So intense was the perfume, that it wafted over to us from there. 17 The inhabitants of that place were clothed in angelic robes, and their clothing was appropriate to their residence. 18 Angels strolled about beneath them. 19 All the inhabitants of that

> place had the same brilliance, and with one voice they praised God the Lord, they were joyful in that place. 20 The Lord spoke to us: 'This is the place of your high priests [brothers?] the just ones.'

The second example is from the same source, at verse 27:

> And other [men] and women stood up to their waists in flames and were thrown into a dark place and were beaten by evil spirits and their innards were eaten up by tireless worms. These were the ones who persecuted the just and handed them over.

That both texts conform to our theme is shown by the continuity between the eschatological fate of each named group and their way of life. By associating the judgment of particular people with their past doings, virtual stories develop. Furthermore, the intention of the revealing consists above all in showing that the plot of these stories is a 'sequence arranged according to an organizing principle'.[7] If, with Edwin Muir, we understand a plot to be 'the chain of events in a story and the principle which knits it together',[8] then in both these examples it is without doubt God's righteous judgment which makes a unity out of the events in the story (behaviour and outcome) and causes them despite their different character to be two parts of a complete story.

1.3 Let me now explore the reason for the particular affinity between 'revelation' and 'story' in the literary context of apocalyptic in order to determine especially the cognitive, argumentative and pragmatic functions in the stories revealed in apocalyptic texts. As a basis for these reflections I will take Daniel 7 and Revelation 13, two texts where there is intertextuality. But first, I offer some presuppositions.

2 Israel as Story, Israel's Story and Israel's Stories

This formulation is intended to signal two things: it signals that in what follows (2.1) three different levels of meaning are distinguished within the concept of story and that (2.2) the identity of Israel as the chosen people of God constitutes the decisive frame of reference for the coordination of 'revelation' and 'story' in early Jewish apocalyptic, sketched at the beginning of this chapter.

2.1 A typology of story is considered below.

2.1.1 A story is a linguistic rendering of sequences of events (Lat. *narratio,* Greek, διήγησις). The tersest definition I have found for this use of the word 'story' comes from E.M. Forster, for whom a story meant 'a narrative of events arranged in their time sequence'.[9]

2.1.2 The concept 'story' can also be applied to identity-forming events in the past, which are present now in the form of collective or individual memory and which can be kept alive through 'commemorative figures'.[10] So I will in what follows call them 'remembered stories'. Dietrich Ritschl calls this 'meta-story' and characterizes it as a 'possibly not-tellable or "never fully expressible" story'.[11]

2.1.3 I here distinguish from the above a third type of story and call it experimentally a 'story experienced in the present' or 'open story'. It is characterized by individuals and groups being able to perceive the specific experiences of reality confronting them as elements of a story's web of events, without being able to see them as completed. Here the interesting question is: what criterion is making the outcome of the story experienced in the present be seen as still undecided or open?

2.2 The self-understanding of Israel as the chosen people of God was doubtless based on the type of story described in section 2.1.2. The special relationship between God and Israel is rooted in a story, the story of Israel's election. This is plain above all in the predications of God which refer to the Exodus event (Yahweh as the God of Israel is the One 'who led Israel out of Egypt'; see Ex. 20:2; 29:35; Lev. 22:13; Deut. 5:6; Judges 12:12; 1 Kings 9:9 and so on). This identity-forming collective memory is continually kept alive through what Jan Assmann calls 'cultural formation (texts, rituals, monuments) and institutionalized communication (recitation, celebration, reflection)',[12] so that texts then emerge like the type of story represented in section 2.1.1, texts which make this story present as narrative. Deuteronomy 26:5–9, and Deuteronomy 6:20–25 are examples:

> 5 And you shall make response before the LORD your God, 'A wandering Aramean was my father; and he went down into Egypt and sojourned there, few in number; and there he became a nation, great, mighty, and populous. 6 And the Egyptians treated us harshly, and afflicted us, and laid upon us hard bondage. 7
> Then we cried to the LORD the God of our fathers, and the LORD heard our voice, and saw our affliction, our toil, and our oppression; 8 and the LORD brought us out of Egypt with a mighty hand and an outstretched arm, with great terror, with

> signs and wonders; 9 and he brought us into this place and gave us this land, a land flowing with milk and honey. (Deut. 26:5–9, RSV)

> 20 When your son asks you in time to come, 'What is the meaning of the testimonies and the statutes and the ordinances which the LORD our God has commanded you?' 21 then you shall say to your son, 'We were Pharaoh's slaves in Egypt; and the LORD brought us out of Egypt with a mighty hand; 22 and the LORD showed signs and wonders, great and grievous, against Egypt and against Pharaoh and all his household, before our eyes; 23 and he brought us out from there, that he might bring us in and give us the land which he swore to give to our fathers. 24 And the LORD commanded us to do all these statutes, to fear the LORD our God, for our good always, that he might preserve us alive, as at this day. 25 And it will be righteousness for us, if we are careful to do all this commandment before the LORD our God, as he has commanded us.' (Deut. 6:20–25, RSV)

It has normative significance here that the testimonies, statutes and ordinances mentioned in verse 20 receive their enduring meaning from a story. This corresponds to the way that in the history of the canon the Sinai Torah has become an integral part of a story.

The third story type (see section 2.1.3) can also be found in the Old Testament. The final redaction of the Deuteronomic historical work provides an example. While it sees the exile as punishment for Israel's apostasy from her God, it does not see this as the end of the story of Israel as God's people. This conception is also found in many other texts, the exilic addition to the book of Amos, for example (9:7–15). Psalm 89 is a national lament in which the covenant promise and the grace and loyalty of Yahweh are named (see vv.2–5, 20–30, 34–8) as criteria for the certainty being communicated that Israel's present disaster is part of an as yet unconcluded story.

This has brought us to the threshold of apocalyptic. Approaching the apocalypses from the standpoint of our story typology, it becomes clear right away that their real authors, exactly like those of the Deuteronomic history and Psalm 89, locate themselves within stories experienced in the present, and that they perceive these stories to be open stories. It is possible for us to determine the standpoint of the real author and the implied reader because we are able to distinguish within stories told by fictive authors between prophecies after the event (the so-called *vaticinia ex eventu*) and 'genuine prophecies'.[13] We do so on the basis of our historical knowledge got from outside the texts and so are able to place each author fairly exactly at the point at which prophecies after the event give way to real prophecies.[14]

The differentiating feature of the apocalypses is (a) that their authors narrate this story as a revelation which can be mediated only by way of esoteric unveiling, and (b) that they cover up their standpoint (which is identifiable by the implied readers on account of their historically being there) in a literary way by telling stories that carry on without break beyond that present standpoint and qualify the web of events experienced in the present as a still open story.

The following text analyses are intended to show that and why these two peculiarities are inextricably linked.

3 Daniel 7

3.1 This chapter assumed its present form between the end of 167 and the beginning of 164 BCE in Palestine.[15] The text consists of two parts, a vision (vv.2–15) and an audition (vv.16–27), which repeats the last portion of the vision (vv.19f.) or continues it (vv.21f.). To begin with, the story of four beasts is told, beasts which, one after another, rise out of the sea, become ever more powerful, wreak increasing havoc, but are then deprived of their power, whereas universal and eternal kingship is handed over to one who looks 'like a son of man'.

Through the last sentence in v.14 ('his dominion is an everlasting dominion, which shall not pass away, and his kingdom one that shall not be destroyed') it is made clear that this story has reached a definitive end and cannot be continued any further. This dream–vision is then interpreted in an allegorizing way by an audition as referring to contemporary history. The four animals are interpreted as symbols designating four empires (v.17), taking up again the four kingdom scheme of the vision in Daniel 2:31ff. Conspicuous in chapter 7 is the narrative compression with which the fourth beast is presented. This beast is expressly distinguished from the first three and it alone is individually interpreted (vv.19–25). The telling of this partial story is then even further intensified in the presentation of the eleventh and final horn, the eleventh king (vv.8, 20f., 24b–25). In contrast to the other horns/kings, only *his* actions are individually described. It here becomes apparent that the special interest of the final redactor of our text is directed to *this* story, which begins with the appearance of this person.

3.2 We can now attempt to locate the text in terms of my story typology.[16]

3.2.1 We have a story as text, that is to say, a *narratio* which is twice told: first encoded symbolically and then in an allegorizing interpretation. Both versions of the story are the content of esoteric revelation.

3.2.2 Further, the type of story experienced in the present as a web of events within which both the real author and the implied reader are located, as introduced in section 2.1.2, can be identified without difficulty. It is evident in the contemporary historical allusions, written as prophecies after the event, which are compressed into the actions of the eleventh horn/king of the fourth beast/empire.[17] Whereas the identity of the kings symbolized by the first 10 horns cannot be established for certain,[18] we can determine that of the eleventh king, and so see the events of the story experienced in the present. It refers to the Seleucid ruler Antiochus IV Epiphanes (reigned BCE 175–164), who in BCE 169 had plundered the temple treasury in Jerusalem and entered the holy of holies (1 Macc. 1:21–3; 2 Macc. 5:15f.). In the autumn of BCE 167, he issued a decree forbidding observance of the Jewish sacrificial cult, sabbath and circumcision (1 Macc. 1:41–58). Observant Jews who held fast to their religious observances were mercilessly persecuted. He had the sacrificial altar in the Temple of Jerusalem given a top and dedicated to Zeus of Olympus. There is no doubt that Daniel 7:25 alludes to these religiopolitical measures because we find specific indications of these events in other parts of the book (see 8:11f.; 9:27; 11:31; 12:11). In reaction to this, there was the revolt of the Maccabees, to whose circle we assigned the final editor of the Book of Daniel. It is also important that the story experienced in the present is expressly qualified, with the help of the temporal indicators given in vv.12b and 25b, as an open story. The restriction of the contemporary tyranny to three and a half times in v.25b finds its explanation in Daniel 9:24–7, where the author uses the 70-year terminus found in Jeremiah 25:11; 29:10 and periodizes the time from the beginning of the Babylonian exile up to the final elimination of alien hegemony as a succession of 70 weeks of years. Antiochus appears at the beginning of the last week. In 9:27. his measures are expressly placed at the mid-point of this week. The date in 7:25 has no contemporary historical meaning, but rather belongs on the plane of the revealed story. It serves to keep the story experienced in the present open, as well as saying that the duration of the current crisis is already limited in advance.[19]

3.2.3 But how do things stand with the second story type mentioned above (see section 2.1.2) that is the identity-forming story of Israel's election preserved in a collective memory? This also will be taken up in our text, in the frequently recurring language about the 'saints (of the Most High)' and the 'people of the saints of the Most High' (7:18, 21, 22, 25, 27). These titles refer to the identity-forming election story of Israel, as is evidenced by their being firmly anchored in the *narratio* of this event. Leviticus 11:45 can be quoted here as an example: 'I am the LORD who brought you up out of the land of Egypt, to be your God; you shall therefore be holy, for I am holy' (see also Ex. 19:6; 22:31; Lev. 11:44; 19:2; 20:26; Deut. 7:6–8 and so on).

According to these passages, Israel's holiness is based on her election, that is, on the holiness of Yahweh who has chosen Israel to be his peculiar people and so allowed her to participate in his own holiness.

The decisive hermeneutic function within the revealed *narratio,* however, belongs primarily to a completely different story of this type. Greek rule, and in particular that of Antiochus IV, symbolized by the fourth beast, is marked off from the first three beasts, yet it is of the same type and of identical origin as the first three, because like them it is presented as a beast that climbs out of the churning sea. This means that, despite its individuality, the frightful reign of Antiochus IV symbolizes a single hostile force and is presented as its climax and high point. It emerges clearly from the beginning of the vision which power is being described, in the understanding of the author. The description of the surging sea, which brings forth the four beasts, harks back to the traditional descriptions of Chaos. There the sea is absolutely *the* primordial element of chaos which was overcome and tamed in the process of the creation of the world (see also Gen. 1:2; Job 38:8–11; Ps. 65:8; 89:10; 104:6f.; Prov. 8:29; Isa. 51:9f.; Jer. 5:22 and so on).[20] The proximity to this myth is detectable also in the saying about the four winds of heaven (v.2b) which designate the cosmos as a whole by heaven's four directions. It shows an unmistakable similarity to Gen. 1:2 as here the chaotic primordial deep is set astir by a 'breath of God'.[21] It is therefore the story of the primaeval battle with chaos that helps encode in symbols the story experienced in the present so that this story can be told as an eschatological new edition of that story.[22]

3.3 The hermeneutical interaction of these last two story types within the revealed *narratio* can be described on two levels. It depends on the question of what function this interaction has for the guidance of the implied reader.

3.3.1 By reverting back to the story of the battle with chaos, the story experienced in the present can be told in such a way that the two stories converge and this serves to establish meaning. First of all, the possibility of establishing a convergence between the two stories is created by means of esoteric revelation, because only this makes it possible to encode the action so that (a) the real character of the story is recognizable to the implied reader and (b) the author can continue the story to a future outside the standpoint of the author and the implied reader. In this sense the mythological metaphor of the animals climbing out of the sea has not simply the task of denouncing the hostile opposing force but, rather, is intended to influence the readers. It gives reasons for the superior power of the adversary and so explains their own defencelessness and defeat by this by taking the present experience of disaster outside historical causality and attributing it to metahistorical powers (the elements of Chaos). The convergence of the stories thus has an *unburdening* function. It assures the reader of the powerlessness of the enemy, because, as the reader of course knows, in the creation event

God has shown that God can overcome the power of the elements of chaos. God will furthermore do this now because, not only is the work of creation endangered, but God's very being is under attack (see v.25; the fourth beast raises itself up against God). The convergence of the stories thus has also a *consoling* function because it imparts the confidence that God will intervene victoriously against the hostile power.

3.3.2 On the other hand, there exists here, between the identity-founding story of Israel's election and the author's story experienced in the present, a *relationship of divergence*, or perhaps better, a conflict between stories. This conflict consists in the plot of the story experienced in the present seeming to suspend the election story, which gives Israel its religious and social orientation. In the time of Antiochus IV it was specifically the pious and righteous who, because they held fast to the Torah, had to endure suffering and persecution and be overcome by a hostile power (see Dan. 7:21). Contrary to the assumptions of the Deuteronomic school and Psalm 89, the connection between guilt and punishment integral to the election story could not be seen as forming the plot of the story being experienced in the present. So this was bound to call into question the plausibility of the story of Israel's election, the story which gave Israel its character and its norms. (In section 2.2, see the example quoted from Deut. 6:20–25.) This basic challenge meant that the continuity of the election of the people of God was also called into question. This experience of a difference was bound to make the story experienced in the present feel like a dead end, because the paradigms already established in the story of Israel's election denied any possibility of theological revision in the light of the present crisis situation. It was not possible to understand the interaction of the two stories as a convergence, because the available model of a remembered story proclaimed a causal connection between sin and punishment which was no longer able to make intelligible the plot of the story being experienced in the present. It was therefore bound to seem that God was no longer in control of the story of Israel.

3.3.3 At this point the story experienced in the present begins to interact with the story told as revelation. That the contemporary crisis is also a component of God's salvation story with Israel can be verified in face of the dead end outlined above only by the story experienced in the present being told further and being extended beyond the immediate position of its actors into the future. In Daniel 7, this occurs as in the animal vision and in the Apocalypse of Weeks in the form of esoteric revelation, which makes it possible for the authors of the apocalypses to show that the story being experienced in the present is open, and to integrate it as such into an apocalyptic *narratio* which overcomes its currently dead-end character. Only in this way is it possible, in view of the experience of difference discussed above, to perceive the contemporary crisis as an integral part of an order established by God in history, and to eliminate its divergence from the story of election present as collective memory, and so finally to guarantee that, on account of God's justice and faithfulness, God remains steadfast to his promise. In this way, the continuity of the salvation story of Israel is not disrupted.

We will now ask how this web of stories making contact with one another is adopted within a Christian apocalypse by looking at Revelation 13.

4 Revelation 13 (and 19:11–21)

4.1 That Revelation 13 is to be seen as a reprise of Daniel 7 is clear especially from the description of the first beast. Like the four beasts in Daniel 7, it arises out of the sea (Rev. 13:1), and its description in vv.1–2 goes back to the characteristics of the four different beasts in Daniel 7. It has 10 horns like the fourth beast (Dan. 7:7,20); in its appearance as a panther it is similar to the third beast (Dan. 7:6), it has its feet from the second beast, the bear (Dan. 7:5) and its mouth from the first beast, the lion (Dan. 7:4). This summarizing of the characteristics of the four different beasts, which in Daniel 7 appear sequentially, into a single one doubtless serves the purpose of intensification. In one beast is combined the destructive impact of the four. Elements of the presentation of the eleventh horn in Daniel 7 are also present in Revelation 13: the beast which rises out of the sea has a mouth speaking haughty things (Dan. 7:8,20 – see also v.11; Rev. 13:5); it blasphemes God (Dan. 7:25; Rev. 13:6); it wages war against the saints and overcomes them (Dan. 7:8, 21, 25; Rev. 13:6) and in specifying the duration of its rule as 42 months (three and a half years, Rev. 13:5) takes up the 'three times and a half' from Daniel 7:25. When we also bring in the beast which rises out of the earth (Rev. 13:11) it is clear that the author of Revelation is also adopting the reference to the myth of the battle with Chaos. The similar origin of the two animals, one from the water and one from the land, refers to the ancient Chaos monsters, Leviathan and Behemoth: the former dwells in the depth of the sea, the latter was thought of as a land animal (cf. Job 40:15ff., 25ff.; 4 Ezra 6:49–52; Eth Enoch 60:7–9; Syr Baruch 29:4).

It is interesting in this connection that the author of the Book of Revelation dehistoricizes the presentation of Daniel 7 even as he mythologizes it. This is to be seen first in the function of the 10 horns: in Daniel 7:24 they are identified with the predecessors of Antiochus IV, so they served to identify the contemporary ruler. In contrast to this, the 10 horns in Revelation 13:1 have lost this function and become merely part of the conventional description of the opponent.[23] The transformation from history into myth is further recognizable in that in Revelation 13 the sequence of the four beasts (that is, kingdoms) from Daniel 7 is not historically related to the seer's own present. Instead, the author of Revelation usurps the historical sequence of the four beasts in Daniel 7 for his own purposes, to symbolize the enemy. Essential historically particular elements of the *narratio* in Daniel 7 migrate from the level of the story experienced in the present to that of the remembered story.

4.2 Let me now try fitting the text of Revelation 13 too into our story typology (see above, section 2.1).

4.2.1 To begin with, we have a revealed *narratio* in which the activity of two beasts is described. On the level of the text, this narrative ends with v.18, because at 14:1 the author of Revelation makes a change of narrative characters and venue with the vision of the lamb and the 144,000 on Mount Zion. The special character of the narrative consists in its ending hanging in the air. This is recognizable in the use of different tenses in the main verbs: the presentation of the first beast begins in the aorist but ends in the future tense, which here expresses a continuing action (and all that dwell on the earth 'shall worship him' (v.8)) whereas the activity of the second beast is consistently described in the linear present: in Revelation 13:12, 13 it 'works'; in v.14 it 'deceives'. In this way, the story loses its dynamic energy and reaches a resting point which at the same time points to the story experienced in the present, in the time of the implied reader (see section 4.2.2).

However, the *narratio* about the activity of the two beasts is not yet concluded. It finds its continuation in 19:11–21, where likewise a revealed *narratio* is related that a heavenly rider who is called 'faithful and true' (v.11) that is, 'the Word of God' (v.13), together with his host, does battle with the beast from the sea with all his vassals, vanquishes them and throws the two beasts from chapter 13 into the lake of fire. The aorist is again employed here (vv.14, 17, 19, 20, 21) to carry the *narratio* to its end.

So, unlike Daniel 7, the *narratio* here does not form a micro-textual unit. It is divided into two partial stories, whose unity is established only at the macro-textual level. A quite calculated, and (for the total meaning of the story) decisive, narrative intention is apparent here. In 19:11–21, not only is the narrative thread begun in 13:1 taken up again, but a different story is also resumed and linked together with that of the two beasts into one total story. We find the decisive clue to the beginning of this second story at 19:15, where it is said of the heavenly rider, referring back to Ps. 2:9, that 'he will rule them [the nations] with a rod of iron'. We have to see here a cross-reference to 12:5, where the same thing is said about the son of the woman appearing in heaven clothed with the sun, the one who, immediately after being born, is taken up to the heavenly throne of God. Through this cross-reference, readers are given three pieces of information: (a) that the two figures are the same; (b) the child and rider, respectively, are identified as the Messiah (cf. Ps. 2:2, 7);[24] (c) together, both stories form a total story. But now we go back to Revelation 13.

4.2.2 To identify the story experienced in the present, revised in the light of the narrated story, is no problem. It is recognizable in the elements of the presentation which go beyond Daniel 7. The seven heads of the beast from the water (v.1) refer to the seven hills of Rome (see 17:9) and the 'blasphemies' on them have in view the titles of the Roman Caesars, with which since the time of Caligula they expressed their claim to cultic worship. Domitian himself had taken the title 'Lord and God' (*dominus et deus*: Suetonius, *Dom.* 13:1f.). The image which the second beast had made for the first one (v.14) points in all probability to the religious symbols which in this context, namely under and by Domitian, were put up (see Cassius Dio 67:8.1). In the cella of the temple of Domitian at Ephesus, that is, in the geographical catchment area of Revelation (cf. 2:1ff.), there was a larger than life statue of this emperor. And finally, verse 15b speaks of Christians being subjected to the force of the emperor cult, as 20 years later Pliny (Ep. 10:96) could record as normal practice. The interlacing of conventional and contemporary elements also shows how the accents have been shifted in comparison with Daniel 7. In the Book of Revelation it is above all the successful imposition of cultic worship of the Roman emperor that the author sees as standing at the middle point of the story. The standpoint of the author and the implied reader in the course of the story probably coincides quite closely with the situation which is described by means of linear verb forms (present and future).

4.2.3 What is the case with remembered stories? Apart from the myth of the Chaos battle there is here a further story, which is used to encode the adversary. It is the myth, widely spread at that time, regarding *Nero redivivus*, a myth based on the peculiar circumstances of the death of the emperor Nero. It suggested that Nero was still alive and would return.[25] We find allusions to this myth in the gematric symbol of a name which is given in the number 666 (v.18). This is exactly the sum of the numerical value of the Hebrew words *nron qsr* (Nero Caesar). Support for this notion can be found in verses 3 and 14 where the author of the Book of Revelation, presumably playing on Nero's suicide, speaks of a mortal wound being sustained by this beast (that is, to one of his heads), and being healed later on (see also 17:8, 11).

If we ask even here about the interaction between the two specimens of this story type, on the one hand, and the story being experienced by the author or the implied reader in the present, on the other, a convergence can be seen which broadly corresponds to that of Daniel 7 (see above, section 3.3.1). It is not so sharply profiled, but cannot be missed. So in this case the revelation story of the Book of Revelation does not speak any differently from Daniel 7.

4.3 We now consider interaction between the stories. In Daniel 7 the intention of the revealed *narratio* was to overcome the conflict between the story experienced in the present and the remembered story (in Dan. 7 the story of the election of Israel) and so to take away the former's dead-end character (see above, sections 3.3.2–3). If this assumption is to be accorded a validity that goes beyond the text, it must be verified by reference to the revealed *narratio* of the Book of Revelation which we have discussed here. So the following questions have to be answered. What in Revelation 13 is the remembered story which corresponds to the identity-forming story of Israel's election in Daniel 7, the story which diverges from the story experienced in the present (section 4.3.1)? What does this divergence consist in materially (section 4.3.2)? How does the revealed *narratio* from the Book of Revelation overcome this story conflict (section 4.3.3)?

4.3.1 In Revelation 13 explicit allusions to the remembered story are to be found in the presentation of the two beasts. It cannot be overlooked that they are given attributes which caricature Christ's attributes.[26] It is Jesus who appeared 'as one killed' (5:6) and became alive again (1:18). Like Christ before him who received universal power from God and rules over 'all tribes, languages, peoples and nations', which he has redeemed with his blood and which worship him (5:7–14), Christ's counterpart receives power from the dragon (that is, the devil) and rules 'every tribe, language and nation' (13:2, 7). The second beast likewise has the appearance of a lamb (13:11) as a counterfeit of the lamb who is Christ (5:6; 6:16 and so on); and the signs of the beast (whose name or number name – 13:16f.) correspond to the name of Christ, with whom the elect have been sealed (7:3; 14:1). That is to say, it is the story of Christ that is referred to here. Its paradigms guide the presentation of the actors in the story experienced in the present.

4.3.2 So it is not difficult to answer the second question. It is the conflict between *the story of Jesus Christ* and the story experienced in the present which emerges and is reworked theologically in Revelation 13 by means of the apocalyptic *narratio*. This also shows, however, how the accent has shifted in comparison with Daniel 7. Naturally, here as there, what is happening is that an experience of reality determined by an alien force is being mastered. But in Revelation 13 it is the success story of the imperial power of the Roman emperor which stands in competition with the success story of Jesus Christ. The experience of difference evoked through the story experienced in the present consists materially in the demonic ruler being able successfully to push through his claim to cultic worship: 'All who dwell on Earth will worship him' (v.8), even though on the basis of the story of Christ which the author of Revelation remembers, only the 'firstborn of the dead and ruler over the kings of the earth' (1:5) can be given exclusive cultic worship.

4.3.3 With that, the function of the specific literary design of the revealed *narratio*, provided to solve this story conflict (see above, section 4.3.1), becomes clear. This solution is only possible if the two competing stories are united into a total story in which Jesus Christ definitively establishes his claim to rule over the forces opposed to God which are currently in power. This then happens by means of the narrative in 19:11–21. Because this story will end only in the future, and above all on account of its mythical character (it begins in Heaven: 12:1, 3, 7–12 and ends coming down from Heaven: 19:11), it can only be told as revelation.

5 Summary

The pair of concepts 'revelation' and 'story' makes the biblical scholar think immediately of apocalyptic, because this literary genre proposes a special affinity between 'revelation' and 'story'. On the literary level of the apocalypses there is a transitive relationship between the two concepts. One of the most important concerns of the apocalyptic writings is to reveal stories.

5.1 Using Daniel 7 and Revelation 13 as an example, I have tried to interpret the relationship between revelation and story in apocalyptic in terms of its context, that is, as the reworking of a story conflict. I have taken for granted that human experience of reality is often perceived as an interaction between two differing stories: the 'remembered story' and the 'story being experienced in the present'. Both stories are related with a view to allowing a point of convergence to be recognized. This makes it possible to integrate the story being experienced in the present into the paradigms of the remembered story and to make it understandable from the perspective of these paradigms. There are of course contexts in which so deep a conflict arises that it is impossible to carry out this desired integration from these alone. The hermeneutical assistance of a third story type is then required. If it is to overcome the sharp story conflict, this can only be a revealed story like those told in the apocalypses. These narratives are undoubtedly planned by the apocalyptic writers as 'open narratives'. So they belong to the type presented in section 2.1.3: the allegorizing coding of the actors in the narratives of Daniel 7 and Revelation 13 are offers of 'disclosure' by the authors of the two apocalypses.[27] They are meant to make 'disclosures' possible insofar as they bring about a deindividualizing typification of characters which the readers can, on the basis of their prior knowledge, read into their own story. They can thus rediscover themselves and the actors in their own story as 'characters' with the help of the narrative. The reason why 'ought' and 'can', that is, perspectives drawn from the aesthetics of production and reception, are not here distinguished is that the implied readers[28] of the apocalypses and their real first readers stand together with the real author in an actual community. Communication is here based on a shared cultural heritage.

5.2 This shared community is now undoubtedly broken, on account of the historical distance between historical readers today and the real author of the apocalypses. The question of what holds the possibility of disclosure for *us*[29] pulls us up sharp against the phenomenon that apocalyptic narratives no longer say anything to us. We cannot, however, blame the texts for this. For in cases where understanding a text[30] involves the story of the readers themselves, we must turn the question round. The difficulty which modern readers of the Bible experience in finding 'disclosures' in apocalyptic texts then becomes a question about how we perceive our own stories. The history of the influence and reception of Revelation 13 shows how the narrative related here has, right down to the present time, generated a history of fresh 'disclosures' for all readers of the Bible who have read their own story into Revelation 13 and so had their own story changed.

This brings us to the question of what it is about our own stories that makes this seem no longer to happen. Why do we see the apocalyptic texts only as aesthetic objects or closed narratives? Is it perhaps our enlightened view of the world and history that makes us incapable of living with myths, with the result that we can no longer see our own stories as part of a cosmic drama? Or is it the political misuse that has been made of these narratives? But then we are quietly introducing an ethical distinction between legitimate and illegitimate 'disclosures', and have to give some account of our criteria.

Finally, do we not too hastily make the intentions of the literary phenomenon 'apocalyptic' into something foreign and primitive when we smooth out the form of the apocalyptic texts? When the author of an apocalypse narrates a story in the form of an esoteric revelation he gives the readers a significant pointer for perceiving their own stories. The postulate that the revelation which the readers are supposed to read into their stories has a *heavenly origin* gains a quite definite theological quality because what is expressed here is nothing less than a hermeneutical *extra nos*, something which comes from outside ourselves. In face of an experience of crisis in which the reader's story can no longer be perceived as part of a meaningful world created and guaranteed by God, the form called 'revelation' gains the important function of assuring readers confronting the collapse of their available possibilities of 'disclosure' that God is still the author of their story.

5.3 This is the background for interpreting the theological intention of the relation between revelation and story in apocalyptic: that the view of history[31] which lies behind the apocalypses makes it possible to gain insight into the continuation of the story experienced in the present, as this already exists in heaven, and so to continue it into the future that it finally converges again with the remembered story. The authors of the apocalypses are thus in this context quite determined to communicate to their readers a contrafactual hope for the intervention of God who orders the world. This hope is based in faith on the faithfulness of God and the reliability of God's word of promise.[32]

Notes

This chapter was translated from the original German by Mary Deasey Collins and Robert Morgan.

1 Cf. K.I. Nitzsch, *Bericht an die Mitglieder des Rehkopfschen Prediger-Vereins über die Verhandlungen i.J. 1820* (Wittenberg, 1822). Cf. also, however, J.S. Semler, 'Vorrede' in G.L. Oeder, *Christlich freye Untersuchung über die sogenannte Offenbarung Johannis* (Halle, 1769, o.S.); s.a. J.M. Schmidt, *Die jüdische Apokalyptik*, 2nd edn (Neukirchen, 1976), pp.98f.; W. Zager, *Begriff und Wertung der Apokalyptik in der neutestamentlichen Forschung* (Frankfurt a.M., 1989).

2 See also J.J. Collins, *The Apocalyptic Imagination* (New York: Crossroad 1992), p.4; K. Koch, *The Rediscovery of Apocalyptic*, (London: SCM Press, 1972).

3 D. Ritschl, 'Theology as Story', *'Story' als Rohmaterial der Theologie* (Münich: Chr. Kaiser, 1976) Theologische Existenz Heute (TEH) (192), 7.

4 On this concept, cf. below, section 2.2.1.

5 K. Müller, 'Apokalyptik/Apokalypsen. III. Die Jüdische Apokalyptik. Anfänge und Merkmale', *TRE* 3 (1978) 202–51.

6 Translation by D. Hill from C. Maurer in G. Hennecke, W. Schneemelcher and R.M. Wilson (eds), *New Testament Apocrypha*, vol. II (Cambridge: Clarke, 1991–2), pp.681–2 and 675.

7 E. Lämmert, *Bauformen des Erzählens*, 6th edn (Stuttgart, 1975), p.25.

8 E. Muir, *The Structure of the Novel*, 5th edn (London: Chatto & Windus, 1949), p.16.

9 E.M. Forster, *Aspects of the Novel*, 8th edn (London: Edward Arnold, 1947), p.116.
10 J. Assmann, 'Kollektives Gedächtnis und kulturelle Identität', in J. Assmann and T. Hölscher (eds), *Kultur und Gedächtnis* (Frankfurt: Suhrkamp, 1988), pp.9–19.
11 Ritschl, *supra*, n.3, 19.
12 Assmann, *supra*, n.10, 12.
13 K. Koch, *Das Buch Daniel* (Darmstadt: Wissenschaftliche Buchgesellschaft, 1980) (Erträge der Forschung (EdF) 144) p.159.
14 In this sense the prophecies (*vaticinia*) of the animal vision allow us to see that their author is living in the fourth period of the 70 shepherds (Eth. Enoch 90:6–19) whereas for example the standpoint of the author of the Apocalypse of Weeks (Eth. Enoch 93:3–10; 91:12–17) stands within the seventh week (93:9).
15 Cf. R. Smend, *Die Entstehung des Alten Testaments* (Stuttgart: Kohlhammer, 1978) (Theologische Wissenschaft (ThW) 1) pp.223f.
16 See above, 2.1.
17 Daniel 7 as a whole narrates the story of Israel's subjection to foreign powers: the first beast (the winged lion) stands for the neo-Babylonian empire (626–539 BCE), the second (the bear) for that of the Medes (626–550 BCE), the third (the panther) for the Persians (550–333 BCE), and the fourth for the empire of Alexander the Great and the Diadochoi (since 333 BCE). Cf. Koch, *Das Buch Daniel* (*supra*, n.13) p.187.
18 Cf. the attempts listed by Koch (ibid.), pp.188ff.
19 Cf. Müller, 'Apokalyptik', *supra*, n.5, p.217.
20 Cf. O. Kaiser, *Die mythische Bedeutung des Meeres*, 2nd edn (Berlin: A. Töpelmann, 1962); C. Kloos, *YHWH's Combat with the Sea* (Amsterdam: G.A. von Oorschot, 1986).
21 Cf. on this C.Westermann, *Genesis*, vol. 1 (London: SPCK and Minneapolis: Augsburg, 1984), pp.104ff.
22 The definitive annihilation of the chaos monster by God's eschatological intervention on behalf of Israel is also expected in Isaiah 27:1, a text in origin roughly contemporary with Daniel 7.
23 This is not contradicted by the author of Revelation trying to secure its symbolic character by making the 10 horns in 17:12–14 into 10 vassal kings. The historical reference is here extrapolated from the picture, whereas exactly the opposite is true for Daniel.
24 On 'iron rod' as an attribute of the Messiah, see also Psalms of Sol. 17:24.
25 Cf. on this U.B. Müller, *Die Offenbarung des Johannes* (Gütersloh: Mohn Würzburg: Echter Verlag, 1984) (Ökumenischer Taschenbuch Kommentar zum Neuen Testament (ÖTK) 19), pp. 297ff.
26 Cf. the combination in O. Böcher, *Die Johannesapokalypse*, 2nd edn (Darmstadt, 1980) (EdF 41), p.83.
27 This is nicely described in the title of D.S. Russell's book, *Divine Disclosure. An Introduction to Jewish Apocalyptic* (London: SCM Press, 1992).
28 The 'implied readers' here are what the author's consciousness faces when planning a narrative strategy. So they are something purely internal to a text.
29 Cf. J. Barton, in Chapter 3 of this volume.
30 See above, p.130.
31 See above, p.131.
32 See also Russell, *supra*, n.27: 'The apocalypticists at heart were men of faith who firmly believed, despite all signs to the contrary, that God was indeed in control' (p.135); and 'The apocalypticists, it is true, looked beyond history for the fulfilment of the divine purpose; but for them history was still the arena of God's activity on behalf

of his people. In this present age evil still prevailed and oppression was still commonplace; but the ultimate power lay in the hands of God and he would in the end prevail.'

Eight

Does the Gospel Story Demand and Discourage Talk of Revelation?

Robert Morgan

He came down to earth from heaven
who is God and Lord of all,
and his shelter was a stable,
and his cradle was a stall;
with the poor and mean and lowly
lived on earth our Saviour holy.

Mrs C.F. Alexander's Christmas carol provides a convenient reminder that the bottom line of Christianity is a story and that this story is an amalgam of myth (line 1), doctrine (lines 2 and 6), history (lines 5 and 6) and (especially prominent in the Christmas story part of the Christian story) legend (lines 3 and 4). The story of Jesus is itself part of the larger biblical and Christian story of God and the world which stretches from creation to a still expected future, but, far from being merely the central part of this, it is the all-controlling centre. How Christians understand the larger biblical and Christian story, and understand themselves as located within it, is (or should be) determined entirely by their response to the story of Jesus, his life, death and resurrection, the gospel of God proclaimed by the Christian church and acknowledged in faith, hope and love within the worshipping community.

Mrs Alexander's hymn also makes clear the paradox which Kierkegaard and Bultmann rightly insisted stands at the heart of Christian belief. Talk of 'revelation' in this context is not straightforward, not so clear and distinct as the word might suggest. The doctrine of the incarnation asserts a paradoxical identity of the divine and human in Jesus Christ. God is hidden *sub contrario*.

Since the sixteenth century a few, and since the nineteenth century many European theologians have found it impossible to believe the ecclesiastical dogma as expressed in the historic creeds and conciliar definitions. They have therefore either abandoned or radically revised or rethought the doctrine of the divinity of Jesus Christ. Some, like F.C. Baur, have withheld the notion of 'divinity' from the man Jesus, and attached it to the idea of Christ (or even in the case of Strauss to the idea of humanity) abandoning what the hypostatic union sought to preserve; others have reinterpreted his divinity to mean his perfect humanity; and others have interpreted it afresh in Johannine terms to mean that Jesus perfectly *reveals* the Father.

Since it is arguably appropriate to interpret conciliar statements in the light of the scripture they aim to be interpreting (rather than by reference to authorial intention), and both in the light of the Gospel to which they intend to bear witness, that third approach seems legitimate. For Anglicans, Scripture contains all things necessary to salvation. The New Testament insists on a high Christology, but does not compel anyone to explicate this in patristic theological categories. We should rather ask what these are getting at by attending to the Christian readings of Scripture which they claim to reflect and aim to guide. A good example of this is Schleiermacher's readiness to criticize the two-natures doctrine while affirming its belief in the divinity and humanity of Christ, interpreting that central belief afresh in a somewhat Johannine way. Whether or not Schleiermacher succeeded in reformulating Christological belief credibly for a new age (Baur and Strauss thought he did not), his construction maintains the Greek fathers' conviction, drawn mainly from the Fourth Gospel, that Jesus is the revelation of God. How that historical and universal revelation is mediated needs explaining, but retelling the gospel story and evoking the memory of Jesus is surely essential. It can be repeated and perhaps improved, but surely never replaced.

Talk of 'revelation' was eclipsed when modern rationalism destroyed precritical ideas, but returned to centre-stage in Barth's reaction against nineteenth-century liberal theologies. Most systematic theologians in the West remain deeply influenced by Barth, but even here some have become wary of inflating the notion of revelation and reticent about using the word. This is not to deny that the idea itself is essential to any Christian talk of God which continues (as it must) to point insistently and passionately to Jesus. If the baseline of Christianity is that, in having to do with Jesus we have to do with God, there is no avoiding the concept of revelation. And since we have to do with Jesus in part by hearing his story, an obvious way to start unfolding what Christians mean by the word is by turning again to that.

Not that the story itself, or the act of retelling it, are themselves the revelation of God. These necessary vehicles of that saving revelation of God in Jesus mediate what Christians assert is its saving significance for the whole world. This claim about the life and death of Jesus is made on the basis of a conviction that God vindicated Jesus in a divine event or mystery which (metaphorically) Christians call his resurrection or exaltation. That claim has been and still is mediated by Christian witness which appeals to both experience and Scripture and cannot dispense with either. But Scripture and preaching are human words, however closely associated with the revelation event of God in Christ. Human formulations are fallible and our use of the word 'revelation' to affirm God's activity in the world today needs to minimize the risk of claiming divine authority for what may be human misunderstandings.

Christian talk of the revelation of God in Christ makes claims about the present. Christians claim to live in the presence of God who can be known and responded to in faith, hope and love. They interpret their experience of life in the body of Christ as being drawn into the life of God, and their understanding of God as Trinity underwrites all that and leads them to look for signs of the Spirit in the world. It is hard to avoid speaking of revelation in this context, at least in a general way. The event of God in Christ has a universal dimension, embracing (as some theologians hold) the whole of nature and history, and responded to in the present. Central and essential and foundational as the now scarcely visible history of Jesus remains, it is the contemporary communication and appropriation of that event which demands most attention when Christians reflect on what they have to say about God's self-revelation in Jesus.

It is in the present-day reference of claims to divine revelation that the dangers inherent in these claims become visible. On the one hand, the need to broaden the scope of talk of revelation to correspond to the universal scope of any monotheistic talk of God threatens the particularity of the Christian claim about Jesus. We talk about 'disclosures', perhaps even disclosures of God, but these cannot easily all be associated with the revelation of God in Christ. This tends, then, to be reduced to merely a paradigm of God's self-revelation, rather than the decisive event that Christians have claimed it to be. Alternatively, where that universal claim is maintained, talk of revelation sounds imperialistic and exclusive.

In view of these difficulties with the word 'revelation' (not with its substantive meaning) there is perhaps a case for again talking in more public terms of the Christian 'religion' and 'tradition', reserving the believer's inflated word 'revelation' for the foundation already laid, that is, Christ (1 Cor. 3:11) and the presupposition that as God's decisive saving event this qualifies the whole of history. Such a claim cannot be established by argument; it can only be asserted by witnesses. But it evidently does impose itself upon participants in its tradition and community, elusive though the notion of faith remains. I therefore propose reserving talk of revelation for the general affirmation that is constitutive of Christianity and summarized in the dogma of the divinity of Christ: that in having to do with Jesus we have to do with God. How that mediation of God's self-revelation in Jesus Christ occurs today is best explained without talking too easily about revelation, even though the truth and reality of that mediation presuppose that God does reveal God's self in such a way as to be responded to in the present.

Talking less about a revelation in which one nevertheless believes is one way of avoiding the dangers of such talk. Instead, we shall talk more about the tradition which has mediated and still does mediate the revelation of God in Christ, in particular the Gospel story which is the essential and quite basic vehicle communicating the Gospel of God. What Christians assert is the universal event of God in Christ is the presupposition of Christian faith and must be called revelation, but beyond that fundamental and framing assertion, found in the Johannine Prologue for example, the Gospel story can be told without much direct appeal to that category, revelation, which constitutes its meaning. It is possible to be sceptical, and critical of the mythological elements in the Gospels, without denying what they affirm, that this life and death is the revelation of God to faith.

What John expresses partly in the mythological language (echoed in the first line quoted from Mrs Alexander) of the Father sending the Son, can be taken as Christologically equivalent to the Church's doctrine of the divinity of Christ on the grounds already adumbrated: they express the same Gospel of God's saving presence in Jesus, without explicating this theologically. Even doctrines need theological elaboration if they are to make sense, and the myth also needs explaining, when it is not taken literally. The theological category of revelation, which Bultmann rightly saw to be the *Grundkonzeption* of John's Gospel, serves both purposes. It provides a theological link between the myth and the doctrine, justifying the claim that they are both saying broadly the same thing, expressing the same Gospel in different kinds of religious language for different purposes.

What Christians mean by the doctrine of the divinity of Christ is (following John) that in having to do with Jesus they have to do with God, the God of Israel, Creator and redeemer and judge of the world. John expresses this conviction by retelling the story of Jesus in a new way, developing it in terms of a myth of incarnation and ascent, and composing discourses which interpret the history and the myth. The functional identity of God and the envoy who reveals God is clearly stated (1:1; 5:17; 10:30). It is as the revelation of God that Jesus can be called Lord and God (20:28). Revelation is the central idea of the Gospel, even though the word itself scarcely occurs (12:38 is a quotation): 'If you knew me you would know my Father also' (8:19); 'He who believes in me believes not in me but in him who sent me. And he who sees me sees him who sent me' (12:44f.); 'He who has seen me has seen the Father' (14:9).

The language of 'seeing' cannot be intended literally in this talk of revelation. 'No one has ever seen God; the only Son [some manuscripts read 'God'], who is in the bosom of the Father, he has made [God] known' (1:18). The visual connotations of 'revelation' are not a barrier to talking of the saving revelation of God in Christ. Etymologically, this 'unveiling' word (*velum* = veil) implies sight, but the derivative meaning, 'to make known' a secret, usually through words, and primarily words spoken, is equally everyday language. However, Christian talk of the revelation of God in Christ remains paradoxical whether it is understood visually or orally/aurally, and this helps explain why 'in many circles the mere use of the word "revelation" will serve to have its user classified with those who yet believe the earth is flat' (R. Hart, *Unfinished Man and the Imagination*, New York: Herder and Herder, 1968).

Another popular carol expresses the paradox in Christian belief in revelation:

> Veiled in flesh the Godhead see:
> hail, the incarnate Deity,
> pleased as Man with man to dwell
> Jesus, our Emmanuel.

If this is revelation, the 'unveiling' is veiled, says Charles Wesley. It will remain so (adds Mrs Alexander) until 'our eyes at last shall see him ... Not in that poor lowly stable, with the oxen standing by.' Turning from the visual to the aural and oral sense of revelation does not reduce the paradox. The mystery of God in Jesus Christ is no less ambiguous when communicated through the word of preaching than it was to those who saw him in Galilee and Jerusalem. Proclamation is no more straightforward or direct communication of information which can be verified than the sight of Jesus to his contemporaries. The communication of his religious meaning and significance is indirect. Some information was and still is necessary to identify the man in whom those who follow him claim to know God and find their salvation, but proclamation is more than this. It includes an appeal and aims to elicit a response beyond what can be rationally justified.

The paradoxical character of the revelation of God in Christ, this veiled unveiling, is properly preserved by all four canonical Gospels, but most interestingly by Mark and John. All four make the paradox visible by lifting the veil, whether at particular points in the synoptic epiphanies, or constantly in the Johannine signs, discourses and passion. But Mark keeps this door closed with his *motif* of the disciples' failure to understand, and John slams it violently on the 'world' of Jesus' opponents who do not see the light. The disciples in John believe on him (2:11) (however imperfectly: 14:9a) as in Matthew they understand, despite their 'little faith', but all four evangelists have their readers or hearers in view. *We* beheld his glory (John 1:14) and blessed are those who have not seen, yet have believed (John 20:29).

All this supports the claim that the idea of revelation is omnipresent in the New Testament, even where the *apocalypt* root is relatively rare (*contra* F.G.

Downing, *Does Christianity have a Revelation?*, London: SCM, 1963). However, it differs from ordinary everyday uses of the word in that what is supposedly revealed is still concealed, at least for the present. In short, the revelation of God in Christ implies as its correlate faith in Christ, itself an elusive category involving trust and confidence, and the will as much as the mind.

This reception aspect is so strong that talk of revelation (and faith) refers more naturally to the present than to the past, and to personal experience rather than to inherited tradition. The dogmatic assertion of the divinity of Christ or the revelation of God in Christ is essential to Christian identity and specifies the shape of Christian belief and practice, but in Christian theology the category of revelation referring to the revelation of God in Jesus Christ has a strong present-day reference. Essential as the claim to 'foundation revelation' in Jesus undoubtedly is, this remains quite formal, without much specific content beyond what is necessary to identify the man who loved his own unto the end. The idea of revelation in Christian theologies says more about the present time in which believers acknowledge God in Jesus Christ. It signals that God in Jesus Christ is (or becomes) a present reality for people today, while also insisting that this 'risen' Jesus is identified with the man from Nazareth. All this is elaborated in the doctrine of the Trinity which asserts that God was and is present in Jesus and operates as Spirit in the world. So this belief in the revelation of God in Jesus presupposes (a) some knowledge of the historical figure from the distant past, which must stem from the traditions about him which have been preserved, and (b) some sense of who God is, which also depends upon a scriptural tradition and upon participating in the religious community. It involves the receiver or believers as well as the sender (God) and the person in whom God is acknowledged.

Claims to revelation are powerful and persuasive only when made by people for whom they are real now. We may talk at second hand about other people receiving a revelation, but only on the basis of their personal testimony, which we cannot verify. That is acceptable: we take other people's word for most things in life, including religion, but we cannot claim too much for it. Christian talk of ongoing revelation of God in Christ is a broad inference from a multitude of moments like Peter's confession depicted at Matthew 16:16, or the call of the fishermen at Mark 1:16–20, and less dramatic, persistent convictions of the present reality of God known from knowing Christ – convictions classically expressed in the Johannine language of mutual indwelling. Those who saw in Jesus enough to leave their nets and follow were already presumably the recipients of an as yet unarticulated revelation of God in Jesus. Subsequent Christian history is the history of belief in a revelation of God in Jesus, beginning with the experiences of his risen presence in the days following his crucifixion. Those resurrection experiences convinced their recipients that they were experiences of *Jesus*, and led them to infer that God had indeed been present in Jesus – and still was.

However, once the weight of the idea of revelation is transferred from the formal and foundational claim which Christians make about God in Jesus, and applied to the personal existential appropriation of this by believers, reservations begin to be heard. Some Christians hesitate to invoke so powerful a word as 'revelation' in connection with their own faint flickerings of faith. We do not deny that God is present in the world today and that God's will can be known, God's love responded to, God's future struggled for. But this often remains more a formal belief than a matter of personal experience. Many Christians are content to be carried along by the examples of the saints and spiritual masters, satisfied with standing in a tradition, joining in the community's common prayer, and are slightly suspicious of most pretensions to revelation. We are content to make the inference from the witness of others whose word and experience we trust, and so to speak of the revelation of God in Jesus, without ourselves claiming to be recipients of revelation in the direct and powerful sense which the word seems to require. We *accept* the reality of the revelation of God in Christ in the world today, without being able to say much about it. Their belief offers no short-cuts through the intellectual jungle which has to be traversed in determining what things we ought to do and say and hope. We *believe* in 'God the Father Almighty … and in Jesus Christ our Lord who was born, suffered under Pontius Pilate' and was vindicated by God, but hesitate to echo Paul's language about God being pleased to reveal his Son in us (Gal. 1:16).

The reason for our hesitation is that it seems to claim more than some sober Christians can truthfully echo. Enthusiastic Christians claim to know Jesus rather intimately, and no one need question their personal experience or label it self-deception – so long as it remains private. But the Church's attempts to know and publicly to proclaim God's will in the world today require careful scrutiny. The experience of believers is shared and tested, not short-circuited by private illuminations such as that vouchsafed to Paul. Even Paul had to support his intuitions by rational theological arguments. Belief in the revelation of God in Christ in the world today is the presupposition of theological reflection, not a substitute for it. This reference to revelation is more formal than material because, while we rightly refer to Jesus, or God in Jesus, we do not have Jesus in our hands or even in our heads. We have only a handful of traditions, heads full of a story frequently retold and needing to be further retold, a story that has echoed in the experience of millions, including ourselves. As the revelation of God in Jesus Christ was veiled in his life and death, the veil on occasion partially lifted, so it has remained for those who have not seen, yet have believed. When so much is still uncertain the dangerous rhetoric of revelation had better be kept at a minimum. The notion of story will fulfil some of its roles in the morphology of Christian witness to God in Jesus.

My suggestion thus far has been to insist upon the reality of the revelation of God in Christ and in the world today, but to resist saying much about it. Human responses to divine revelation in Christ presuppose the event, but need to be clearly distinguished from it if idolatry (including bibliolatry) is to be avoided. Whereas most of the contributions in this book expect the notion of story to illuminate the idea of revelation, my instinct has been to hold them apart and to allow the notion of story to do some of the work usually done by the idea of revelation. Disclosures happen, and some are interpreted as disclosures of God, thanks to a religious tradition which instructs us where to find such revelation, that is, in Christ, mediated by a tradition, within a worshipping community. Personal conviction is the life-blood of a religion, and shared convictions shape the body within which this life-blood flows. Shared belief in God in Christ, active as Spirit in the world today, implies the idea and event of revelation, but does not justify extending it further to cover the means by which Christian faith is communicated. Barth's threefold form of the Word of God seems to me an unnecessary and dangerous extension, not warranted by the Gospel story. This plea for caution and reticence in talk of revelation, necessary as such talk is within the limits already prescribed, can now be reinforced by a series of further considerations.

One reason for some decline in the talk of revelation that was so common in the kerygmatic theology of mid-twentieth-century German protestantism is surely its deficit in experience, even among the minority of Christians who faithfully listen to the Word of God preached on Sunday mornings. Barth's account in 1919 of the awesome responsibility experienced by the preacher would be echoed by many preachers even today, but it scarcely matches the experience of most hearers in the pews. The necessity of recipients' experience for credible talk of divine revelation today is illuminated by Michael Wolter's penetrating contribution. He gives us *stories* of revelation from the scriptural part of our Christian tradition. But, as he makes clear, these are not revelation for us. They are tradition (and not even a central part of the scriptural tradition). What he was able to show by means of the intertextual relationship between Daniel 7 and Revelation 13 was how a story might become a vehicle for revelation to a later generation – and how it might not. John the seer was able so to identify with the community and its destiny narrated in Daniel 7 as to draw upon that story in addressing his prophetic word to his own generation of persecuted believers, and so to maintain their identity and give them hope.

Some modern Christians are still able to identify with the story of the people of God unfolded in their Old Testament and in some way (bristling with discontinuities) continued in the New and beyond. Some form of 'people of God' ecclesiology is perhaps inescapable, but for Christians to identify with Israel and to associate this claim with revelation is at best artificial and often morally and politically suspect. The only 'larger' biblical story which we should be willing to associate with the idea of revelation is the story of Jesus himself. For Christians this is the focus of the overarching story of God's engagement with the world from Creation to eschaton. Smaller units of biblical tradition, Old Testament as well as New, may become vehicles of religious disclosure, but primarily on account of their relationship to that larger story of Jesus. The Old Testament prophets are on any account at times inspiring and may make us want to join in the struggle for human justice and liberation, rather as a political orator might persuade us to do the same. That on its own is not called Christian revelation of God. Only in connection with a larger pattern of judgment and grace, focused for Christians in the reality of God in Jesus, is it likely to trigger a response which might be attributed to revelation.

The modern history of the idea of revelation in Christian thought does not encourage its overuse. Protestant orthodoxy's identification of revelation with Scripture was discredited in eighteenth-century Europe when rational investigation of the Bible showed this to be a human book, or rather collection of books, subject to historical, scientific and even moral error. At first some of its contents were still assumed to be divinely revealed, and for as long as German idealism remained popular it was possible to combine advances in historical understanding with a belief in God's Spirit moving through the historical process, especially the history of religion. A more positivist philosophical climate later in the nineteenth century eroded the plausibility of seeing God in history, and such metaphysical beliefs were further discredited by the First World War. But this decline in the fortunes of the concept was dramatically reversed after the war, when revelation in 'the Word' (written and/or preached) replaced the idea of God in history. Barth and Gogarten persuaded even the liberal Bultmann that the Reformers' kerygmatic idea of revelation had been rehabilitated and that, after a century's talk of the human, Christian theology was again on course and talking of God, albeit by talking of humanity *coram Deo*.

Schleiermacher's theological strategy, and even Luther's, could easily be represented as running dangerously close to Feuerbach. Bultmann's similarly anthropological orientation was open to the same reduction, as Jaspers, Buri and Braun were soon to show. Revelation occurs in the ear of the hearer or the eye of the beholder, and not all Bultmann's admirers have acknowledged God in Jesus as the source and substance of Christian revelation today. Talk of revelation or word events sometimes lost the Christocentricity of Luther (or Käsemann); the identity of Jesus is unclear when the narrative of his life and death is reduced to near vanishing point. Barth's talk of revelation appeared more robust, but the price paid for this has been a reversion among his more conservative followers to identifying revelation with the text of Scripture. Barth's own resistance to Bultmann's *Sachkritik* contained a trace of biblicism, though in general he stressed only the importance of Scripture for Christian witness. Scripture remains tradition, not revelation, but it has a central place in the life of the Christian community, lived in the presence of God, privileged to participate in a knowledge of God whose will can be known today.

Both Barth and Bultmann located revelation in the Word of God, in true Reformation spirit insisting on the importance of the biblical witness and on preaching, but recognizing both as mediating, and thus subordinate to, the Word of God who had been incarnate in Jesus Christ. This emphasis was in reaction to their teachers' finding revelation in history and it brought with it an underestimation of the place of history in Christian understandings of the revelation of God in Jesus Christ. Barth's failure to come to terms with modern critical history and Bultmann's reduction of the concept to the historicity of human existence scarcely do justice to the way most Christians think about Jesus.

Pannenberg's reaction against these theologies of the Word took history more seriously, but was not entirely persuasive. Its view of revelation hinged on treating the resurrection of Jesus as a historical event anticipating the end of history, and that seemed to many as arbitrary as those authoritarian and mythological ideas of the Word of God that he justly criticized. It is in the context of this and other widely perceived failures to speak credibly of 'revelation in history' that our theme, 'revelation and story' is to be understood.

On the one hand, the new theme sounds promising. It allows the idea of revelation to remain closely connected with Scripture while evading the problems about historicity involved in locating revelation in real history. It also avoids the pejorative connotations of the related word 'myth'. The 'literary turn' in recent biblical studies has directed attention to biblical narrative, and advances in these disciplines of Old and New Testament have sometimes in the past proved fruitful for systematic theology. The new (or newly promising) category of 'story' redirects attention to the *text* of Scripture instead of reducing this to a collection of sources for a reality behind it, and at the same time invites analysis of the relationship between text and *readers*. Those brought up on Luther or kerygmatic theology may, like Papias, still prefer to *hear* the word than read it, but either way an emphasis on present-day believers trying to live under the guidance of God without claiming too much for their glimmers of insight is rightly preserved. This new focus on a transaction 'in front of' the text (that is, interpretation) promises to clarify the relationship between the religious community and its Scriptures better than theories of revelation in the history behind the text. Like kerygmatic theology, this alternative interest in the Word preached or in the story avoids claiming doctrinal precision or historical accuracy for Scripture. It also, however, avoids the kerygmatic theology's ambitious claims for what happens at 11 a.m. on Sundays *ubi et quando Deus vult* ... (*quod non est saepissime*, as some would add).

Most Christians' religious experience is less punctiliar and individualistic than that model implies. The formation of Christian character and growth in holiness, or even the discovery of a Christian identity within a Christian community, is more gradual, less dramatic, at least for once-born believers. It is also more dispersed through the variety of human experiences, among which listening to sermons may not be the most formative. The attraction of the 'story' theme for elucidating Christian talk of God is not only the fact that it avoids making implausibly authoritative claims, but also the way it dovetails with how we most naturally talk about 'the story' of our own life. Here too Michael Wolter's discussion in Chapter 7 was most suggestive. The idea of readers or hearers being drawn into a story which comes to define their personal and communal identity and motivate their behaviour is both attractive and initially illuminating. It also opens up points of contact with other literature, as Paul Fiddes' chapter beautifully illustrated, and so avoids isolating the Bible in ways which to many no longer appear credible.

On the other hand, it is precisely the 'implausibly authoritarian' aspect of kerygmatic theology which constituted its claim to communicate (as *Anrede*) the revelation of God. 'Story' is softer than the 'word preached' and sometimes it draws listeners into its web, but its relationship to the revelation it is supposed to communicate remains less clear and less tight than that of the kerygmatic theology's sermon.

Some negative vibrations about our collocation of 'revelation' and 'story' should also be acknowledged. It accepts the centrality of the idea of revelation in Christian theology and invites us to think about it in new ways. But the most important aspect of claims to revelation is their claim to truth, and fictions are commonly thought of as untrue, at least in any literal sense. This objection can be answered and the potential of stories for communicating truth reasserted, but how the truth of stories is related to the truth of revelation remains unclear.

These initial misgivings are confirmed when the phrase 'revelation and story' is heard as a change from 'revelation and (or *as*, or *in*) *history*'. Despite recent appreciation of its narrative quality, history writing is still widely thought of as reporting and interpreting *facts*. Even where positivism is repudiated (and that is not everywhere) history seems cognitively 'harder' than the 'softer'-sounding notion of story. Recent shifts in biblical study to a more literary frame of reference are at best ambiguous in the messages they send to systematic theology. Historical research is sometimes devoid of theological interests or interest, but it was thought to have a solidity on which theology and apologetics were pleased to build. Literary study finds the Bible less factual, and makes it seem more subjective, and this partly accounts for the theological coolness towards it exemplified long ago by the professional unease (noted by John Barton) with the once-popular *Bible Designed to be Read as Literature*.

Again the objection can be answered and the suspicion that our collocation of 'revelation' and 'story' threatens the truth claims of revelation parried. Fresh approaches which acknowledge the elusiveness of religious truth are as likely to rehabilitate as further to undermine the idea of revelation. The question is at least worth exploring. Regardless of the question of truth, the category of story, like that of myth, is evidently more appropriate than 'history' for describing narratives of God or the gods engaging with humans. As usually understood, the term 'history' describes human reality and action. It may be believed to be the field of divine action, but that is not a category applicable without question in history writing. It is precisely these questions and doubts which have undermined talk of revelation in history and given to the word 'revelation' itself what Ray Hart in the paragraph from which I have already quoted (above, pp.148–9) called 'a graveyard-bell ring of supernaturalism'. Whether or not revelation in or through story is any more promising, it avoids the immediate definitional barriers confronting any identification of particular historical events as divine actions. We do at least possess stories of divine revelation. Whether or not they are credible or illuminating (and whether these are the right criteria to be invoking) remains a question.

Most Christian theologians now accept the necessity of some theory of revelation: to speak religiously of God is to speak of revelation. This is now virtually axiomatic. The concept of God may be defined in a purely formal way as 'what one sets one's heart on' or by negations of the human experience of finitude, but for the reality of God to be known, God must communicate or reveal God's self. The doctrine of God is no longer separated (as it was in some older scholastic textbooks) from the doctrine of the Trinity.

The intuition that human talk of God can derive only from God's self-disclosure, coupled with the perception that some sense of God is found outside positive religious traditions, lies behind the contrast once commonly drawn between 'general revelation' and 'special revelation'. St Paul's echoes of Stoic natural theology at Romans 1:19–20 (cf. 2:14–15) provide a precedent (and who needs a warrant?) for interpreting human experience theologically. It is natural to suppose that something of God can by known quite apart from Christian proclamation if God is the creator and Lord of all, and this idea of 'general revelation' (like Rahner's idea of an original revelation in creation) avoids some of the problems in the older natural theology's contrast between *reason* and revelation. Reason is presumably God-given – and its judgments are less universal than once was thought. Reason is normally necessary for the reception of revelation, and the receiver's knowledge and experience make an impact upon the terms in which any revelation of God is understood. Contrasting these terms in the eighteenth-century manner of 'natural religion' was discredited by Schleiermacher. But if we accept that the sense of God outside religious traditions is usually a residue from these, it seems better to talk descriptively about *religion,* and to reserve the normative truth-claims implied by the word *revelation* for the system in which one is oneself a participant. That is not to deny that other religions may be responding to a revelation of God, but to insist that only participants can credibly make that religious confession because a religious response belongs to the grammar of 'revelation'. If what is meant by 'God' religiously is above all that God is worshipped (or rebelled against) then God's self-revelation can be spoken of in direct speech only by the participant (or rebel) not (except in brackets) by the neutral observer, analyst, sociologist, phenomenologist or even a certain type of philosopher of religion. Christians may from their own perspective assume that God is making God's self known in all religions and in other human experience, and they will then want to call it 'revelation' because knowledge of God is (axiomatically) based on God's self-revelation. But they cannot go beyond this formal statement and draw material conclusions about God from what they see of other religions because one's theological statements are internal to one's own religious system.

Contemporary religious pluralism is inadequately addressed by those older distinctions between kinds of revelation. The vitality and evident value of several religious traditions, each making its own claim to revelation(s), and some of these conflicting, invites the fair-minded observer to admit the possibility of many revelations, and to oppose the narrow exclusiveness of much past and present religious discourse. But that exclusivism was itself a recognition that religious talk of God, that is worship and the doctrinal and moral thinking which this may generate, is internal to a religious tradition. It was based on a particular revelation responded to in a particular religious community. Outsiders do not share 'our' truth. It was natural, until we got to know them, to consider their alternative ideas false. Now we are more tolerant, but the logic of religious claims has not changed. They are still internal to some particular system, though open to all available knowledge and experience. We *assume* that

God is active everywhere, but *acknowledge revelation* only by faith, and so only in our own religious contexts.

However polite and positive we wish to be about other claims to revelation, our lack of this personal existential engagement means we are not speaking of God but assessing religious traditions. Judgments about their divine character may be made by comparing them with one's own religion, based as this is on a self-involving acknowledgment of revelation, but such judgments cannot expect to do full justice to the religion in which one is not a participant. Respect for other people demands reverence for their religion, except where it conflicts with one's moral or intellectual insights (a limit set also to one's own religion), but that is not to call other religions 'revelation'.

This modern shift in the idea of revelation, binding it so closely with the reality of God who reveals God's self that it can be used only in tandem with the notion of faith, both sidesteps the plausibility problems posed by modern pluralism and is one way by which some Western theology has responded to the loss of its older philosophical foundations over the past 200 years. It seems that claims to a knowledge of God, even (for some) a conviction about God's existence, are inseparable from the practice of religion; and that is typically seen as human response to divine self-disclosure. It builds into the concept of revelation the element of human transformation, however difficult that may be to measure empirically. A revelation of God that does not *change* its recipient is hardly worth the name. But none of this emphasis on faith and practice minimizes the place of human reason and understanding in the reception of a revelation of God. The place of human language in most acknowledgment of God implies rather that reason and revelation belong together.

We have taken it as widely agreed that God's self-revelation or self-communication is a precondition of God being known at all. In this purely formal sense (apart from the material issue of God in Christ, or God revealing Himself through the Koran or Herself in nature or as spirit in history) the category of revelation is included in what believers mean by 'God', the mystery beyond human comprehension. The decisive question of where and how God makes God's self known to us only arises because this is said by specific religious communities to have happened already. The old answer that reason could take us so far, and so prepare us to receive the special revelation which is necessary for salvation, is no longer persuasive. Neither in its traditional form (such as Aquinas' five ways), nor in its modern analogues (for example, some theologians' use of Kant's postulates of practical reason) does such a natural theology seem to provide a foundation for talk of revelation today. Much that seemed commonsense even a century ago now appears culture-specific; belief in God today is likely to be as much the *result* of religious practice as its cause.

The views of revelation implied by the old 'revealed theology', which identified part of the tradition as itself revelation, are even less defensible. They introduce unnecessary conflict with modern scientific and historical reason, and, where combined with understanding revelation as God's self-revelation, they infringe the otherness of God, or God's non-objectifiability. They are also rightly suspected of ideological misuse; claiming to 'possess' the true revelation or its true interpretation has been a way of silencing opposition and free enquiry. All these factors have led to drastic revisions of the idea of revelation over the past 300 years, including its devaluation in late nineteenth-century liberal theology.

Reassertions of revelation in early and mid-twentieth-century theology avoided those conflicts with science and history and preserved God's transcendence. The Bible and Christian proclamation are seen as essential to any Christian understanding of revelation, but only as *witness* to the revelation of God in Christ, not as in themselves revelation. Even so, these appeals to an authoritative word of witness stand in some tension with human autonomy, and those who, like Barth, say so much the worse for human autonomy have not convinced more liberal Christians. A gentler or less bullying account of revelation and its communication may be more true to the spirit of the Gospel, or at least to the synoptic Gospels. We are today rightly suspicious of absolute claims to authority, and of all exercise of power which is not subject to rational scrutiny and criticism. Yet this is what some appeals to revelation seem to resist. This kind of talk has accordingly declined in recent English-language theology, or has retired from the field of public statements to the subjectivity and private decisions of individual believers. Even there we are uneasily aware of the dangers of self-deception. Against that flight from the very idea of revelation (and the very idea of God) it is important for Christian theology to reassert the idea within its proper limits while rejecting its improper extensions.

The study of religion, including both empirical study and philosophical theories of religion, fulfils the necessary functions of a natural theology in making talk of God intelligible and credible by drawing attention to such features of the human condition as the search for meaning, and the necessity of symbols in meeting this need. *Homo sapiens* may not often be wise or even rational, but is surely *homo symbolicus,* the symbol-making animal. In addition to raising the question of God without itself answering it, this historical and social scientific enterprise provides descriptions and analyses of the answers given to this question in particular religious traditions. It therefore provides data that any modern Christian account of revelation will need to take account of. But it is impossible now to identify revelation with any *part* of the tradition, whether Scripture alone or including also some subsequent church pronouncements. It is the echo of that pre-critical identification which has done most to discredit the idea of revelation today. If it remains an essential presupposition of Christian talk about God, and therefore an important category in Christian theology, it needs to be purged of those pre-critical elements.

The theme 'revelation and story' hints at a way out of the impasse into which the idea of revelation has fallen. It suggests how the two main (and rival) categories with which the idea of revelation and its communication have been associated in the present century (revelation in history, and revelation in the 'Word') might be combined. Despite Barth's denials, both these frameworks continued the trend of protestant theology since Schleiermacher to associate revelation with religion, and indeed with a particular or 'positive' religion, namely that of the theologians concerned, as Bultmann pointed out in 1922, in his review of *Römerbrief.* Both approaches also contained resources for taking a wider view of God's self-revelation, whether through world history or through language as such. But both frameworks expected the idea of revelation to do too much, in particular to solve the epistemological problems of religion in the modern world. The notion of 'story' makes more modest claims to truth and universality than either language or history. It therefore offers a less close 'fit' with the idea of revelation. But that might be helpful, because it encourages us to limit talk of revelation to the contexts in which it belongs, instead of expecting it to dominate the entire theological agenda.

Instead of first forging a concept of revelation which will solve its epistemological problems, Christian theology can simply consider the story through and in which its specific claim to revelation is communicated: the story of Jesus, already discussed.

This story is retold in four different ways within the New Testament, and endlessly outside it, by witnesses who share the tradition's basic conviction about God's eschatological involvement in the life and death and resurrection of Jesus. It is the story rather than this history behind it which, retold from this (its own) theological perspective, becomes the vehicle of a power to transform and liberate. This happens through some kind of merging between the story of Jesus and hearers' own stories. The fictional elements in this story are part of its religious power and truth. When Wallace Stevens wrote that poetry is the supreme fiction, he was far from denying that it may be a vehicle for the most important matters confronting humans, and myth too may be a bearer of life-shaping truth. But some relationship between the story of Jesus and the history behind it is also a truth condition of this story. Believers whose lives are transformed by it do not think it is mere history, but they certainly and rightly assume some historical basis to it. No doubt God could have saved the world through a book, and some think He yet might, but the Christian claim is that God did so through a human life and death. God's self is revealed in the love and suffering of a human being, not in a novel, tragedy or farce, even in a holy book, according to the Christian message.

The resurrection claim is also part of the story and means several things, including strong reference to the history of Jesus. It is 'the power of [Jesus'] earthly mission extending beyond its moment in time and manifesting itself in the church's proclamation as well as in sacrament and in acts of faith and love' (Dan O. Via, *The Revelation of God and/as Human Reception*, Harrisburg: Trinity Press International, 1997). Some strong connection with Jesus' historical ministry and mission is thus presupposed by the Gospel story of God's veiled self-revelation in Jesus Christ. That is the Christian claim and it does not have to be justified by theology. It is enough for the Church to bear witness and allow the story to draw others into its web where they may experience (say Christians) the power of God.

Christian retelling of the Christian story is a form of preaching: persuasive discourse by those who are persuaded of the truth and importance of the message. But it is not only preaching. Believers themselves live with it in its endless variations which are ignited and controlled by the four canonical retellings. Sometimes believers can improve on one or another detail in the New Testament retellings without presuming to substitute an alternative narrative of Jesus controlled by something else, as R.W. Funk and others propose. This story retold in the Church in the power of the Spirit draws old and new hearers into its symbolic world. This can be analysed in terms of reader-response theory, even though the spoken word which carries the preacher's engagement and advocacy is primary.

In Jewry (or Judaea) is God known, says the Psalmist; in Christ, says the Christian, Christ mediated through Christian witness and accepted in faith. But to understand the story of Jesus as the story of God's self-revelation we have to know who God is. That is why at least the Hebrew Bible is a necessary part of Christian Scripture alongside the New Testament. The story of Jesus in the Gospels is a story of the fulfilment of God's promises and, however conceptualized, for all humans the decisive moment in the eschatological self-revelation of this same God of Israel, the Creator and Judge of the world. The revelation of God is for the time being veiled in the life and death of this human Jesus, acknowledged only in faith and hope, anticipating a future in which God's rule will be manifest. But this veiled revelation, communicated in a variety of literary and theological strategies, is enough to allow those who are called and apparently chosen to respond in faith and hope.

The story of Jesus, variously retold and presupposed in the New Testament and in the subsequent history of Christianity, is not itself revelation, because the divine event cannot be identified with any part of the tradition through which it is mediated. These elements of tradition and witness must be complemented by the element of contemporary reception, and even then we may hesitate to speak of revelation of God in Christ to favoured individuals in the present. A formal acknowledgment of revelation is sufficient to bring the tradition to life and make possible a joyful response to God in Christ, such as seems to be implied by Paul's apparently revelation language ('received from the Lord') at 1 Corinthians 11:23. A 'material' revelation conveying new information is probably not implied in that context, despite the invitation to read it that way. Revelation events make new connections, linking Christian memory and tradition with what Paul as a Jew already knew of God, rather than uncovering new information. The foundational revelation event for Christians is Jesus himself, and the resurrection teaches us to see in it a universal event which has bearing on our own present and the future of the world. But we do not have direct access to this man, whom Christian tradition calls the incarnate Son of God, or this God made known in Jesus, whom we believe to be active in the world today. We read the tradition and hear Christian witness, made on a basis of Christian tradition, mainly scriptural traditions, and some speak of revelation in connection with the transformative event in which God in Christ is acknowledged and confessed, whereas other Christians hesitate to use this word in such direct connection with their own experience, while insisting that the revelation of God in Christ is the necessary presupposition of their Christian experience and understanding of themselves, the world and God.

Where twentieth-century protestant theology has spoken most insistently about revelation in the present, or 'word events', these have been said to occur through preaching. St Paul's words at Romans 10:17 are paradigmatic: 'faith comes from hearing and hearing through Word of Christ' and v.14: 'For how are they to call on one in whom they have not believed? And how are they to believe in one of whom they did not hear? And how are they to hear without someone proclaiming?'

This Pauline model of revelation authorizing proclamation and faith is interpreted by kerygmatic theology one-sidedly in a way that is open to criticism. Paul does on occasion (1 Thess. 2:13) virtually identify his own preaching with God's act of revelation in the present, though even here he avoids being too punctiliar by adding that 'God *is* at work in you who believe'. One objection to a punctiliar account of revelation and faith is that it denarrativizes the Christian message, which is plainly at odds with the Gospel story. The more we appreciate the place of narratives in shaping human identity the less attractive it becomes to insist on self-understanding being changed dramatically by a call to decision. Christian identity is shaped by the believer's alignment with the story of Jesus and this is typically a gradual process of growth in faith and love.

Bultmann's kerygmatic account of revelation is also more individualistic than Paul's and even than that of the Fourth Gospel, where strong emphasis is placed on the individual decision character of believing, but where the community of disciples, dwelling in Christ, is also presupposed. Attention to the *story*, demanded by John's Gospel form itself, makes more room for the historical and corporate dimensions of faith without making the unwarranted claims to knowledge about the past presupposed by 'revelation in history' frameworks, and without driving the concept of revelation's centre of gravity from the present back into the past, as Jeremias did. Recent emphasis upon the narrative character of historiography has in any case brought history and fiction closer together, rather as von Rad's concern with the history of traditions had moved away from the illusory solidity of brute historical facts. Personal and communal identity owe much to history, but that means to historical memory mediated by narratives, not by naked uninterpreted facts.

But attention to the story rather than the kerygma removes the temptation to identify human words with divine revelation. Talking of revelation events in connection with proclamation and faith gives to proclamation a starkly authoritative character which is no doubt intended but also dangerous and unattractive. The notion of story is gentler. A parable may challenge the hearer, but its indirection is less open to the charge of religious and moral bullying. For Christians, only God has absolute authority. All human authority depends on consent. In proclamation the lines get blurred and it is tempting for the preacher who hopes to speak in God's name to act as though his word has more authority than it has. The Thessalonians received Paul's word as Word of God and Paul was sure they were right to do so. But he appeals to their own experience (1 Thess. 2:13), not to his apostolic authority. Others have been less scrupulous. Paul persuades and exhorts even when he is sure he is right; some clergy show less tact.

My point is not to deny that God's self-revelation in Christ stands behind and authorizes Christian witness, but to note the dangers of fusing the fundamental Christian claim to revelation of God in Christ at work in the world today with specific events of fallible human Christian witness or discernment. The idea of revelation is better held at a distance from the mechanics of proclamation and contemporary Christian experience. We believe and celebrate God's saving presence but dare not make of it a weapon of ecclesiastical power play. The word 'revelation' is in any case so freighted with pre-critical assumptions and so open to ideological misuse that many Christian theologians prefer to avoid it, beyond the purely formal and axiomatic place it has in any Christian talk of God. The main reason why some continue to call the contemporary event of disclosure and faith 'revelation', even though that description is rightly denied to scriptural traditions and human proclamation as such (that is, apart from the act of God it may mediate and the response of faith or rejection which it makes possible) is to insist on an integral relationship between contemporary Christian experience and the foundational event (now only indirectly accessible through traditions and proclamations) in which Christians see God's decisive saving revelation. The notion of story, that is, the story of Jesus, threatens to weaken that integral relationship by sitting lightly to the historical facts, but when qualified by our insistence on some loose relationship between the story of Jesus narrated in the Gospels and the now largely invisible historical reality, this relationship is preserved.

Another reason for avoiding the word 'revelation' in connection with the contemporary communication and reception of the Christian Gospel mediated through the story of Jesus is that it may tempt the unwary back into a biblicism which identifies revelation with the canonical retellings of that story. The plurality of the Gospels affords some protection against that misunderstanding, and the elements of concealment and paradox, indirection and irony built into the Gospels' retellings also prevent a fundamentalistic attitude to the Gospels doing much damage to the Christian community. A fundamentalistic attitude to the more direct and more often objectionable statements in the epistles, or to the fantasies of the Apocalypse when taken literally, has been more damaging. It is less easy to overestimate than to underestimate the Gospels' foundational character for Christian faith and witness.

Some believers still want to speak of God's revelation to or in themselves, as Paul did at Galatians 1:16, in order to insist that the Christian claim about the saving presence of God in Jesus has become an existential reality for them. The claim itself is fundamental to Christianity and so is the necessity of existential appropriation. Christ might be born a hundred times in Bethlehem and die a thousand times on Calvary, but if the holy child of Bethlehem is not born in us today it is not a lot of use to us. Christians need to discover or construct some connection between the foundational events of their religion, where (they claim) God engaged with the world by identifying God's very self with a human baby (presumably – despite the legendary birth stories – some years before anyone knew what was happening), and their own commitment and experience. The question is whether it is necessary to make this claim in terms of personal revelations, or whether such language is not rather better avoided. The point at issue in our reflection on the 'story' of Jesus is how this concept helps us to make sense of that connection between God in Jesus and ourselves without employing this dangerous extension of the idea of revelation. How believers come to accept the Christian claim is part of the question, but it also includes the nature of faith's response to God and membership of the religious community.

Other stories of revelation in the Judaeo-Christian tradition have no comparable foundational significance for the Christian sense of God and salvation. It is not the notion of story as such which is so important for Christian theology, but the story of God's self-revelation in Jesus. One of the dangers of the category is that it might focus attention on the wrong story, since the biblical story is not self-evidently focused on Christ. It can be read ecclesiocentrically as the story of God's people in history, and there is truth in that reading, but it is a truth derived from the revelation of God in Christ. The story of Israel and the Church is not the Christian story of revelation, nor even, except brokenly, the story of the reception of revelation. Christians should read the Old Testament as witness to the God of Israel whom we Gentiles know through knowing Christ, not in the first place as the story of God's people and so their own story. Though common in Calvinism, that is morally and politically dangerous and theologically one-sided.

There are also in the Judaeo-Christian tradition many stories of conversion, that is, of other people's experiences. Any of these may on occasion become vehicles of new disclosure for later believers, as may other stories of faith. They can be called vehicles of a divine revelation if they help actualize the tradition of God's self-revelation in Christ for some later believer, so that the believer claims a personal revelation of God in Christ. But most Christians will shrink from making any such extravagant claim and will allow their faith in God in Christ to rest on less dazzling apprehensions mediated with some authority by the Church's Scriptures, traditions and representatives. Enthusiasm *can* be a very horrid thing.

We turn now again to the four canonical representations of the story of Jesus, having denied they are themselves revelation and having reduced talk of revelation to the level of being the necessary presupposition of all Christian belief and action rather than expecting it to provide its content. The gospel story is the bottom line of Christianity even if we reduce talk of God's self-revelation in Christ to a necessary minimum.

A few religious thinkers and others in North America are hostile to the constraints which the New Testament canon places upon modern retellings of the Gospel story. They prefer to create new and very different narratives of Jesus' life and death in the interests of some private political, social or religious agenda. So-called 'historical' Jesus research provides an opening for this by drawing upon new sources (and sometimes claiming they are better than the old ones) and by proposing a variety of Jewish contexts for Jesus which place the elements of Jesus tradition accepted as authentic in a new and different light.

An element of such construction is always present in Christians' reception of the Gospel message, and nobody should deny its legitimacy or the place of historical judgments in responsible theological accounts of Jesus today. New sources and new proposals about Jesus' historical context may well shade our reading of the Gospels and affect even believers' mental pictures of Jesus. They may highlight aspects of the Gospels' pictures and provide grounds for criticizing other aspects of those portraits (such as Jesus' hostility to 'the Jews' or to some pharisees). It is possible to welcome a few such modifications to one's picture of Jesus while still belonging to a community which defines itself by reference to Scripture rather than by all the sources available, including those deliberately rejected by the Church as it gradually formed its canon. If our worthy desire for justice to those who were excluded leads us to believe that emergent orthodoxy was deeply mistaken about Jesus, we shall modify our own pictures accordingly and perhaps part company with the Christian Church. Those who have done so recently are mostly those least willing to speak of the revelation of God in Jesus in any case.

Each must follow his or her own conscience in constructing a faith picture of Jesus, and biblical scholars will naturally give more weight to their conclusions as historians than most. But even biblical scholars may respect the weight of a historic tradition and the experience of countless others in their own religious community when making their theological judgments. Even when the old constraints of the house of authority have become weakened, the canon may reasonably be thought to give the best guidance on Jesus.

So we return to the story of Jesus retold in the Gospels and in Christian tradition, the Gospel story with which we began, not because this is itself revelation, but because it reflects or refracts the saving revelation of God in Jesus in ways which have enabled that hidden event or mystery to become light and life to millions. There is no reason to suppose that the study of these witnesses will verify the Christian axiom about the revelation of God in Jesus. That foundational event is no longer directly accessible and was never directly or unambiguously visible. The supposed revelation of God was always veiled and has remained so as the evangelists' lifting of the veil has come to be seen as their way of bearing witness to the religious truth about Jesus as this presented itself to their faith.

Because Christians find God pre-eminently in the life, death and resurrection of Jesus and in the activity of the Spirit which derives from him and testifies to him, the Gospels enjoy a privileged position within Scripture. We may judge Paul the best theologian in early Christianity and the most important missionary or apostle. But his witness presupposes and depends on a narrative which we know best from its four later instantiations in the canonical Gospels. It is therefore to these human documents that we must turn first if we want to understand the Christian claim to know God by knowing Christ.

Christians claim to know God by knowing Jesus Christ whom (following John) they say God 'sent', thus identifying him as God's envoy who speaks with the full authority of God. It is uncertain how quickly the first followers of Jesus recognized in him more than a prophet and teacher, God's agent in a sense that stretched all available categories to breaking point. It is uncertain and unimportant, because what matters is not how they became convinced of this, but how *we* do, and it is clear that we (unlike them) are dependent on traditions which plainly point to the particular identifiable first-century Jew that they knew personally. These traditions enable us to identify Jesus but do not simply reflect the historical reality. That largely forgotten historical reality has been transfigured and/or distorted by the memories and experience of those who came to worship him.

Some symbolic heightening and (from a historian's perspective) distortion was to be expected. It is not a problem for Christianity until the historical figure has thereby become unrecognizable and unidentifiable beneath the rewrites. Christians do not claim to find a revelation of God in the fragile reconstructions of contemporary historians whose methods (and often their aims too) have little to do with the question of God. The quest of the historical Jesus only ever made Christological sense (as opposed to being merely an apologetic necessity) because most of its nineteenth-century and some of its twentieth-century protagonists injected into the mix so much of their own liberal Christian faith.

How much and what historically secure knowledge of Jesus is essential for Christianity is hard to specify. In history nothing is absolutely certain. That makes it as impossible for historical research to disprove as to validate Christian faith. It can make some theological constructions look implausible and can massively erode confidence in a faith which fails to adjust to modern knowledge and sensibilities, but believers live with their pictures and stories of Christ without needing a licence from historians, including biblical scholars. Whether or not the first disciples were right to find in Jesus what they found, historical Christianity is predicated on the assumption that they were broadly right, and that the stories preserved in the four canonical Gospels accurately convey something of their seminal memory and understanding. We have paraphrased their experience very loosely as a conviction that, in having to do with Jesus, they had to do with the God of their fathers, and we judge that John's Gospel expresses this conviction most accurately through discourses (cf. John 8:19, 12:44f., 14:9), and that these Johannine discourses deviate dramatically from anything Jesus actually said, and that this revelational unity of the Son with the Father, which they assert and in which the evangelist claims believers somehow participate, is what Christians mean (or ought to mean) by their doctrine of Christ's divinity, whose implications for the doctrine of God were worked out further in their doctrine of God as Trinity.

All this confirms the importance of the idea of revelation for Christianity, but warrants its application only in the restricted context of the doctrine of God and Christology. It does not encourage its extension to Scripture or proclamation, essential as both are to the mediation of God's self-revelation in the communication and persistence of Christian faith. The hiddenness of God's self-revelation in Christ, witnessed to by the Gospel story, rather discourages extravagant talk of revelation in other contexts. Making Christian doctrinal and moral decisions is a theological task which cannot be bypassed by appeals to biblical or charismatic authority.

The Jesus in whom Christians find their saving revelation of God has been defined dogmatically, but that was a secondary development, however necessary and however true in its own terms. The primary way in which Jesus (like anyone else) is spoken of is by narrative. Christians have developed mythical narratives of Jesus in order to express pictorially their conviction that, in speaking of him, they are speaking of God, or that the story of Jesus is the focus of a larger story of God's engagement with the world. Some Christians have found these mythical narratives unhelpful, and have tried to say what they are getting at in other ways. They are at least right that mythical narratives have proved misleading by being taken literally, and rightly insist that myth be called by its name, not identified with history. But some who found mythic narratives objectionable mistranslated them and ended up saying something different. Like poetry, myth is not readily translated, least of all into philosophical categories, but not into history either. We may be content with retelling the Gospel *story*.

New *historical* narratives of Jesus respond to the spirit of the age and have been more or less satisfying and more or less speculative. They cannot claim much certainty, but become anti-Christian (or at least anti-orthodox) by definition only when they claim to interpret Jesus more accurately and truthfully than the New Testament writers themselves, because (orthodox) Christianity is defined by reference to the New Testament interpretations of Jesus, imperfect as these are. The Gospels may be less attractive than some of the 'alternative narratives' of Jesus produced by some modern theologians and anti-theologians, but it is possible to call them less *Christian* only if we redefine Christianity (as some of course have wanted to do over the past 300 years).

The limitations of history writing as a vehicle for expressing Christian faith are evident. A discourse which cannot speak of God (and such is most historians' definition of their craft) is by definition inadequate for Christology. It is legitimate in its own theological fields, but these fields are apologetics and Church history, not proclamation or Christology. For these the Gospel story provides the better starting point. It is the product of a belief in revelation and does not make much sense apart from that belief, but it does not compel us to say more about revelation than the basic Christian affirmation that Jesus is the revelation of God, with all that that implies about the past, the present and the future of the world. The unfolding of Christian belief and proposals for action does not have to be constantly appealing to supposed revelation, whether in the text of Scripture or elsewhere. It is rather a faithful response to the story within the community of believers.

That story retold in the four Gospel portraits of Jesus is scarcely a historical narrative, even though it is the narrative account of an identifiable historical figure. Little is gained by classifying the Gospels generically as 'biographies', despite their similarities to ancient 'lives'. Any generic classification has to do justice to their religious character, most clearly evidenced in the fact that the resurrection of Jesus is integral to these narratives. This mystery, unhelpfully objectified as a quasi-historical event, marks the point where the person Jesus becomes a symbol of God available for all and powerful in many, the second Adam, a life-giving Spirit. It is an essential component, with the cross it is *the* most essential component, of the story of *Jesus* which controls and shapes the whole Christian story of God and the world, not merely part of the story of the disciples and their faith, which is where the modern historian must place it. But it says nothing more about revelation than that Jesus was and is and will be the decisive saving revelation of God. This is the shape of the Christian religion, whether or not it is in any important sense true, and whether or not many people remain willing, indeed eager, to understand their own lives in terms of this system of symbols. Christianity continues to exist through the Christian story of Jesus (which presupposes, and is itself, a story of God and the world) being retold and persuading others to become part of that story by themselves becoming disciples. God's self-revelation is the presupposition of the story and what it ultimately points to, but the story has its own integrity which must not annihilate the history by swallowing it up in the myth – a danger which becomes visible in John.

The canonical Gospels are instantiations of the story of Jesus accepted by the second-century catholic Church as best preserving the story and message of salvation. Most twentieth-century Christians identify with that historic community, however fractured, and accept the decisions made over a period of time in the formation of a canon. That does not preclude taking seriously new sources of information about early Christian groups and perhaps about Jesus himself, such as the Gospel of Thomas. If these writings are thought to contain some reliable historical information about what Jesus said or did, those grains will be pressed into some theologians' Christian accounts of and witness to Jesus, and so may ultimately influence the larger community. Again, in turning to the Gospels we are turning not to 'revelation' but to traditions consisting in a larger story of Jesus, made up very largely of smaller stories, some more or less historical, others fictional, whether admittedly so (parables) or not (legends). Christians believe in God's self-revelation, but can retell the story of Jesus without wanting the category of revelation to support the details, only to constitute the framework. Christians read the Gospels expectantly because they have already heard and believed that Jesus is the revelation of God. They expect their own stories to be illuminated by this story of God in Jesus because that *tua res agitur* is part of what is meant by 'God'.

The Gospel story of Jesus, the decisive manifestation or revelation of God has been preserved and is constantly reread in four canonical (that is, normative, measuring-rod) instantiations. These consist of many smaller units, some of them short stories (apophthegms, *Novellen*, parables), some of them collections of sayings or aphorisms. John's Gospel contains revelatory discourses, as well as reports of signs which are said to have manifested Jesus' glory. The synoptic miracle stories can also be called epiphanies, and Dibelius illuminatingly called Mark a 'book of secret epiphanies', catching neatly the dialectic of revelation and concealment in that narrative. The narratives of Jesus' baptism and transfiguration describe revelatory events or experiences, and some of Jesus' sayings tell of future revelations. The resurrection traditions report self-revelations of Jesus after his death and, however historically unreliable these are, they point to what must be called the revelatory event *par excellence*. However it happened (and it would be absurd to expect to penetrate the mystery of the resurrection), and however the first disciples became convinced that it had happened (the evidence permits only guesses), one can reasonably call what Paul reports (1 Cor. 9:1, 15:4–5) revelatory experiences, revelation for the disciples and himself, though only tradition to later generations. In all these examples we must put the word 'revelation' in brackets, not to deny the reality of God in them, but to insist that they are 'revelations' only to their recipients. Revelations of God to some people are not a revelation to anyone else, even though as tradition they may contribute to others' faith by illuminating the person of Jesus and being the occasion for their being persuaded to respond to what they sense God is doing in the world. We are drawn into the story of Jesus by hearing it read and by coming to know it. We come to understand ourselves as part of God's family, as disciples, friends, or followers of this Jesus who (we say) was dead and is alive. We confess Him our Lord and God, finding in Him the key to our understanding of God and the world: the way, the truth and the life. That is what we mean by calling Him the saving revelation of God.

So the Gospels are shot through with this category, 'revelation', with its absolute claim to truth. But it does not add to the story of Jesus, only state and communicate its meaning, inviting the hearers or readers to respond by acknowledging a total claim upon their own lives. Those who risk the wager and make this story the key to their life's meaning, and that a small part of the continuing story of God's engagement with the world in Christ, will, according to the famous concluding words of *The Quest of the Historical Jesus*, 'know in their own experience who He is.'

It is the whole religious system, including rituals, spiritual and moral practices, and institutions, as well as stories of different kinds (myths, histories, parables) which illuminates (or fails to illuminate) human lives and proves to be a vehicle for the holy, the power that Christians and others call God. Within this whole Christian bundle of traditions and practices, the Gospel story of Jesus as the saving revelation of God is the hub from which everything radiates. It has to be articulated in a more systematic form that relates Christian belief to the rest of human knowledge at any particular time or place and its credibility depends on the success of these attempts to weld faith and rationality. Elements of falsehood in the way the story has been retold or understood need to be purged by prophetic and theological criticism. The story of the self-revelation of God may evoke powerful experiences, but is generally accepted on the authority of the wider community, whose judgment is distilled in a few poetical and theological texts and lived with in a quite undramatic way. Belief in revelation shapes the telling and the hearing of the story, and is elaborated in the doctrine of the Trinity, but itself needs to be spoken of very little. It is the story which has to be constantly retold and re-enacted, and which constantly draws new hearers into its web, and constitutes every Christian account of God's mysterious (that is, hidden) presence in the world. It is the story of God in Jesus that occasions new responses of discipleship, and draws believers on to a still unseen future.

The preceding discussions have not encouraged much talk of revelation beyond insisting on its axiomatic place in any Christian doctrine of God and Christ, including the Spirit of God operative in the world today. The Gospel story in its scriptural instantiations presupposes revelation but requires very little theory to back it up. It is possible to see how these human stories contribute to human transformation without inflating them with the hot air of 'revelation'. Of course, Christian Scripture and other Christian traditions bear witness to God in Christ, and that cannot even be asserted without the concept of revelation, but talk of revelation that goes beyond formal delineations of the structure of Christian belief in (and response to) God as Father or Creator, Son or Redeemer, Spirit or Sanctifier, Perfector or Renewer seems open to the charge of idolatry: identifying human traditions and (worse) human authorities with divine revelation.

The peculiar danger of the notion of revelation when applied to anything 'given' in the world, as opposed to the inaccessible event or mystery of God in Christ, is that where it is accepted there is no place for questioning. We only scrutinize claims to revelation if we do not religiously believe them. If we passionately believed we would worship, not scrutinize. This belief belongs in the private and semi-private realms of personal conviction and the shared worship of a like-minded community, not paraded as an argument in the public arena of theology, or used to solve theology's epistemological problems. All our first-order talk of God is talk of revelation, but to say that the category is part of the grammar of religious talk of God is not to say much. Actual Christian belief in God stems from the Christian story of God's self-revelation, not from the idea of revelation as such. That second-order category insists on the reality that is constitutive of the Christian story, but does not supply its content. Believers live from the story and symbols, exposed to the dangers of idolatry inescapable where God is known through human traditions and institutions and responded to by sinners. The task of theology is to minimize those dangers by identifying, criticizing, and uprooting perversions, and to help the system of symbols to direct worshippers to God.

The bare assertion of the revelation of God in Christ contains little content until articulated in the Gospel story. Even the love and reverence and humility in the face of God, and love, forgiveness and self-denial in face of the neighbours, which some would propose as the content of the revelation in Christ, or the victory of suffering love, are abstractions until communicated through the story of Jesus and in the witness of Christian character, drawing others to respond. The story of Jesus is retold by men and women whose lives are shaped by it. All they need in order to bear witness are the biblical traditions about Jesus which tell the story of Jesus as the revelation of God and the context of biblical and Christian faith in God which makes that story intelligible. That means tradition and community, not further talk of revelation. The Gospel of John asserts the revelation of God in Jesus, but the First Epistle writes of tradition: 'that which was from the beginning, what we have heard, what we have seen with our eyes, what we beheld and our hands handled'. Yesterday's revelation is sedimented in today's traditions, which become the raw material of new disclosures, making possible what that epistle calls a fellowship among believers which is a fellowship with the Father and with his Son Jesus Christ. The writer's fullness of joy depends on the event of revelation but is communicated through tradition and story, exhortation and doxology. Faith acknowledges God in and through human words, but human speakers and writers ought not to play God by claiming too much for their efforts to pass on the tradition and invite others into the community. The word 'revelation' is a dangerous one to use in this context.

Extending it beyond its statement of the self-evident (that God can be known only because God makes God's self known) and the foundational claim of Christianity that to know Jesus is to know God (what I have called the axiomatic use of this category) gives unwarranted power to the institution's leadership. The idea of revelation has too often claimed divine authority for our own all too human theology and sometimes sub-human politics. Cutting the category back to its formal assertion of God in Christ and denying it to human traditions and even to the dangerous rhetoric of proclamation except where this is accepted as such by free individuals is a way of minimizing those dangers.

Among theologians from different traditions trying to understand one another the category has not identified as much common ground as was hoped and has threatened to become an umbrella camouflaging different agendas. Not even the fruitful notion of story seems able to restore this theological category to the dominant position it occupied earlier in the twentieth century at the centre of all Christian discourse.

To summarize: from Barth's threefold form of the Word of God, only the Word incarnate can properly be called divine revelation, God's revealing of God's self in Jesus. The main value of the category lies in preserving the theocentric and Christocentric character of Christian theology against the natural tendency of a legitimate anthropological orientation to become an anthropocentric theology. The necessary derivatives by which the Word of God is communicated, Scripture and proclamation, are human words or traditions. They include many stories, but only the Christian story of Jesus is foundational for the Christian claim about God's engagement with the world, because it is only in this man's life and death and 'resurrection' by God, that this Christian claim to revelation is made. The alleged self-revelation of God remains hidden, its reality now offered in the story of Jesus which is an amalgam of myth, history and legend. The paradox of God's self-revelation in Jesus can be stated doctrinally (the divinity of Christ), unfolded by theology, or narrated in the retold story of Jesus – and sung in Charles Wesley's already quoted echoes of the Johannine and Matthean prologues:

> Veiled in flesh the Godhead see:
> hail, the incarnate Deity,
> pleased as Man with man to dwell,
> Jesus, our Emmanuel.

There is revelation for us, *pro nobis*, there glory.

Nine

The Productive Vagueness of an Untranslatable Relationship

Caroline Schröder

The Oxford–born symposium on the theme 'story and revelation' began in the spring of 1995. The participants were looking, without any programmatic intentions, for a theme that could offer many opportunities for encounter to people belonging to different churches and representing various theological disciplines. However, at the beginning there had to be efforts at mutual comprehension. Attempts to translate 'story and revelation' into German had a certain distancing effect, since the possible variant '*Geschichte und Offenbarung*' pointed to a quite different meaning ('history and revelation') which certainly would have been programmatic. Thus linguistic complexities accompanied the discussion, and compelled us again and again to revise and make more precise our own use of language, and to listen for undertones and overtones.

But the progress of our conversations was also made more difficult by a certain vagueness in the matter under discussion. What exactly is supposed to be clarified by discussing the relationship of 'story' and 'revelation'? Is it the reading of the Bible (Sauter, Maurer, Fischer) or the inner dynamic of a process which can (for good theological reasons) also be encountered with non-biblical texts (Fiddes)? Is it perhaps a matter of describing and evaluating how the elemental assertion of life involved in reading discloses possibilities for human existence (Barton), so that human beings respond to these possibilities with practical knowledge (Ward, Morgan)? Or is it rather that people are drawn into a – quite specific – story precisely because the biblical text has priority over its other possible instantiations, and shows this – since it frees the story from itself and gets it a hearing – by being its own interpreter (Maurer)? Is 'revelation' an event which can be presupposed with a certain theological self-evidence yet which, once it becomes a concept and passes into currency as a much misused slogan, invites silence rather than speech (Morgan)? Or, on the other hand, does it not show us a more appealing aspect, once it becomes clear how it impinges on men and women: as experiences in which something important for life is disclosed, experiences which are connected with our handling of 'open stories' (Fiddes)? Is this openness a structural characteristic of stories, or is it more a matter of the reader's expectations (Wolter, Barton)? What can we learn from certain specific biblical genres of text in which stories are disclosed in order to make hope arise anew, against all appearances (Wolter)?

It was the very fuzziness of the theme that challenged us to interrogate the concept 'story'. What gain in precision could it provide for the way we handle texts? Which texts could be up for discussion, and what consequences would our observations have for clarifying 'Scripture and Revelation'?

1 Revelation, Story, Disclosure

The participants in our discussions shared a general reserve towards the classical doctrine of revelation. Insofar as 'revelation' characterizes an event which affects men and women from above, from outside, it cannot be brought into relationship with the structure of their experience. But it is such structures to which the concept of 'story' draws attention. Its intention is precisely to remove the distinction between the event of remembrance and retelling, and every facticity that is distinct from that event. Facticity which has not yet itself come to be spoken of is not comprehensible: it remains fundamentally withdrawn from human understanding – just as, indeed, nothing at all can be experienced without being spoken of, even if only in the virtual wording of something which is concealed in silence. Hence the concept of 'story' marks out, in a sense, the beginning of human knowledge. Any knowledge which is posited by revelation, in whatever way, cannot be an exception to this rule, but represents a confirmation of it.

The question arises whether this knowledge, as the experience of a disclosure, points us to an event which has left traces in the text. Is it the possibility of becoming a 'story' that discloses something designed to be there in the text, and the history of its reception? So the interest in our discussion was directed in the first instance towards clarifying a complex relationship, a relationship in which 'story' formed the middle term between 'revelation' and 'disclosure'.

2 An Unstable Consensus: We May Not Go 'Behind' the Text

Very early on, one point of consensus was formulated. We were to a great extent at one in thinking that the relationship between 'story' and 'revelation' mandated a particular orientation to the text. As a first description of this orientation, we quickly arrived at the formulation that an appropriate understanding of a text is one that does not reach 'behind' the text and try to 'get to the back' of it. However, it was soon to become apparent that this consensus left certain open questions, especially when the biblical text was the text under discussion.

What principles does the theological distinction between the spirit and the letter yield for our handling of biblical texts? Is an orientation to the literal meaning of the text the ultimately irreplaceable opportunity for new theological knowledge (Maurer), or is it, on the contrary, a practically heretical narrowing of a much wider practice of reading, according to which meaning was able to multiply in a stimulating way without justifying human claims to possess the text (Ward)?

3 Loyalty to the Text and the Problem of Authority

However the intention of 'not going behind the text' was understood by the individual participants in the discussion, there were always in the background two possible reasons for it which, once expressed, stood in a certain tension with each other. On the one hand, it is possible to say that we cannot go behind the text because in the flux of remembrance and retelling it has itself equally become fluid, has become 'story', part (and a part that cannot be definitively marked off) of a communicative space in which, in spite of any conceivable critical technique, I am already standing. Consequently, I can do justice to the text as 'story' only if at the same time I take account of this communicative space, which cannot be 'gone behind' and which forms the space in which the text exists. Anyone who wishes to listen to the text in this sense will hear the many-voiced witness of the tradition at the same time (Morgan). The emphasis here lies on saying that we *cannot* go behind the text.

But another reason for not going behind the text is the Reformation principle *sola scriptura*, according to which the texts of the Old and New Testaments form a unity or at least a whole; and this whole *can* be seen from the point of view of the formation of tradition, but its decisive quality really lies somewhere else. The *sola scriptura* of Protestant theology is an expression of the theological insight that God's Word makes *itself* perceptible (Sauter). It is to this principle that the theological concept of 'revelation' corresponds. This concept emphasizes the distinction between God and humanity. By contrast with this, the question *how revelation happens* moves rather into the background, and is perhaps not immediately answerable. But what, on the other hand, certainly can be said is how (that is to say, according to what rules) the theological insight that God's Word makes itself perceptible continually renews the realization that God and humanity are distinct), and thus characterizes a certain way of reading and a certain expectation in reading (Sauter, Maurer, Fischer). This expectation is then directed in a particular way to biblical texts, which are read as 'canonical', that is, with the assumption that there is a difference between them and any other texts one might choose. With regard to the Church's understanding of itself, a special authority is ascribed to these texts. They point to the fact that the Church is *creatura verbi* and therefore may not take as its starting point anything other than the Word of God, insofar as this word makes itself heard. Now the emphasis of this justification for our point of consensus lies in recognizing that it is certainly *possible* to look for another starting point: the Church has over and over again drunk from other fountains, and in doing so has continually risked losing its true shape. Reference to the *sola scriptura* principle reminds us of the possibility that one *can* go behind the texts in which God makes himself knowable: but it also reminds us that it is in this very possibility that the Church is most seriously jeopardized.

Recourse to the concept of revelation rules out the idea that human beings have any natural access to God. But this cannot be shown on the basis of any particular passages in the text; it is to some extent a way of reading the text. The insight that people are being told something that they cannot tell themselves (Sauter, Barton) is a discovery that has something to do with the structure of stories, with the way retelling and remembrance continually start up and break off again.

The fact that 'revelation' is anchored in certain elements of the structure of the text makes it possible to escape the limits of the biblical canon. It also suggests an understanding that emphasizes the human reply to God's self-disclosure. And, consequently, it is thinkable that the relation of story and revelation is in principle expressed in all literary texts (Fiddes). So can this direction in the Church's reading or hearing of the Bible alert us to a reality concerning non-biblical texts and stories, too? Or does it entail attachment to a 'closed' canon, which we risk abandoning if we look over its 'edges'? In that case it would be legitimate to ask whether this attachment to the limits of the canon is capable of providing guidance for an expectation in reading that is faithful to Scripture at all. For, surely, this can only arise when we enter into the texts, that is, into a space whose inner vitality is disclosed more and more over time? This in turn produces a richness of perspective (Fischer) which is capable of recognizing such vitality elsewhere, on the other side of the 'edges'. And in that case we ought to take the trouble to discover the rules for such recognition.

How, then, can the concept of revelation mark out the Church's dependence on the Bible in a way that does not involve a levelling down? Or, rather, should we not continually ask who it is that gains a hearing in the

Church, and by what means? Does *sola scriptura* settle the dispute about authority, or really only instigate it?

4 The Question of What is Binding

Even if we regard a plurality of stories, both inside and outside the Bible, as pointing the way ahead; even if we should like to hear and renarrate stories only for the sake of new ways of reading, derived from seeing how they intermesh with each other and are open to supplementation; even if we think that we can escape the problem of authority through this kind of participation in them – even then we shall come up against problems. Are there not stories that have absolutely nothing to do with God, or even stories that can lead us on false trails, stories which support the human tendency towards self-deception, manipulation and oppression, rather than warding it off? Are we not confronted in certain texts by a particular factor which cannot be reduced to a formula, but which can be recognized in a certain pregnant and simple quality (Fischer) – and perhaps also in other, similar stories, to which we feel drawn with a certain legitimation, even if this is a legitimation which is fundamentally open to criticism? (Compare the theme of 'forgiveness' in Fiddes' chapter.) Does this repeated recognition regulate itself, simply through the medium of 'stories', or does it not heed other (normative, rule-like) elements of language, however much these for their part can also be aspects of a story (Wolter), and however little these 'rules' can *guarantee* communication free of interference (Maurer)? Where does anything's binding character come from? Or, to put it more bluntly, what is the relationship between the idea of *story*, with its emphasis on an unassuming power to carry conviction, and the 'harder' idea of *doctrine*, which remains awkwardly alien to human experience and yet claims validity for it?

Are there presuppositions for understanding which are indispensable, even though they may be silent and only need to be verbalized in cases of conflict, which yet shape the process of retelling and remembrance without themselves making an appearance in the condensed form of doctrine, which always appears so polemical: presuppositions of understanding which mostly (that is, in the normal states of life in the Church) are simply 'meta-narrative'? Is doctrine a symptom of illness in the Church?

5 Open Questions

So much for the consensus we have arrived at; it is noticeable that describing it has already led to further questions. First, does opening up the concept of 'story' provide a new access to the idea of 'revelation', or do we, perhaps, in the end learn something quite different? And if so, what theological judgment can be passed on what we have learned? Second, what does the consensus that we are to agree not to go 'behind' the text actually exclude? If we *were* to go 'behind' the text, where would we be going? Third, does our experience with stories help us to say, and to describe, *how* God becomes knowable to us: unmistakable *and* unprotected, reassuring yet without arousing fantasies of possession? And finally do 'stories' provide a complete account of what is to be said, heard and read within the arena of the Church? Do other forms of speech jeopardize the health of the Church's life; or should we, putting it less sharply, be content with the insight that it would be good for doctrine, too, if it were to base its self-understanding on stories?

Despite the differences between the terms 'revelation' and 'story', they share the role of guarding against certain conceptions. Invoking the concept of revelation avoids linking God to anything that is not God, whether this is only cultural progress or the suggestive power of an experience that forms a society. God is God, not a human being or a created being, and that is why human beings cannot bring themselves up to God's level. There is no *experience* through which they are led to God.

However, this use of the concept of revelation seems to bury a whole line of tradition which was concerned not to allow human life to be barred from absolutely any sight of God. According to this tradition, too, God is beyond our reach: but not completely alien, 'for in him we live and move and have our being' (Acts 17). This sentence from Cleanthes the Stoic and Luke's Paul operates with the *immanence* of God, which as human beings we cannot evade. Or take Romans 2: all human beings, irrespective of the fundamental distinction between Jews and Gentiles, are inexcusable, because God, after all, continually lets himself be seen, and because humans cannot deny this perception of God. This perception, which no human life can avoid and yet which no human life can do justice to, is also 'revelation'. Expressed as 'natural revelation', this has provided the occasion for 'natural theology', which is disputed, but by no means disputed on every side. This, too, can be seen in either of two ways: 'grace perfects nature' or 'even "nature" is never without "grace"'. Perhaps only the emphasis is different: but differences of emphasis have a claim to be heard.

Revelation is a theological concept which has made history especially in German-speaking areas. In the history of dialectical theology recourse to 'revelation' became the hammer of liberal culture-Protestantism, whose concern was mediation. Against this, 'revelation' became the characteristic of God's reality, which remains fundamentally alien to human experience. There is no gradual approach, but only ever an irruption into the contexts of human experience: no traces, but only a meteor striking from another world. Revelation then means that God lays waste the contexts of meaning belonging to human life, confronting them as the wholly Other. A theology which takes this understanding of revelation as its orientation will see itself as obliged to emphasize this confrontation. Meeting God is of its nature confrontation. In it something is torn apart: everything that was previously known and relied upon, everything that had proved itself and been taken for granted. People who let the concept of revelation melt on their tongue develop a taste for this confrontation, and learn to recognize this taste wherever human beings experience discontinuity, shock, disturbance ('and, behold, we live!'). A hole is torn open before which the range of human possibilities has to capitulate; and everywhere in it we sense God the wholly Other. But, on the other hand, is it necessary to link the fact that God exists over against us with the image of a frontal assault? And is the opposition of story and revelation not a sign that even the dramatic comes with time to have a rather insipid flavour, and that it is time to reflect more on the traces and less on the craters?

The change in taste showed itself in our discussions in our liking for saying that 'disclosure' situations are those in which people are 'surprised'. 'Surprise' presupposes expectations, even when these are updated against experience, contradicted or newly minted. A surprising experience is in any case a very much more moderate 'shock' than a strike by a meteor. Thus this description was widely accepted for a long time, with only one objection: that, bound up with it, was the questionable idea that the insight given through the disclosure, and the change brought about in the recipient of the story, were thereby reduced to a dateable moment.

Revelation is linked to stories: it is recorded in stories, or anyway in the way in which stories are heard and read. What occurs through this link causes *surprise*. But is it enough to characterize this event as an experience of surprise? In my opinion this description is still much too weak. But the alternative is not to underline the violence of the effect. The problem lies elsewhere. People may be receptive to stories. But there are also resistances. For example, Jesus tells parables ('stories') which show the resistance that Israel always manifested towards God. But the punch line is that his contemporary hearers are no different from their forebears, who had the life of the prophets on their conscience. Jesus ascribes to his hearers exactly the role in a story which they would never seek for themselves. This is the point at which the punch line hits home to us.

In my view a substantial question is therefore as follows: do we not have to do, first and last, with a quite specific story, whose peculiarity perhaps consists precisely in the fact that we do not want to be part of it? We feel drawn to all manner of stories; but do we not bear within ourselves an obstinate resistance which constantly hinders us from seeing ourselves as actors, or even marginal figures, in this story? And would it not be revealing to communicate with each other about the scale of, and reasons for, this possibly fundamental reserve? To hear, yet not to hear; to see, yet not to see; to welcome Jesus of Nazareth as the awaited Messiah, yet then to turn away from him, so as not to be brought into connection with him: is not this the tension in which we, the most faithful hearers of this story, remain caught up? What is the role of stories when they confront us with ourselves and with the way in which we always deny God's presence in our midst? Is not the problem of *homines narrantes* that they constantly feel drawn to the wrong stories, or are unwilling or resistant to recognizing themselves in the 'right' stories, the ones where they really belong? There are a good many stories we may experience as opening reality to us, but which are in fact only an expression of our own self-deception and guilt.

Human beings live by telling stories, by remembering. In a time when it is an everyday necessity that boundaries should break down, it seems sensible to call attention to the fact that the authority of stories is anchored not only ecclesiologically but also, indeed, anthropologically. The conception of 'story' sensitizes us for ourselves as the Church *alongside* and *together with* communities with a different character, communities that deal with stories and whose existence is dependent on their dealings with stories. It is not only inside the Church that handling stories has something creative about it: it sets something free, it lets something new come to be, it opens up fresh perspectives and opportunities for perception which did not exist before. Handling stories immunizes us against the danger of categorizing reality, and also against the danger of dividing people into 'insiders' and 'outsiders'. The way stories intermesh has already reached too high a degree of complexity for such a schematic division.

Furthermore, it is important to bear in mind that it is the very 'insiders' in the Church who remain unprepared for the openness of their story. They may be marked by a particular expectation of reading, but so long as they stay with their stories, they also stay with the experience that these stories might contradict their expectation. How can openness then be tracked down? How does it come about that we experience certain stories as open but others as closed? Does closure mean that such stories no longer have anything to say to us? Or may it be a question of our culpably closing the stories off, something that lies more on our own side than on the side of the story or the text?

In addition there are stories that are not told, even though they are remembered. But these have no plot, they are fragmentary and they confirm the fact that only a minority of our stories actually ever are told. A story which is told or staged is the exception which breaks the general rule of baffled silence, linguistic inadequacy and guilty concealment. Does this observation settle anything? The major part of human reality is not opened up by 'stories': it is only occasionally that I am dragged out of my silence by a (modest) confrontation with someone else's story. That is why telling stories is so important.

'Story' is the side of reality that is turned towards us, or towards which we can turn. In this sense the concept of story marks a difference from the understanding of history in which the concern is the reconstruction of historical events. It forms the provisional end of a development in the humanities which has taken leave of the notion of an objective, demonstrable history of hard facts, and which assumes instead a plurality of stories which we cannot get behind – neither behind the stories, so as to be able to discover what really happened, nor behind the plurality, in order to advance through it to a unifying core of reality. 'History' is always in the plural, and stories are always *told*, whether orally or in writing. They are tied to language and memory, both of which can only be apprehended within a speaking and remembering community. The Church is understood to be such a community. Thus we are made aware through the concept of story of a web of connections, in the face of which any '*sola*' will have difficulties in making itself comprehensible.

The spatial metaphor in the formula 'not going "behind" the text' really means nothing other than faithfulness to Scripture, to which theology is fundamentally committed, even though in various different ways, partly determined by confessional allegiance. It does not, for example, rule out critical discussion of biblical texts, but warns against going astray, which can easily happen if one fails to begin with the text and does not keep returning to it. The attention we are paying to 'story' also, after all, expresses the insight that the biblical text is not to be reduced or rendered down, whether into its constituent parts, into some intellectual substratum, into something that packs a greater punch or is more 'portable', in short into something that would make the text itself superfluous.

Thus 'story' no less than 'revelation' shows us where we can begin. We do not need to look for a reality behind the stories that are given us, or to compare what is told and heard with the unexpressed facts, in order to distinguish true from false. We can entrust ourselves to the structures, the dynamic, the gradient and direction of a story; then we shall be doing justice to the story, and all questions about 'what really happened' will fall silent.

Or will they? Are there really not legitimate occasions for getting 'to the back of' the text? Where, for example, am I going if I get to the back of the text in the sense of going 'beneath' it, and where if I go 'behind' it? 'Beneath' indicates a greater measure of closeness and faithfulness to the text (cf. 'into' the text). I get aboard the text, get involved in a text's various dimensions and perspectives. A text after all is not flat, and so I can penetrate the surface of the text without at the same time abandoning it. 'Behind' indicates that there is something which can be distinguished from the text yet acts as a control on it: there is a whole range of things that the text itself does not express, but which must have been there and have been tangible, at least in the original situation to which the text owes its existence, and these things must then at least have regulated the way the text was received by its implicit readers. This self-effacing reality 'behind' the text, which emerges only indirectly, has left traces behind – otherwise a text would not have come to be at all. If one understands the text as a trace, then one is soon on the way to getting on the tracks of the text, by constructing the reality to which this text can lead us back. And thereby we can find out this or that about the original conditions of the text's understanding. The question is whether this can succeed. That it is only approximately possible is true, but no objection. The problem is not a hermeneutical so much as a theological one: is it not the case that in the Bible we are dealing with texts which, if they are understood as merely historical sources, are not understood at all? This does not mean that it is not worthwhile sometimes to look behind the text. There are certain texts that actually demand this – texts in which a reality topical at the time is encoded. Where the text works with code, two things are both essential: first, an attempt at decoding, so that one 'gets to the back of' what is really intended, and secondly, application. Wolter begins with the reconstruction of a 'topical' story and demonstrates in an exemplary way that one certainly can get 'behind' texts – and *thus* come to an increased knowledge which does justice to what is happening *inside* the text.

So is the question of 'what really happened' actually dispensable, once we espouse the cause of an orientation to the text, to Scripture? Reality is always reality mediated through narration. Reality is always fictive. It is true that there are differences of degree, but still: of degree! In everyday dealings with different genres of text, people – people who read, people who hear, people who face reality yet also flee from it – know instinctively the difference between a fictive story and a newspaper report. Both may be expressed in language, but they differ where their relation to reality is concerned. The newspaper report relates to something which can be presented according to certain categories on which a consensus is possible, and may also be checked (the date, place and name of the people involved can be recorded). A fictive story does not claim this relationship. Of course I can assert that a poem has a higher degree of reality than a piece of television reporting. But this higher degree of reality is connected more with the fact that a poem releases reality from within – that it is creative, brings forth something new by considering and representing what is, or what has happened, from a disturbing perspective. The superficial aspect of a newspaper article has a different effect, connected with the socially acceptable myth that what happens can be portrayed in a 'watertight' way, and from a more or less neutral perspective. *But we do not really know what has happened.* We never see deeper than the surface, and even this looks different at this or that moment, depending on the direction from which we approach it.

Firmly as this insight, which shakes the myth of neutral reporting, has established itself, it is dangerous in my view for it to be linked to a growing scepticism in inspecting public, political life. Scepticism overcomes those who feel themselves to be increasingly shut out of this life. There is a whole new genre of stories which underpin this scepticism. The 'brute facts' have long since evaporated. Distrust, cynicism, the feeling of being deceived on all sides, these make all 'facts' seem at the same time ambiguous and opaque. At the end of the day there is an enemy behind every friend. (Cf. Isaac Singer's tale of a Jewish woman who, following a series of 'revelations', converts to Christianity, falls into deep despair because of this and eventually dies without ever having found any foothold. Her whole life becomes a continual slide into a bottomless abyss, linked with the constantly disappointed hope of finding the ground of truth beneath her feet.)

What, then, is gained by introducing the concept of 'story'? A revaluation of narrative history, based on a constitutional openness but purchased at the cost of a growing loss of any sense of security? Or simply the erosion of an understanding of history that loses a fundamental point of reference by giving up the unattainable strangeness of the event – a point of reference to which narrative history must always relate if it is to remain open to checking?

There is, of course, nothing for us to fall back on but our experience, insofar as it has found linguistic expression. Human beings make discoveries through which they are led beyond themselves, that is to say beyond their horizons of expectation. They can experience and express this movement as confrontation, as a clash between contrary 'stories' in which something gets broken. But even then this is a moment of experience ('disclosure') and this seems at the same time to be the expression human beings assume before God, when God communicates himself to them. If we ask what happens when God reveals himself, then we are speaking about the human side of an event much of which must remain hidden to us. But does not such a way of speaking stand in a certain tension with a concept of revelation which is meant to lead us to speak of *God*, in the expectation of His acting, and not of *ourselves*?

Perhaps, finally, it is right to reflect on the following. Faithfulness to Scripture in the sense of the (disputed) *sola scriptura* principle is actually only possible because Scripture points beyond itself (it is only in that way that we can say it is its own interpreter). It does not stand alone; and yet the difference between it and other literature cannot be levelled out. The irreducible rules of Bible reading proceed from the text itself (Sauter): the biblical texts are already in movement *before* we receive them. It is into this movement we are drawn when we are drawn into biblical 'stories'. This movement, or turbulence, is not produced only when there is a confrontation with other 'stories' or even 'contexts'.

Thus faithfulness to Scripture causes men and women to begin with biblical texts and to stay with them even beyond this beginning: not to remain 'stuck' to them, but constantly to come back to them. And this is possible because we are not alone with these texts. That we are not alone with them cannot, however, be expressed only as a 'story', but is a matter of doctrine. Thus eschatology, the doctrines of the Trinity and of creation, and also the Reformation doctrine of justification, can be understood as aids to reading which keep alive a quite particular expectation, and in this way guard our reading against falling asleep or into idolatry. In this sense doctrine gives a foundation to the freedom of the letter. In this freedom the texts continually gain authority, in a new and inventive way, for the life of a community.

And perhaps this is because we do not simply tell stories, but when we tell them and remember them we are confronted, as on an Easter walk, with the insight that something *had to* happen like this; and because in that 'had to' there lie the roots of the Church's obligation to read the text; and perhaps that is why there is a need for doctrine – doctrine of a particular character, which encourages openness.

In looking at the 'stories' which have entered into the history of this colloquium it has turned out that reference had again and again to be made to 'doctrine'. But what is taught in doctrine? Forgiveness? Love? That forgiveness and love cannot be compelled (Fiddes)? That God does not meet human beings irresistibly, but in freedom? That people who get drawn into stories get involved in them, and experience this as 'liberation', because everything compulsive is removed from the way they receive them? This may indeed be one element of truth in 'story', as against the reception history of 'doctrine': the decisive thing does not permit of authoritative mediation. The authority of biblical texts will not allow itself to be presented through human claims to authority: to attempt one is to lose the other.

Nevertheless, 'disclosure' and 'closure' cannot be distributed respectively to 'story' and 'doctrine' as 'good' and 'evil'. Stories can be used just as much as doctrine to close men and women up, and then more is needed than to refer them to different forms of speech. Then only God can help: God, who in a plurality of speech forms breaks silence, and mints anew the form of our reading and hearing, whether they are full of expectation or despair of it.

Translated from the German by John Barton.

Bibliography

Albus, Michael (1976), 'Geist und Feuer. Ein Gespräch mit Hans Urs von Balthasar', *HerrKorr*, 30, 72–82.

Alexander, Loveday (1993), *The Preface to Luke's Gospel*, Cambridge: Cambridge University Press.

Alexandre, Monique (1976), 'L'exégèse de Gen. 1.1–2a dans l' *In Hexaemeron* de Grégoire de Nysse: deux approches du problème de la matière', in Heinrich Dorrie, Margarete Altenburger and Uta Schramm (eds), *Gregor von Nyssa und die Philosophie*, Leiden: Brill, pp.159–92.

Anderegg, Johannes (1985), *Sprache und Verwandlung. Zur literarischen Ästhetik*, Göttingen: Vandenhoeck & Ruprecht.

Arens, Hans (1984), *Aristotle's Theory of Language and its Tradition*, Amsterdam: John Benjamin.

Arnheim, Rudolf (1972), *Visual Thinking*, London: Faber, 1970; German translation by the author, *Anschauliches Denken. Zur Einheit von Bild und Begriff*, Cologne, pp.150ff., 181.

Asad, Talal (1993), *The Genealogies of Religion: Discipline and Reasons of Power in Christianity and Islam*, Baltimore: Johns Hopkins University Press.

Assmann, J. (1988), 'Kollektives Gedächtnis und kulturelle Identität', in J. Assmann and T. Hölschner (eds), *Kultur und Gedächtnis*, Frankfurt am Main: Suhrkamp.

Auden, W.H. (1974), 'The Sea and the Mirror', II, in *Collected Longer Poems*, London: Faber, p.212.

Augustine, *Confessions*, trans. Henry Chadwick (1992), Oxford: Oxford University Press.

Balas, D.L. (1985), *Theologische Realenzyklopädie*, vol. XIV, Berlin: De Gruyter, p.177.

Balthasar, Hans Urs von (1942; English trans. 1995), *Presence and Thought: An Essay on the Religious Philosophy of Gregory of Nyssa*, trans. Mark Sebane, San Francisco: Ignatius Press.

Balthasar, Hans Urs von (1959), *Das betrachtende Gebet*, 2nd edn, Einsiedeln: Johannes Verlag.

Balthasar, Hans Urs von (1961), *Herrlichkeit. Eine theologische Aesthetik*, I: *Schau der Gestalt*, Einsiedeln: Johannes Verlag.

Balthasar, Hans Urs von (1965), *Herrlichkeit. Eine theologische Aesthetik*, III/1: *Im Raum der Metaphysik*, Einsiedeln: Johannes Verlag.

Balthasar, Hans Urs von (1970), 'Die christliche Gestalt', reprinted in H.U. von Balthasar (1974), *Pneuma und Institution. Skizzen zur Theologie*, IV, Einsiedeln: Johannes, pp.38–60.

Balthasar, Hans Urs von (English trans. 1991), *The Glory of the Lord*, V, trans. Oliver Davies *et al.*, Edinburgh: T.&T. Clark.

Barth, Karl (1975), *Church Dogmatics*, I/1.5, trans. G. Bromiley and T. Torrance, Edinburgh: T.&T. Clark.

Barth, Karl (1985), *Church Dogmatics* (11th edn), I/1 (German title: *Kirchliche Dogmatik*, 1/1), Zurich: Zollikon: Verlag der evangelischen Buchhandlung.

Barthes, Roland (1990), *The Pleasure of the Text*, trans. R. Miller, Oxford: Blackwell.

Barton, John (1995), 'Reading for Life: The Use of the Bible in Ethics and the Work of Martha C. Nussbaum', in John W. Rogerson, Margaret Davies and M. Daniel Carroll R. (eds), *The Bible in Ethics: The Second Sheffield Colloquium*, *Journal for the Study of the Old Testament* supplement series, 207, Sheffield: Sheffield Academic Press, pp.66–76.

Bauckham, Richard (1993), *The Climax of Prophecy: Studies on the Book of Revelation*, Edinburgh: T.&T. Clark.

Bayer, Oswald (1988), 'Oratio, Meditatio, Tentatio. Eine Besinnung auf Luther's Theologieverständnis', *LuJ*, 55, 7–59.

Beintker, Michael (1991), *Anmerkungen zur Kategorie der Texttreue* (Comments about the Category of Faithfulness to the Text), in Hans Heinrich Schmid and Joachim Mehlhausen (eds), *Sola Scriptura*, Gütersloh: Carl Bertelsmann.

Benjamin, Walter (1977), *The Origin of German Tragic Drama*, trans John Osborne, London: New Left Books.

Böcher, O. (1980), *Die Johannesapokalypse*, 2nd edn, Darmstadt.

Booth, Edward (1983), *Aristotelian Aporetic Ontology in Islamic and Christian Thinkers*, Cambridge: Cambridge University Press.

Brecht, Martin (1967), 'Johann Albrecht Bengels Theologie der Schrift', *ZThK*, 64, 99–120.

Brown, Raymond E. (1970), *The Gospel According to John (xii–xxi)*, The Anchor Bible, New York: Doubleday.

Buber, Martin (1963), *Das Buch der Preisungen*, Cologne and Olten.

Buber, Martin (1964), *Die Schrift und ihre Verdeutschung*, in *Werke*, vol. II, *Schriften zur Bibel*, Munich and Heidelberg: Kösel-Verlag, pp.1093–1186.

Bultmann, Rudolph (1971), *The Gospel of John. A Commentary*, trans. G.R. Beasley-Murray, Oxford: Blackwell.

Cadbury, H.J. (1922), *The Beginnings of Christianity*, vol. II, ed. F.J. Foakes-Jackson and K. Lake, London.

Calixt, Georg (1619), *Epitome Theologiae*, reprinted in Inge Mager (ed.) (1982), *Dogmatische Schriften*, Göttingen: Vandenhoeck & Ruprecht.

Cixous, Hélène (1990), *Reading with Clarice Lispector*, trans. Verene Andermatt Conley, Hemel Hempstead: Harvester Wheatsheaf.

Clark, Stephen R.L. (1975), *Aristotle's Man: Speculations upon Aristotelian Anthropology*, Oxford: Clarendon Press.

Coakley, Sarah (1996), '*Kenosis* and Subversion', in Daphne Hampson (ed.), *Swallowing a Fishbone: Feminist Theologians Debate Christianity*, London: SPCK, pp.82–111.

Collins, J.J. (1992, *The Apocalyptic Imagination: An Introduction to Jewish Apocalyptic Literature*, New York: Crossroad.

Cunningham, Valentine (1994), *In the Reading Gaol. Postmodernity, Texts and History*, Oxford: Blackwell.

Daniélou, Jean (1970), *L'Etre et le temps chez Grégoire de Nysse*, Leiden: Brill.

Danneberg, Lutz and Friedrich Vollhardt (eds) (1996), *Wie international ist die Literaturwissenschaft? Methoden- und Theoriediskussion: Kulturelle Besonderheiten und interkultureller Austausch am Beispiel des Interpretationsproblems (1950–1990)*, Stuttgart: Metzler.

Dawson, David (1992), *Allegorical Readers and Cultural Revision in Ancient Alexandria*, Berkeley: University of California Press.

Derrida, Jacques (1976), *Of Grammatology*, trans. G. Spivak, Baltimore: Johns Hopkins University Press.

Derrida, Jacques (1978), 'Structure, sign and play in the discourse of the Human Sciences', in *Writing and Difference*, trans. A. Bass, London: Routledge.

Derrida, Jacques (1982), 'Of an apocalyptic tone newly adopted in philosophy', trans. J. Leavey; reprinted in H. Coward and T. Fosby (eds) (1992), *Derrida and Negative Theology*, New York: SUNY Press.

Derrida, Jacques (1984), 'No Apocalypse, Not Now', *Diacritics*, 14 (2), Ithaca, NY: Cornell University Press, pp.20–32.

Dodd, C.H. (1963), *Historical Tradition in the Fourth Gospel*, Cambridge: Cambridge University Press.

Dorrie, Heinrich (1983), *RAC*, XII, Stuttgart: Anton Hiersemann.

Downing, F.G. (1963), *Does Christianity have a Revelation?*, London: SCM.

Ebeling, Gerhard (1958), 'Geist und Buchstabe', Religion in Geschichte und Gegenwart (RGG), 3rd edn, II, Tübingen: J.C.B. Mohr, pp.1290–96.

Ebeling, Gerhard (1985), 'Einfalt des Glaubens und Vielfalt der Liebe. Das Herz von Luthers Theologie', in *Lutherstudien*, III, Tübingen: Mohr, pp.126–53.

Else, Gerald (1986), *Plato and Aristotle on Poetry*, Chapel Hill: University of North Carolina Press.

Fiddes, Paul S. (1991), *Freedom and Limit: A Dialogue between Literature and Christian Doctrine*, Basingstoke: Macmillan.

Fish, Stanley (1980), *Is There a Text in This Class? The Authority of Interpretive Communities*, Cambridge, MA: Harvard University Press.

Fitzek, Herbert and Wilhelm Salber (n.d.), *Gestaltpsychologie. Geschichte und Praxis*, Darmstadt.

Forster, E.M. *Aspects of the Novel*, 8th edn (1947), London: Edward Arnold & Co.

Foucault, Michel (1981), *The History of Sexuality*, vol. 1, trans. Robert Hurley, London: Penguin Books.

Frank, Manfred (1985), *Das individuelle Allgemeine. Textstrukturierung und - interpretation nach Schleiermacher*, 2nd edn, Frankfurt am Main: Suhrkamp.

Gadamer, Hans-Georg (1990), *Wahrheit und Methode. Grundzüge einer philosophischen Hermeneutik*, 6th edn, Tübingen: Mohr.

Gellrich, Jesse M. (1985), *The Idea of the Book in the Middle Ages: Language, Theory, Mythology and Fiction*, New York: Cornell University Press.

Gregory of Nyssa (1978), *The Life of Moses*, trans. Abraham J. Malherbe and Everett Ferguson, New York: Paulist Press.

Greshake, Gisbert (1964), 'Review of H.U. von Balthasar, *Herrlichkeit*, I and II', *US*, 2, 370–73.

Grimm, Jacob and Wilhelm Grimm (1897), *Deutsches Wörterbuch*, IV, Leipzig.

Gross, Sabine (1994), *Lese-Zeichen. Kognition, Medium und Materialität im Leseprozess*, Darmstadt: Wissenschaftliche Buchgesellschaft.

Hamann, J.G. (1988), in *Aesthetica in nuce* (1762), reprinted in *Sokratische Denkwürdigkeiten*, ed. S.A. Jørgensen, Stuttgart.

Handreichung für Mitglieder der Landessynode, der Kreissynoden und der Presbyterien in der Evangelischen Kirche im Rheinland (Instructions for members of the Regional Synod, the District Synods and the Presbyteries in the German Protestant Church in the Rhineland) (1988), no. 44, Austeilung von Traubensaft beim Abendmahl in Ausnahmefällen (Distribution of Grapejuice at Holy Communion in special cases), Düsseldorf: Archiv der evangelischen Kirche im Rheinland.

Hart, R. (1968), *Unfinished Man and the Imagination*, New York: Herder & Herder.

Hartmann, Michael (1985), *Ästhetik als ein Grundbegriff fundamentaler Theologie. Eine Untersuchung zu Hans Urs von Balthasar*, St Ottilien: EOS Verlag.

Hartshorne, Charles (1967), *Creative Synthesis and Philosophic Method*, London: SCM.

Hebel, Johann Peter (1839), *Schwänke aus dem Rheinlandischen Hausfreund* (Comic tales from a Rheinlandish friend of the family), I, Stuttgart; reprinted 1979, Dortmund.

Heerbrand, Jacob (1587[1573]), *Compendium theologiae; De sacrosancta scriptura*, Leipzig.

Heinz, Hanspeter (1975), *Der Gott des Je-mehr. Der christologischer Ansatz Hans Urs von Balthasars*, Berne and Frankfurt a. M: H. Lang.

Henckmann, Wolfhart (1992), 'Gestalttheorie', in W. Henckmann and K. Lotter, *Lexikon der Aesthetik*, Munich: Chr. Kaiser.

Hennecke, Edgar, Wilhelm Schneemelcher and Robert McLachlan Wilson (eds) (1991–2), *New Testament Apocrypha*, Cambridge: Clarke.

Hoeps, Reinhard (1988), 'Das Gefühl des Erhabenen und die Herrlichkeit Gottes. Studien zur Beziehung von philosophischer und theologischer Ästhetik', Habilitationsschrift, Bonn.

Ignatius Loyola (1973), *The Spiritual Exercises*, trans. Thomas, S.J. Corbishley, Wheathampstead: Anthony Clarke.

Ivanka, E. von (1936), 'Vom Platonismus zur Theoriemystik. Zur Erkenntnislehre Gregors von Nyssa', *Scholastik*, 11, 163–95.

Jaeger, Werner (1966), *Gregor von Nyssa's Lehre vom Heiligen Geist*, Leiden: Brill.

Josipovici, Gabriel (1988), *The Book of God. A Response to the Bible*, New Haven and London: Yale University Press.

Jüngel, Eberhard (1976), *The Doctrine of the Trinity. God's Being is in Becoming*, trans. H. Harris, Edinburgh: Scottish Academic Press.

Jüngel, Eberhard (1986a), 'Das Dilemma der natürlichen Theologie und die Wahrheit ihres Problems', *Entsprechung: Gott – Wahrheit – Mensch*, Munich: Kaiser Verlag, pp.175f.

Jüngel, Eberhard (1986b), 'Gott – um seiner selbst willen interessant. Plädoyer für eine natürlichere Theologie', in *Entsprechungen: Gott, Wahrheit, Mensch: theologische Erörterungen*, Munich: Chr. Kaiser, pp.196–7.

Jüngel, Eberhard (1989), 'Metaphorical truth. Reflections on theological metaphor as a contribution to a hermeneutics of narrative theology', in J.B. Webster (ed. and trans.), *Eberhard Jüngel: Theological Essays*, Edinburgh: T.&T. Clark.

Kähler, Martin (1895), *Unser Streit um die Bibel*; reprinted in Ernst Kähler (ed.) (1967), *Aufsätze zur Bibelfrage* (ThB 37), Munich: Chr. Kaiser, pp.17–83.

Kähler, Martin (English trans. 1964), *The So-called Historical Jesus and the Historic Biblical Christ*, Philadelphia: Fortress Press.

Kaiser, O. (1962), *Die mythische Bedeutung des Meeres in Ägypten, Ugarit und Israel*, 2nd edn, Berlin: A. Töpelmann.

Kant, Immanuel (1798), *The Conflict of the Faculties*; reprinted in Wilhelm Weischedel (ed.) (1964), *Werke*, VI, Darmstadt: Wissenschaftliche Buchgesellschaft; English trans. 1979, Lincoln, Nebraska: University of Nebraska Press.

Karpp, Heinrich (1980), 'Bible', IV, *TRE*, 6, Berlin and New York: Walter de Gruyter.

Karpp, Heinrich (1992), *Schrift, Geist und Wort Gottes. Geltung und Wirkung der Bibel in der Geschichte der Kirche – von der Alten Kirche bis zum Ausgang der Reformationszeit*, Darmstadt: Wissenschaftliche Buchgesellschaft.

Kloos, C. (1986), *YHWH'S Combat with the Sea: A Canaanite Tradition in the Religions of Ancient Israel*, Amsterdam: G.A. van Oorschot.

Koch, K. (1972), *The Rediscovery of Apocalyptic*, London: SCM Press.

Koch, K. (1980), *Das Buch Daniel*, EdF, 144, Darmstadt: Wissenschaftliche Buchgesellschaft.

König, Johann Friedrich (1699[1664]), *Theologia positiva acroamatica*, Rostock.

Lacoste, Jean-Yves (1994), *Expérience et Absolu*, Paris: Presses Universitaires de France.

Lämmert, E. (1975), *Bauformen des Erzählens*, 6th edn, Stuttgart: Metzler.

Larkin, Sr Miriam Theresa, CS (1971), *Language in the Philosophy of Aristotle*, The Hague: Mouton.

Leahy, Brendán (1994), 'Theological Aesthetics', in Bede McGregor and Thomas Norris (eds), *The Beauty of Christ: An Introduction to the Theology of Hans Urs von Balthasar*, Edinburgh: T. & T. Clark, pp.23–55.

Lochbrunner, Manfred (1981), *Analogia Caritatis. Darstellung und Deutung der Theologie Hans Urs von Balthasars*, Freiburg-i.B., Basle and Vienna.

Lotz, Johannes B. (1984), *Ästhetik aus der ontologischen Differenz. Das Anwesen des Unsichtbaren im Sichtbaren*, Munich: J. Berchmann.

Luther, Martin (1520), *Assertio omnium articulorum*, *WA* 7.

Luther, Martin 'Answer to the hyperchristian, hyperspiritual and hyperlearned book by Goat Emser in Leipzig', *WA* 7; American edn, vol. 39, ed. E.W. Gritsch (1970), Philadelphia: Fortress Press.

Luther, Martin (*c.* 1516), *Randbemerkungen zu Taulers predigten*, *WA* 9:95–104.

Luther, Martin (1522), *Kirchenpostille*, *WA* 10, I,1:62–6.

Luther, Martin (1523), *Epistel S. Pauli gepredigt und ausgelegt*, *WA* 12, 259–399.

Luther, Martin (1525), *De servo arbitrio*, *WA* 18, 653; English trans.: *On the Bondage of the Will, Library of Christian Classics*, Vol. 17: *Luther and Erasmus*, ed. P.S.N. Watson and B. Drewey (1969), London: SCM.

Luther, Martin (1523–34), *Vorlesung über Jesaja. Scholien*, *WA* 25: 87–401.

Luther, Martin, *Sermon on John 16–20, WA* 28, 43–479.

Luther, Martin (1531), *In epistolam S. Pauli ad Galatas Commentarius, WA* 40 I,391:3–5.

Luther, Martin (1539), 'Preface to the first volume of the Wittenberg edition', *WA* 50, 657–61.

Luther, Martin (1515–16), *Lectures on Romans, WA* 56; American edn, vol. 25, ed. H. Oswald (1972), St Louis: Concordia.

Luther, Martin (1525), *De servo arbitrio*, reprinted in Hans-Ulrich Delius (ed.) (1983), *Studienausgabe*, III, Berlin, pp.177–356.

Man, Paul de (1979), *Allegories of Reading: Figural Language in Rousseau, Nietzsche, Rilke and Proust*, New Haven: Yale University Press.

Man, Paul de (1983), *Blindness and Insight: Essays in the Rhetoric of Contemporary Criticism*, London: Methuen & Co.

Metzger, Wolfgang (1971), 'Gestalt', in Joachim Ritter (ed.), *HWP*, 3, cols. 540–48.

Metzger, Wolfgang (1986), *Gestalt-Psychologie. Ausgewählte Werke aus den Jahren 1950 bis 1982*, ed. M. Stadler and Heinrich Crabus, Frankfurt a. M.

Moltmann, Jürgen (1967), *Theology of Hope*, trans. J. Leitch, London: SCM.

Muir, E. (1949), *The Structure of the Novel*, 5th edn, London: Chatto & Windus.

Müller, K. (1978), 'Apokalyptik/Apokalypsen.III. Die Jüdische Apokalyptik. Anfänge und Merkmale', *TRE*, 3, 202–51.

Müller, U.B. (1984), *Die Offenbarung des Johannes*, ÖTK, 19, Gütersloh: Mohn/Würzburg: Echter Verlag.

Nancy, Jean-Luc (1993), *The Birth to Presence*, trans Brian Holmes *et al.*, Stanford: Stanford University Press.

Nicol, W. (1972), *The Semeia in the Fourth Gospel. Tradition and Redaction*, Leiden: Brill.

Nitzsch, K.I. (1822), *Bericht an die Mitglieder des Rehkopfschen Prediger-Vereins über die Verhandlungen i.J. 1820*, Wittenberg.

Nussbaum, Martha C. (1986), *The Fragility of Goodness: Luck and Ethics in Greek Tragedy and Philosophy*, Cambridge: Cambridge University Press.

Nussbaum, Martha C. (1990), *Love's Knowledge: Essays on Philosophy and Literature*, Oxford: Oxford University Press.

Nussbaum, Martha C. (1994), *Therapy of Desire: Theory and Practice in Hellenistic Ethics*, Princeton: Princeton University Press.

Oelmüller, Willi (ed.) (1982), *Kolloquium Kunst und Philosophie*, II: *Ästhetischer Schein*, Paderborn, Munich, Vienna and Zurich: Schoningh.

Origen (1936), *On First Principles*, ed. G.W. Butterworth, London: SPCK.

Patiz, G. (1979), 'Theology and Ontology in Aristotle's Metaphysics', in Jonathan Barnes, Malcolm Schofield and Richard Sorabji (eds), *Articles on Aristotle*, vol. 3, London: Duckworth, pp.48–9.

Quine, Willard V.O. (1971), *Ontological Relativity and Other Essays*, 2nd edn, New York and London: Columbia University Press.

Rahner, Karl (1978), *Foundations of Christian Faith*, trans. W. Dych, London: Darton, Longman and Todd.

Ratschow, Carl Heinz (1964), *Lutherische Dogmatik zwischen Reformation und Aufklärung*, I, Gütersloh: Gütersloher Verlagshaus G. Mohn.

Ricoeur, Paul (1966), *Freedom and Nature: The Voluntary and the Involuntary*, trans. E. Kohak, Evanston: Northwestern University Press.

Ricoeur, Paul (1969), 'Freedom in the light of hope', in *Essays on Biblical Interpretation*, Philadelphia: Fortress Press, pp.163ff.

Ricoeur, Paul (1974), *The Conflict of Interpretations: Essays in Hermeneutics*, Evanston: Northwestern University Press, 1974, pp.49–50.

Ricoeur, Paul (1978), *The Rule of Metaphor*, trans. Robert Czerny, London: Routledge.

Ricoeur, Paul (1980), 'Towards a Hermeneutic of the Idea of Revelation', in Lewis S. Mudge (ed.), *Essays on Biblical Interpretation*.

Ricoeur, Paul (1985), *Time and Narrative*, vol. 1, trans K. McLaughlin and D. Pellauer, Chicago: University of Chicago Press.

Ricoeur, Paul (1986), *The Rule of Metaphor*, trans. R. Czerny, London: Routledge.

Ricoeur, Paul (1988), *Time and Narrative*, Chicago and London: University of Chicago Press, 1984, pp.52–87.

Ritschl, D. (1976), 'Theology as Story'/*'Story' als Rohmaterial der Theologie*, TEH (192), Munich: Chr. Kauser.

Rose, Gillian (1992), *The Broken Middle: Out of Our Ancient Society*, Oxford: Blackwell.

Ross, W.D. (1955), *Aristotelis Fragmenta Selecta*, Oxford: Oxford University Press.

Russell, D.S. (1992), *Divine Disclosure. An Introduction to Jewish Apocalyptic*, London: SCM Press.

Schlatter, A. (1928), *Hülfe in Bibelnot*, 2nd edn, Verbert: Freizeiten-Verlag.

Schlatter, Adolf (1952), *Rückblick auf seine Lebensarbeit*, Gütersloh: Carl Bertelsmann.

Schleiermacher, F.D.E. (1993), *Hermeneutik und Kritik. Mit einem Anhang sprachphilosophischer Texte Schleiermachers*, 5th edn, Manfred Frank, Frankfurt: Suhrkamp.

Schmidt, J.M. (1976), *Die jüdische Apokalyptik*, 2nd edn, Neukirchen: Neukirchener Verlag.

Schnackenburg, Rudolph (1990), *The Gospel According to St. John*, vol. 3, trans. D. Smith, New York: Crossroad.

Semler, J.S. (1769), 'Vorrede', in G.L. Oeder, *Christlich freye Untersuchung über die sogenannte Offenbarung Johannis*, Halle.

Smend, R. (1978), *Die Entstehung des Alten Testaments*, ThW, 1, Stuttgart: Kohlhammer.

Söding, Thomas (1992), 'Geschichtlicher Text und Heilige Schrift – Fragen zur theologischen Legitimität', in C. Dohmen, J. Jacob and T. Söding (eds), *Neue Formen der Schriftauslegung* (QD 140), Frieburg i. Br., Basle and Vienna: Herder, pp.74–130.

Stegmüller, Wolfgang (1973), *Theorienstrukturen und Theoriendynamik. Probleme und Resultate der Wissenschaftstheorie und Analytische Philosophie*, Bd. 2/2, Berlin, Heidelberg and New York: Walter de Gruyter.

Stegmüller, Wolfgang (1978), *Hauptströmungen der Gegenwartsphilosophie: Eine kritische Einführung*, 6th edn, vol. 1, Stuttgart: Kröner Verlag.

Swinburne, Richard (1992), *Revelation: From Metaphor to Analogy*, Oxford: Clarendon Press.

Twesten, August Detlev Christian (1829), *Vorlesungen über die Dogmatik der Evangelisch-Lutherischen Kirche according to the Compendium of Dr. W.M.L. de Wette*, 2nd edn, I, Hamburg.

Via, Dan O. (1997), *The Revelation of God and/as Human Reception*, Harrisburg, PA: Trinity Press International.

Wächter, O. (1865), *Lebensabriß, Character, Briefe und Aussprüche. Nach handschriftlichen Mittheilungen*, Stuttgart.

Waldenfels, Bernhard (1992), 'Die Fremdheit der Schrift', in M.M. Olivetti (ed.), *Religione, Parola, Scrittura*, Milan and Padua, pp.49–59.

Ward, Graham (1991), 'Biblical Narrative and the Theology of Metonymy', *Modern Theology*, 7 (4), July, 335–50.

Ward, Graham (1994), 'Mimesis: The Measure of Mark's Christology', *Journal of Literature and Theology*, 8 (1).

Ward, Keith (1982), *Rational Theology and the Creativity of God*, Oxford: Blackwell.

Welsch, Wolfgang (1991), *Ästhetisches Denken*, 2nd edn, Stuttgart: Reclam.

Westermann, C. (1984), *Genesis*, I, London: SPCK and Minneapolis: Augsburg.

Williams, Rowan (1990), 'Der Literalsinn der Heiligen Schrift', *EvTh*, 50.

Williams, Rowan (1991), 'The Literal Sense of Scripture', *Modern Theology*, 7 (2), 121–34.

Wolleb, Johannes (1626), *Christianae theologiae compendium*, Basle.

Zager, W. (1989), *Begriff und Wertung der Apokalyptik in der neutestamentlichen Forschung*, Frankfurt a. M.

Zimmerli, Walther (1963), 'Promise and Fulfilment', in C. Westermann (ed.), *Essays on Old Testament Interpretation*, trans. J. Mays, London: SCM.

Index